HOME SAUSAGE MAKING

How-to Techniques for Making and Enjoying
100 Sausages at Home

Susan Mahnke Peery & Charles G. Reavis

Storey Publishing

The mission of Storey Publishing is to serve our customers by publishing practical information that encourages personal independence in harmony with the environment.

Edited by Dianne M. Cutillo
Art direction by Cynthia N. McFarland
Cover design by Carole Goodman, Blue Anchor Design
Illustrations by Elayne Sears
Text design by Carole Goodman, Blue Anchor Design,
    Cynthia N. McFarland, and Susan Bernier
Text production by Jennifer Jepson Smith
Indexed by Susan Olason/Indexes & Knowledge Maps

Printed in the United States by Malloy
10 9 8

Library of Congress Cataloging-in-Publication Data

Peery, Susan Mahnke.
    Home sausage making : how-to techniques for making and enjoying 100
    sausages at home / Susan Mahnke Peery and Charles G. Reavis.
        p. cm.
    Includes index.
    ISBN-13: 978-1-58017-471-8 (alk. paper)
    1. Cookery (Sausages) 2. Sausages. I. Reavis, Charles, 1948– II. Title.
TX749.5.S28 P44 2002
641.3'6—dc21

                                                                        2002015780

Contents

PREFACE

Like the first person to eat an oyster, history's first sausage maker is anonymous. But we owe this person a great debt, for sausage is up there with wine and cheese and bread as one of the world's great foods. Sausage is more than just a way of preserving meat and using up the scraps. Sausage has been made for centuries in nearly every culture and country around the world, with great variation and ingenuity in taking advantage of local conditions and ingredients.

If you have never made sausage before, this book will walk you through the steps to successful sausage. Your neighbors, friends, and relatives will not only be impressed — they will "happen" to show up for supper with amazing frequency! With minimal equipment, anyone can make a simple fresh sausage: It's like meatloaf stuffed into a casing.

For the more experienced sausage maker, we offer recipes for more than 100 different sausages, from fresh pork sausage to Old World cured and smoked specialties. Game sausage from venison and rabbit to bear and boar will please the hunters among us. (Come to think of it, no doubt that first sausage maker was a hunter faced with hundreds of pounds of woolly mammoth, yards of intestines, and the prospect of a long winter.)

If you are a vegetarian or prefer poultry or seafood, we offer more than three dozen recipes for making these new and delicious sausages.

Once you get the hang of sausage making, your own ingenuity will lead you even farther along this culinary path. We hope that you will utilize the response card bound into this book and let us know about your own adventures in sausage making.

Part One

The Techniques

CHAPTER 1

The Story of Sausage

Everything has an end except a sausage,

which has two.

— Danish proverb

SAUSAGE WAS BORN OF NECESSITY, a way of preserving meat in times of plenty to eat when life turned lean. The fact that it tasted good, made efficient use of a slaughtered animal, and could be seasoned and shaped according to the sausage maker's taste meant sausage was a real keeper in the larder, right next to cheese, wine, beer, dried lentils, raisins, and other staples.

When you make your own sausage, fresh or cured, you are in good company. Homer mentioned the Greeks' love for grilled sausage in the *Odyssey*. The legionnaires of Imperial Rome wouldn't march without their little bottles of *garum* (a fermented fish sauce similar to today's *nam pla* from Thailand) and long strings of dried or smoked sausages.

Sausage making really took off in Europe during the medieval period, when an energetic spice trade and returning Crusaders brought exotic seasonings and new cooking techniques to sleepy farms and villages. Medieval towns all across Europe — Bologna, Frankfurt, Vienna, and many others — gave their names to distinctive sausages we still love. In North America, Native Americans dried and smoked venison and buffalo meat to make jerky, and they stuffed meat, suet, and berries into skins to make pemmican.

Sausage, part of the original portable feast, still delights our palates. It is a sturdy, nourishing comfort food, a "link" to the past. And when we make our own sausage, choosing ingredients and styles that please ourselves, our families, and our friends, the possibilities are, well, endless.

SAUSAGE BASICS

There are literally thousands of varieties of sausage in the world, but the United States Department of Agriculture groups them all into two types: uncooked, including fresh bulk sausage, patties, links, and some smoked sausages; and ready-to-eat, including dry, semidry, and/or cooked sausages.

Fresh sausages must be cooked before they are eaten. Like other fresh meat, they are highly perishable and must be refrigerated or frozen until you are ready to cook them. Ready-to-eat sausages are cooked and/or preserved with ingredients such as salt, nitrites (now closely regulated), and alcohol, and they may be dried and/or smoked to further prevent spoilage. These sausages can be eaten out of hand (a slice of pepperoni, for instance), or cooked just enough to heat through (a frankfurter, for example).

By our definition, sausage is a mixture of ground meat and (usually) fat, poultry, seafood, or vegetarian ingredients laced with salt, herbs, and spices. A sausage mixture can be shaped into a patty and fried like a burger or it can be stuffed into a casing. Once stuffed and twisted into links, it may be cooked on the spot or dried, smoked, fermented, or otherwise preserved.

Stuffing may seem like a lot of extra work, especially for fresh sausage, but it is worth it. Beyond giving the sausage its characteristic shape, the casing helps to improve the texture of the finished product and meld the flavors. That sublimely satisfying moment of biting into a hot, juicy homemade sausage doesn't happen when you shape the mixture into patties instead.

It would be futile to try to catalog all of the varieties of sausage in the world, since some kinds are made only in a small region or even in a single household. As you learn to make your own sausages, you will begin to personalize your recipes, perhaps creating your own unique variety, and certainly adding to the dazzling array of sausages that have already been thought up in the human mind to please the human palate.

Homemade sausages are popular among hunters, who like to make good use of the wild game they bring home. People who raise livestock turn to sausage making as a delicious way to make economical use of their animals at slaughtering time. But as our recipes will demonstrate, you can live in a tiny city apartment and shop in a supermarket, and still make your own delicious and distinctive sausage. Sausage making is for everyone.

Varieties of Sausages

Some of the many varieties of sausages that we will make are described below. Included in the description is an indication of whether the sausage is usually a fresh one or falls into the ready-to-eat category. The cooked, dried, fermented, and smoked sausages are always stuffed into casings for ease of handling and processing.

Bavarian summer sausage is a German-style salami mildly flavored with mustard seed and sugar. Whenever I have some, I think of Bavarian beer fests and rye bread. It's a dried sausage.

Bockwurst, a German-style sausage made from veal or veal and pork, is usually flavored with onions, parsley, and cloves and is prepared fresh or partially cooked, then refrigerated and completely cooked before eating.

Bratwurst is a German-style sausage made from pork and veal. It looks like a fat hot dog and is deli-

SAUSAGE CATEGORIES

In the inimitable words of the Food Safety and Inspection Service (FSIS) of the United States Department of Agriculture (USDA), "Sausages are either ready to eat or not."

Classifying sausages into categories is difficult because sausages are produced by so many different methods. Following is a simple classification of various types and how they should be stored and cooked.

Fresh sausages are made from uncooked meats and other ingredients. They must be kept refrigerated, then cooked before serving and may be frozen for 2 to 3 months. Examples include fresh pork and Italian sausages.

Cooked sausages are fully cooked, as by poaching or smoking, during processing and may be eaten without heating, but most are heated again before serving. These should be stored in the refrigerator, as well. Frankfurters and bologna are examples.

Other ready-to-eat sausages, also called *preserved* or *cured* sausages, are treated with salt and other additives to impart different flavors and extend storage time. Some sausages, including pepperoni, are cured, or preserved, by drying, and some are smoked as well during processing. These sausages need no further cooking and keep indefinitely in the refrigerator.

cately seasoned with allspice, caraway, and marjoram.

Braunschweiger, a German-style pork liver sausage, is usually smoked after it is cooked. Onions, mustard seed, and marjoram accent the flavor.

Breakfast or **Country-Style Sausage,** one of the most common in the United States, is known by two names. By whichever name, it is usually made from pork seasoned with thyme, sage, and savory. It can be made into patties or small links.

Chorizo originated in Spain and can be fresh or dried. The fresh variety is similar to Sicilian sausage but much spicier; the dried version resembles pepperoni in size and shape but is much more pungent.

Cotechino is an Italian-style sausage that is best made from fresh, uncured ham. Nutmeg, cinnamon, cloves, and Parmesan cheese give it a unique flavor.

Frankfurter, your plain old hot dog, is the most widely consumed sausage in the world, thanks to the industriousness of American meat packers. In 2000, more than 1 billion pounds of hot dogs were sold at retail stores. Only 5 percent of hot dogs are sold with natural casings. Once you make your own, you may never go back to store-bought hot dogs. Frankfurters are a cooked, smoked sausage.

Garlic ring bologna is lightly smoked and precooked. Its predominent flavor is garlic.

Garlic sausage can be fresh or cooked and smoked. The fresh variety is a finely textured pork sausage flavored with lots of garlic and some white wine. It holds up well in soups and in stews. The cured type has a complex and unforgettable flavor and is meant to be eaten out of hand.

"Italian sausage" that you see in the meat case can be either hot or sweet. As it is traditionally made in northern Italy, it contains pure pork flavored with coriander; crushed red pepper provides the heat. Sicilian-style Italian sausage is basically the same, except fennel takes the place of coriander. These are fresh sausages that must be fully cooked before eating.

Kielbasa is made from coarsely ground lean pork sometimes combined with beef and/or veal. The Polish word *kielbasa* simply means "sausage." Commercial kielbasa is usually an uncooked smoked sausage, but we also offer a recipe for a fresh version that we think you will enjoy.

Liverwurst or **liver sausage** is made from finely ground pork and pork liver, among other ingredients. A fresh sausage, it's usually stuffed into a nonedible casing, such as the muslin casing we teach you to make with our recipe.

Luganega, a fresh, mild northern-Italian-style pork sausage flavored with freshly grated orange and lemon zest, is usually made in long links and broiled or boiled intact. Its Greek sister, **loukanika,** is made with both lamb and pork, seasoned with orange rind, and usually cut into chunks and fried or grilled.

Mettwurst is similar to garlic ring bologna but milder. An uncooked, smoked sausage, it contains ginger, celery seed, and allspice.

Pepperoni, an Italian-style sausage made from beef and pork, is a dried sausage that can be extremely pungent depending upon how much red pepper you dare to throw in. The drying process further intensifies the flavor.

Salami is a generic term that refers to dried sausages made from beef or pork or both. It comes in many shapes and sizes and can be quite hard and dry.

Smoked "country-style" sausage is similar to the "little smokes" you've encountered in the meat case at your grocery store. You can easily make your own using pork and beef.

Summer sausage. Also called cervelat, beefstick, or beer sausage, summer sausage is a beef or beef/pork dried sausage that got its name because it was made in the summer. It resembles some of the drier salamis but usually is milder and somewhat sweeter.

Thuringer sausage is a German-style, lightly smoked sausage. It is semidry and more perishable than are other cured sausages. Coriander, mace, and mustard seed provide the flavor.

Venison sausage is one you'll have to hunt for! It often includes some pork and pork fat because venison — whether from deer, elk, bison, moose, or other large game — tends to be a very dry meat. Sausage made from venison may be prepared as fresh, dried, or smoked.

And Many New Sausage Varieties!

The years since this book was first published have seen an explosion of interest in ethnic foods and flavors. People focused on sausage as both an old-fashioned favorite and a satisfying food with great flavor possibilities. In retail markets, sausage sales have boomed, and the number of home sausage makers has also risen. People want sausage that is both tasty and healthful, and when you make your own, you are in charge of both qualities.

In this edition, contributions from home sausage makers in the United States and Canada have added recipes for pork and pistachio sausage, Portuguese linguiça, Thai-flavored turkey sausage, and an array of vegetarian sausages, just to mention a few. We hope the recipes inspire you to try your own variations.

pemmican

The Cree Indians of the North American woodlands called animal fat *pimyi*, from which we get the word *pemmican*. The Cree and other tribes dried strips of meat from buffalo, deer, rabbits, squirrels, and antelope, creating a product like jerky. This dried meat was nourishing and easy to carry, but it became moldy in wet weather. To solve the mold problem, the Indians made rawhide bags about the size of a pillowcase, filled them with pulverized bits of dried meat, dried berries, herbs, and nuts, and poured in hot melted bone marrow and fat *(pimyi)*. Then they sewed the bags shut and walked on them to compress the mixture and drive out air. The bone marrow and fat cooled and congealed around the meat, effectively sealing it. The Indians had, in effect, created a very large sausage.

Some claim pemmican could last up to 30 years. (Think about it: Would you eat 30-year-old meat soaked in bone marrow? Or would you save it for the next generation?)

CHAPTER 2

Equipment and Ingredients

Laws are like sausages —

it is better not to see them being made.

— Otto von Bismarck

WE BEG TO DIFFER WITH HERR VON BISMARCK! In this chapter, we will explain the basics of sausage making from start to finish. These principles and methods can be used to make any of the sausages in this book.

We will discuss a variety of types of equipment you can choose to make sausage, as well as how the steps vary depending on your choice of equipment.

It's also important to understand the ingredients you will need, as well as how the quality of the ingredients you choose will affect your final product. Generally, we will recommend the best-quality ingredients to ensure that you get the best-tasting sausage.

Our best advice for the sausage maker comes from the French, who have a term for culinary preparedness: *mise en place*. This means you should have everything gathered together and "in its place" before you start a recipe. By "everything" we mean all of the equipment and ingredients you will need. So we begin by describing "everything."

EQUIPMENT

Fortunately, sausage making only requires one or two pieces of specialized equipment: a meat grinder and sausage stuffer, plus a smoker if you are going to take that step. You probably already have the rest of the gear in your kitchen. Please consult our Resources list (see page 272) for mail-order sources for sausage-making equipment. Yard sales, auctions, and flea markets are good places to find used equipment, perhaps exactly what your grandmother or grandfather might have used to make sausage.

Meat Grinders

Unless you are able to wield two razor-sharp knives like a samurai warrior or a chef at a Japanese restaurant, you will need an appliance for grinding the meat. There are several options.

Hand Grinders. An old-fashioned cast-iron hand grinder is still a bargain, even at today's prices. You will find that many are made in Eastern Europe, where they have always taken sausage making seriously. Buy a heavy-duty one with at least two chopping disks: a fine disk with holes about ⅛ inch in diameter and a coarse disk with holes about ⅜ inch in diameter. A new grinder will last for generations.

A hand grinder will either clamp or bolt onto a tabletop. Be sure that you can achieve a sturdy grip either way, for grinding meat does involve a good deal of elbow grease and torque.

If you are lucky enough to have a hand grinder in your family, clean it up, removing any rust with a wire brush. Be sure the grinding disks are sharp and clean.

To sharpen grinding disks, place a sheet of emory cloth (available at hardware stores) flat on a table or board. Rub the disks over the cloth, using circular motions. Or, take the disks to a vendor who sharpens knives.

You may be tempted to buy a plastic grinder in a discount store or from one of the ubiquitous television commercials. The plastic models may look nifty, but we have yet to find one that is sturdy enough for the task. Furthermore, they usually fasten to the table with a suction-cup base, which invariably loses its grip

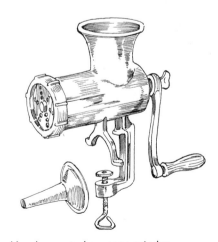

Hand-operated sausage grinder with funnel for filling casings

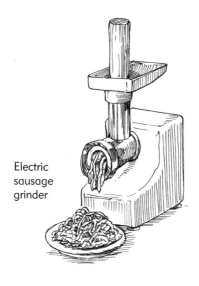

Electric sausage grinder

Food-grinding attachment on a heavy-duty standing mixer

at the most inopportune moment. You will get very frustrated by a grinder that has to be reattached every 5 minutes.

Electric Grinders. If you don't want to get "sausage elbow" grinding meat by hand, or if you intend to make a lot of sausage frequently, an electric grinder is a wise investment. Kitchen stores, restaurant-supply shops, and many on-line sources have a range of grinders starting with relatively inexpensive models and going up to deluxe professional styles (see Resources, page 272).

Some electric grinders come with an add-on kit that includes two or three stuffing tubes (from hot-dog size to salami size) and an extra-coarse disk to make larger sausages.

Heavy-duty mixer grinder attachment. Many of the home sausage makers profiled in this book use a grinding attachment with their heavy-duty mixer for their sausage making. It's a good alternative to purchasing a separate grinder, especially if you've already invested in the mixer.

Food Processors. If you own a heavy-duty food processor, it can do a splendid job of chopping meat. Models with a wide feed tube work best for sausage making. Read your instruction book and warranty to see if the motor on your processor is strong enough for chopping meat. (Models with smaller motors can overheat easily and burn out.)

EASIER GRINDING

Make sure your meat is as cold as possible before you grind it. You can even put it in the freezer for about an hour until it starts to stiffen, with just a few ice crystals. This makes the meat easier to grind and the fat doesn't clog up the grinder disk.

— Michael Ballon, Castle Street Café, Great Barrington, Massachusetts

The major drawback to using a food processor is that you get a very uneven cut of meat and it is very easy to overprocess meat. A few seconds too many, and a pound of meat cubes is reduced to the consistency of toothpaste. In addition, you will need separate equipment for stuffing sausages into casings.

A word of caution: If you are buying a grinding attachment for a mixer or food processor, be sure the motor is powerful enough to handle the heavy work of grinding meat. A hand-operated crank grinder of good quality is a better tool than an ineffective attachment.

Grinder plates or disks. When choosing a grinder or grinding attachment for another appliance, be sure to get at least two disks or plates, one coarse (⅜ inch), the other fine (⅛ inch).

Sausage Stuffers

If your grinder does not have a sausage-stuffing attachment or if you use a food processor to grind your meat, you will need a way to stuff your sausage into casings. There are several types of sausage stuffers, including hand, push, crank, and hydraulic, and they are made from a variety of materials: plastic, stainless steel, and cast iron among them.

Sausage funnels, also called hand stuffers, are handheld funnels that you use to push the meat into casings. The size of the funnel is directly

A food processor may be used to grind meat; be careful not to overprocess. You will need a sausage funnel for stuffing sausages.

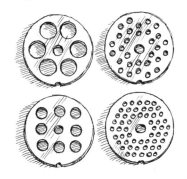

Disks of these sizes — ½ inch, ⅜ inch, ¼ inch, and ³⁄₁₆ inch — are used in making sausage. They are also called the extra-coarse, coarse, medium, and fine disks; only the fine and coarse disks are called for in this book.

Sausage funnels are made in many sizes. A ½-inch funnel, left, is appropriate for hot dogs; a 2-inch model, right, is good for links such as Italian sausage.

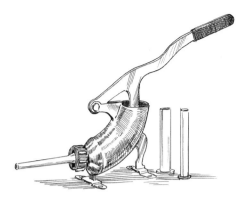

Old-fashioned, but still very practical, is this freestanding push stuffer, which you might use if your grinder does not have a stuffing attachment. Be sure to choose a model with several sizes of funnels.

Crank stuffers come in many shapes and sizes, from 3-pound devices to 25-pound machines.

A water-powered sausage stuffer generally has a 10-pound capacity.

related to the size of the sausage casing. If you have two or three funnels ranging from ¾ inch to 1½ or 2 inches, you will be off to a good start. Sausage funnels are straight, not tapered, and are usually about 5 inches long. Most are plastic and inexpensive.

Don't be tempted to make do with an ordinary kitchen funnel — most are too tapered on the small end and not long enough to gather up the casings. You can make perfectly good sausage at home with these relatively inexpensive hand tools, but you can get fancier to make the job easier. Hand-stuffing sausages takes a long time.

Push stuffers. Quickest to reload, a push stuffer has a small capacity. You must push down on a handle to force out the meat. Though its capacity is relatively small, you may find one easier to use than a hand funnel. These do require a fair amount of muscle power.

Crank stuffer. If you find yourself making a lot of sausage, you may find it saves time to invest in a crank stuffer, which offers a gear ratio to make it easier to crank out the meat. A crank stuffer has more capacity than a push or hand stuffer, too. But it also costs more.

Water stuffer. This type of stuffer, pricier than the crank variety, uses water pressure to push meat through and allows the sausage maker to use both hands to guide the casings.

Hydraulic stuffer. If your hobby turns into a small business, you might need one. It uses pressure to power the stuffer, and it accommodates the greatest capacity. But it will lighten your wallet considerably.

Mixer attachment. If your heavy-duty electric stand mixer has a grinding attachment available, the manufacturer probably also sells a sausage-stuffing attachment, though the range of casing sizes that mixers can accommodate is generally more limited.

Measuring Tools

Scales. A reliable scale for weighing meats and other ingredients is essential. For small batches of sausage, a scale often termed a "1 by 11" (1-ounce increments, up to 11 pounds) should suffice. For the more ambitious, a "2 by 22" (the standard meat scale, 2-ounce increments, up to 22 pounds) may be more desirable. You will find many other uses for the scale around the house once you have it (weighing loaves of bread, puppies, maybe even babies).

Some older or European recipes may call for seasonings and cures in terms of grams or ounces. For this, you will need a smaller scale, particularly if you are measuring curing chemicals by weight, where precision is vitally important. USDA recommends that home sausage makers who are making cured sausages have

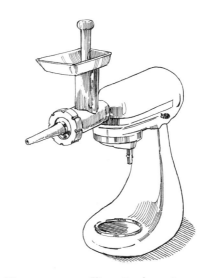

The sausage-stuffing attachment on a heavy-duty standing mixer works well for small-batch processing.

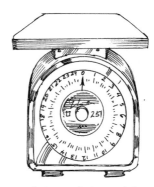

A meat scale is needed to weigh meat to the nearest pound.

a scale that can weigh curing ingredients (primarily sodium nitrite) to the nearest one-tenth of a gram. (For more information about curing agents in sausage, see page 22.)

Measuring Cups and Spoons. A good set of measuring spoons, from ¼ teaspoon up to 1 tablespoon, will come in handy with every recipe. A glass measuring cup for liquids and a set of dry measuring cups, ¼ cup to 1 cup, will also be useful.

A kitchen scale that can weigh curing ingredients to the nearest one-tenth of a gram is helpful for sausage makers who cure sausages.

An instant-read thermometer takes readings in 15 to 20 seconds and is used to ensure that sausage is cooked to a safe temperature.

Thermometers

Instant-read thermometer. This is used in testing fresh sausage for doneness and in making hot-smoked sausage.

This type of thermometer is essential to make sure that sausage is cooked to the proper temperatures to ensure safety. It contains a coil in the probe made of two different metals that are bonded together. According to USDA's Food Safety Inspection Service, the two metals have different rates of expansion. The coil, which is connected to the temperature indicator, expands when heated. This food thermometer senses temperature from its tip and up the stem for 2 to 2½ inches. The resulting temperature is an average of the temperatures along the sensing area. This thermometer has a dial display and is also available as "oven-safe." More accurate — but more expensive — models have digital displays.

For sausage making, you should be sure to get the instant-read type. This food thermometer quickly measures the temperature of a food in 15 to 20 seconds. It is not designed to remain in the food while it is cooking, but should be used near the end of the estimated cooking time to check for final cooking temperatures. To prevent overcooking, check the temperature before you expect the food to be done.

For accurate temperature measurement, insert the probe of the bimetallic-coil thermometer the full length of the sensing area (usually 1½ to 2 inches). If you are measuring the temperature of a thin piece of food, such as a sausage link, insert the probe through the side of the food rather than from above, so that the entire sensing area is positioned through the center of the food. Some models can be calibrated. Check the manufacturer's instructions.

Oven thermometer. If you have a smoker, ideally it will have a built-in thermometer; if not, set an oven thermometer on one of the racks.

Knives

No doubt you already have a prized knife that you keep sharp with a stone or other sharpening device. If you have both a **chef's knife** and a **boning knife,** you are really well equipped. A good knife may be the single most important tool you use in making sausage because so much of the job involves cutting, boning, and trimming the meat, poultry, and fish that will be ground into your sausage.

If you don't already own at least one excellent knife (by this we mean one made from high-carbon stainless steel, which can be sharpened to a razor's edge), now is the time to make an investment. Wash it by hand only and store it in a knife block or separated from other utensils. The high-quality knife will last a knifetime . . . make that a lifetime.

Butcher's Twine

Cotton butcher's twine or kitchen string is used to make some types of sausage links. It can be found wherever professional culinary equipment is sold and at sausage-supply companies; it can also be ordered from your butcher. If necessary, you can use other 100 percent cotton string but it tends to be stiff and difficult to work with. Do not use plastic string or a polyester/cotton blend, as it could melt.

INGREDIENTS

Here's our favorite part about making sausage at home: You control what's in your sausage. Whether you are trying to avoid the high-fat content in many commercially prepared sausages, prefer to limit preservatives or excess salt, or add your own preferences of seasonings, you can ensure your goal by making it yourself. An understanding of the basic ingredients, outlined below, will get you on your way.

The Main Component

Traditionalists (like us) think first of pork when we think of sausage; beef and veal are traditional, too. The last few decades have seen a mind-expanding array of sausages come into our culinary consciousness, and we are happy to offer recipes for the entire range of sausage fillings. In the previous edition of this book, we brought in chapters on poultry and seafood sausage. With this edition, we have added a brand-new chapter on vegetarian sausages, as well as new sausages in all the other categories. You can only imagine how much fun we had during the recipe-testing (and -tasting) process! The possibilities for sausage truly are endless.

When you make your own sausages, be they hot dogs, lobster sausages, kielbasa, or wild mushroom sausages, you choose your own fresh, high-quality ingredients. With meat sausage, you can choose the cut and control the amount of fat.

Pork. The pork cuts we use are the butt (sometimes called the Boston butt or shoulder roast) and fresh hams. On occasion, you might find a rib or loin roast that substitutes admirably for the butt when the price is right. The loin is the leanest of the three cuts, and if you use it, you may want to grind some extra fat into the mix so your sausage isn't too dry.

Beef and Veal. The chuck and rump are the most economical cuts. Since most grocers sell only USDA Choice beef and veal, you can be assured of the quality.

Game. Deer, elk, bison, moose, boar, bear, woodchuck, and game birds from doves to ducks all make excellent sausage. Because wild animals move around more than domestic ones, their meat tends to be dark, lean, and muscular. The quality and food-worthiness of the meat depends on the health of the animal and the skill of the butcher. Game sausages can be cooked and eaten fresh or they may be cured and/or smoked. Making sausage is a great way to use up the carcass.

Poultry and Seafood. Chicken, turkey, duck, goose, lobster, scallops, shrimp, lobster, and many finned fish make excellent sausage, whether prepared as fresh sausages or cured and/or smoked. Ethnic seasonings — Thai, Mexican, Indian, Italian — add to the mouthwatering possibilities for these homemade sausages.

Vegetarian Staples. All the staples of a vegetarian diet — beans, grains, vegetables, fruit, soy, and dairy products — can be used to make delectable vegetarian sausages. Vegetarian sausage is often eaten fresh in patty form, wrapped in an edible casing like cabbage leaves, or stuffed into plastic casing to shape the sausages, which are removed from the casing for cooking and eating.

Herbs, Spices, Salt, and Sugar

Herbs and spices are a small percentage of sausage by weight or volume, but they decide the character and piquancy of the recipe. The variations in the flavorings make the difference between bockwurst and bratwurst, knockwurst and bologna.

Herbs. The best of all possible worlds is one in which you grow and dry your own herbs. If this is not practical, buy fresh herbs at a supermarket, or, better yet, at a farmer's market, where they are likely to be fresher. For dried herbs, be sure to date your containers when you dry your own. And you might do the same when you purchase them from a market. Your herbs should be of recent vintage, lest their reduced potency from old age diminish the glory of your sausage. Air, light, and heat are the biggest enemies of dried herbs. They may be stored in a cool, dark place for up to 6 months. Best flavor is preserved if you refrigerate them after 3 months of storage.

Spices. We like to buy spices in small quantities from a reliable supplier (see our Resources list on page 272 for mail-order spice companies) and store them in a cool, dark place for no more than 6 months. While it may be handy, never store your spices in a hot spot like over the stovetop; they'll lose flavor faster. If you find yourself buying a supply of a spice that will last you for more than 6 months, refrigerate it. Whenever possible, buy whole spices and grind them as needed. They'll have more flavor than the preground variety. Allspice, cloves, and nutmeg are often readily available whole.

Salt and Pepper. For maximum flavor, use kosher salt or coarse sea salt in fresh sausage, rather than salt with any additives — table salt included (it has iodine added). Buy whole peppercorns and grind your own. Freshly ground pepper has a sharper flavor than preground pepper. When *finely ground* pepper is specified, it should be ground until it's uniformly powdery and has no large pieces of peppercorn. *Medium grind* pepper should be in flakes that will pass through a pepper shaker; *coarse grind* pepper pieces should be larger and may be ground in a mortar and pestle instead of a pepper grinder.

Sugar, often added to sausage mixes to balance the sharp taste of salt and other flavorings, contributes its own qualities to the finished product. Plain granulated sugar will do the job, but when you experiment with recipes, you might try brown sugar, honey, or maple syrup for a subtle change of flavor. In the form of dextrose, sugar is an ingredient in premixed cures.

Extenders and Binders

Sausage extenders and binders include soy protein concentrate, soy flour, ground rusks or breadcrumbs, and nonfat dry milk. There is a common misconception that they are added to sausage to "extend" the meat and keep the price down, like watering down the soup. This isn't the case. These ingredients are added to some sausages to make them more moist and juicy or to give them a particular texture.

What homemade sausage *doesn't* include are additives, colorants, extra water, MSG, odd pieces of meat tissue, stabilizers, and other ingredients that go into commercial sausage. No more mystery meat or hunks of gristle in your sausage when you make your own.

Casings

Sausage has to be stuffed into something. If you think of sausage as the world's first "convenience food," and with edible packaging to boot, you can understand why the intestinal tract of a pig, cow, or sheep makes a handy holder for chopped meat and seasonings. But there are alternatives to natural casings.

Natural casings. Before you wrinkle your nose about intestines, rest assured that they are scrupulously cleaned before use. Once flushed out and packed in salt to keep them fresh, the innards — we'll call them "natural casings" at this stage — are usually sealed in airtight bags and kept frozen or refrigerated. Sheep and hog casings are digestible and are permeable to moisture and smoke.

Buy natural casings based on the diameter of the sausages you want to make: Sheep casings are the smallest of the natural casings, ranging from lamb (¾ inch; 20 mm) to sheep (just

---

FRESHNESS: IT'S ESSENTIAL

Whether you buy your sausage meat, raise and butcher your own livestock, bag your own game, or catch your own fish or shellfish, there is one cardinal rule that must be followed faithfully: All meat — any source of protein — must be *very, very fresh*.

Ground-up meat has a proportionately greater surface area than the same weight before it is ground. The more surface area, the larger the breeding ground for bacteria. Bacteria thrive at temperatures between 40 and 140°F (4 and 60°C). This means that your fresh ingredients must be kept refrigerated at all times so that bacteria will not have a chance to reproduce and taint the meat. *Keep ingredients clean, cold, and covered* until you are ready to make your sausage.

For vegetarian ingredients, spoilage is not quite as great a concern, assuming you use common sense, but freshness is always important to the flavor. A sausage is only as good as its components.

The same is true for seasonings. Throw out that dusty tin of powdered sage or the tired curry powder you got from your mother ages ago. Herbs and spices do not keep their flavors for more than 6 months, sometimes less. Fresh, bright-tasting seasonings make a world of difference.

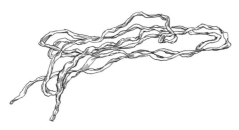

Natural casings look dry and stringy when first taken from the container; they stretch out as you stuff them.

over 1 inch; 26 mm) in diameter. Sheep casings, the most delicate of the natural casings, are often used for hot dogs.

Hog casings come in several sizes for home sausage making. The smallest casings are about 1¼ inches (32 to 35 mm), used for bratwurst and Italian sausage. The intermediate size, approximately 1½ inches (35 to 38 mm), is used for knockwurst. Larger-diameter casings are 2 inches (42 mm) or more.

The recipes in this book generally specify a type of casing; however, you have the option to make a smaller- or larger-diameter sausage than suggested. Hog casings are considered to be the "all-purpose" casing.

The most used beef casings are called *beef bungs*, *beef rounds*, and *beef middles*. Beef casings are larger, 2½ to 4 inches in diameter. Bungs and middles are generally used for bologna, veal sausage, and cooked salami, and the rounds for Mettwurst or ring bologna. Because beef casings tend to be tough, they are usually peeled away and discarded before the sausage is eaten.

Collagen casings are natural in the sense that they are made from edible protein from animal connective tissues and formed mechanically into casings. Collagen casings are made in small sizes ideal for breakfast links, and they can be used for fresh, smoked, and dried sausages. Collagen casings do not stretch the way natural casings do, so you must take care not to overfill them. Collagen casings are usually sold sealed in plastic. You may notice a rather unpleasant odor when you open the package; this will dissipate. Do not rinse the collagen casings or get them wet, as they are easier to work with when they are dry.

Artificial and Inedible Casings. Fibrous casings are popular among commercial sausage makers because they are uniform in size and easy to use. They are not edible and must be peeled away before you eat the sausage.

Cellulose and plastic casings are relative newcomers to the artificial casing field. They can be used for vegetarian sausages, but must be removed before cooking and eating. For sausages that are cooked in water or steam (like braunschweiger), plastic casings work well.

Muslin casings, sometimes used for large salamis and summer sausage, can be purchased or homemade. You need not be a Betsy Ross to stitch up a muslin casing. For instructions, see the box on page 69 following the recipe for Liverwurst.

Researchers are trying to perfect an edible vegetarian casing, but none is available at this writing.

Casings can be purchased from sausage-supply houses, meat-packing companies, butcher shops (although the neighborhood butcher is a dying breed, unfortunately), and ethnic groceries. See our Resources list on page 272 for names and addresses of some suppliers. We recommend natural casings for most sausage.

SAUSAGE AND YOUR HEALTH

Fat. Salt. Chemical additives. For some time now, nutritionists and scientists have been telling us to decrease or eliminate them from our diets. True, we need some fat and salt to survive, but not as much as most people consume. And where does sausage fit into this picture? Many commercial pork sausages derive well over half of their calories from fat and have more than their share of salt and additives. Let's take a closer look at the role of fat, salt, and additives in our diet.

Let's Talk about Fat

The U.S. Department of Agriculture (USDA) and the U.S. Department of Health and Human Services have published *Dietary Guidelines for Americans*, which recommends that less than 30 percent of our diet come from fat. Yet most of us regularly consume far more than that (the "figure," no pun intended, is about 50 percent of the diet for the average American). If that "average American" could be found, he or she would be chubby, pleasingly plump, robust — yet a person whose health may be compromised by the burden of all those extra pounds and the overconsumption of high-fat and high-cholesterol foods.

In the quest for a "healthy" diet, some folks choose the opposite extreme, seeking out fat-free foods in every category. This strategy is rarely effective, often frustrating, and almost never satisfying. (Statistics from the American Meat Institute show that consumers are moving away from fat-free and low-fat hot dogs, with sales dropping 10 percent and 37.2 percent, respectively, in a recent year.)

Some fat is necessary for our health. Fat stores energy, transports fat-soluble vitamins (A, D, E, and K), builds connective tissue, develops new cells, and keeps our skin supple and our hair shiny. In addition, fat is a flavor carrier. It makes food taste better, brighter, and less bland; it also keeps food moist and fresh. So the trick is to eat enough fat but not too much.

Fat is a traditional and necessary ingredient in sausage, helping to bind the various ingredients and carry the flavors of the seasonings. Without a small amount of fat, sausage is too dry. We've modified the recipes in this book to eliminate excessive fat but retain enough to create a good sausage. Most of our sausages are made primarily from lean meat with a small amount of added fat, usually between 10 and 20 percent of the total meat/fat mix. You may prefer the texture of sausages with the traditional 25 to 30 percent fat; experiment. (By way of comparison, many commercial hot dogs and other sausages derive more than 50 percent of their calories from fat.) The seafood, poultry, and vegetarian sausages are particularly lean. Sometimes we add moisture to sausage by adding chopped fruit, vegetables, or tofu rather than extra fat.

Food trends, scares, and fads come and go. In the end, moderation seems to be the best answer.

A Word (or Two) about Salt

Like fat, salt is a double-edged sword. You can not live without it, but too much can kill you. Salt is important in the human diet because it plays a role in how the body balances water and dissolved salts and minerals and regulates them in the cells. Without a proper balance, virtually every bodily function ceases.

On the other hand, about 20 percent of the population is known to be "sodium sensitive," which means that intake of sodium (half of the salt molecule, sodium chloride) makes their blood pressure rise. Even in people who do not have this sensitivity, too much salt in the diet makes the kidneys work too hard.

Our bodies need only a teaspoon of salt a day (that's 2,000 milligrams of sodium), counting salt already in food, plus whatever extra we shake over our plate. Sausage tends to be salty because of the role played by salt as a curing, binding, and flavoring agent. (However, modern sausage is nowhere near as salty as the salt-dried meats of an earlier age, some of which required extensive soaking and rinsing just to be edible.)

We have formulated the recipes in this book so they use enough salt to produce sausages with good taste and good texture. In *fresh* sausages, you can totally adjust the amount of salt to your taste; you can even eliminate it, although you may miss what it contributes to the taste. We recommend using kosher salt. In *cured* sausage, because salt helps dry out the meat and prevent bacterial growth, it is best to use the amounts we recommend as a minimum amount. Pre-mixed cures contain both salt and a curing agent, usually sodium nitrite, usually in a dextrose carrier.

What about Nitrates and Nitrites?

If you plan to make dried or semi-dried sausages, such as pepperoni or others that USDA would categorize as ready-to-eat, you will want to read on. Potassium nitrate (saltpeter), sodium nitrate, and sodium nitrite are used to make many of these sausages (USDA mandates that none of these ingredients may be used in *fresh sausage*). Of all of the additives in food, few have attained the notoriety of the nitrates and nitrite, which in high doses and under certain conditions are known to be carcinogenic.

When this book was first published in 1981, there was great confusion over the role of these chemicals in making cured sausages. Some people advocated eliminating them altogether; others declared them necessary because they retard spoilage (they are particularly effective in stopping the formation of botulism in processed meats) and give cured meat its pleasing rosy color. They also contribute to the flavor of the finished product.

Today, commercial sausage makers must meet strict regulations for the amounts of nitrate and nitrite they add to cured meats. Nitrites are not allowed to exceed ¼ ounce, or 7 grams, per 100 pounds of meat; nitrates must not exceed 2¾ ounces, or 77 grams, per 100 pounds of meat. The use of nitrites and nitrates cannot result in more than 200 parts per million in the finished product. Nitrates are banned from most kinds of bacon and from any food intended for babies and toddlers. In meat-processing plants, nitrates and nitrites used as curing agents are strictly controlled and regulated.

Nitrites and nitrates are still the most controversial cured-sausage ingredients, and the most tightly regulated at the commercial level. They are always handled with great caution. They are regarded as safe as long as they are used at the prescribed levels. USDA has ruled that in curing meats, the known benefits of nitrates and nitrites outweigh the potential risks.

Where Does This Leave the Home Sausage Maker?

It is extremely difficult to meet the federal regulations when you make cured sausage on a small scale at home. You know, for example, that sodium nitrite may not exceed ¼ ounce (7 grams) per 100 pounds of meat. For a batch of sausage using 10 pounds of meat, this would mean weighing out 0.7 gram of pure sodium nitrite and figuring out how to distribute it evenly throughout your meat.

For this reason, we strongly recommend that you use a commercial premixed cure in any recipe for cured sausage. Use the commercial curing mix at the levels recommended by the supplier. Premixed cures replace the saltpeter in older recipes.

One example of a premixed cure is Prague Powder #1, a common "all-purpose" cure containing 6¼ percent sodium nitrite. The recommended quantity is a level ¼ teaspoon per pound of meat, which works out to 2½ teaspoons of the cure mix for 10 pounds of meat.

An example of a less concentrated mix is Morton Salt's "Tender Quick" mix, a fast-cure that contains 0.5 percent sodium nitrate and 0.5 percent sodium nitrite and is used in some recipes at the rate of 1 teaspoon per pound of meat.

Many of the recipes that have come down through the years still call for saltpeter, or potassium nitrate. Most sausage supply companies no longer sell saltpeter, but you may be able to find it in some

HOW TOXIC IS THIS STUFF, ANYWAY?

According to an article called "Nitrite in Meat" published by the University of Minnesota in 1992, the fatal dose of potassium nitrate (saltpeter) for adults is in the range of 30 to 35 grams (slightly more than 1 ounce) consumed as a single dose. (It would be very hard to gag down that much, for the stuff is salty and bitter.) The fatal dose of sodium nitrite is in the range of 22 to 23 milligrams per kilogram of body weight. To be killed outright by sodium nitrite, a 154-pound adult would have to consume 18.57 pounds of cured meat (figuring 200 ppm of sodium nitrite) at a single sitting.

Some say that people normally consume more nitrates from vegetables than from cured meat products; spinach, beets, radishes, celery, onions, and cabbages contain high concentrations of nitrates. (No wonder kids don't like to eat their vegetables!)

As for nitrites, part of the controversy stems from research that showed that, under certain conditions not yet fully understood, nitrites combined with proteins to form compounds known as nitrosamines, particularly when bacon, a cured meat, was overcooked. Nitrosamines are known carcinogens in test animals. Of course, not all cured meats contain nitrosamines. And, a small amount of ascorbic acid (vitamin C) added to a cure mix greatly reduces their formation (USDA now requires adding vitamin C to bacon cures).

The conclusion of the Minnesota report: Nitrite as it is used in meat such as sausages is considered safe because its known benefits outweigh the potential risks. On the other hand, if you are concerned about limiting the amount of nitrites and nitrates in your diet, you may decide to stick with the fresh sausages, of which there are many delicious choices.

drugstores. If you persist in using saltpeter, be sure that it is food-grade. Today, nitrates are used only in sausages that undergo a slow cure. During the curing process, nitrate (sodium or potassium) breaks down to form nitrite. USDA allows nitrates to be used at the rate of only 1 to 3 ounces per 100 pounds of meat, depending on the preparation, or approximately ¼ of an ounce (about 1 teaspoon) for 10 pounds of meat. It is difficult to distribute such a small amount evenly in 10 pounds of meat, hence our recommendation to use a premixed cure instead. If you find an old recipe calling for saltpeter, *do not* exceed using 1 teaspoon for every 10 pounds of meat, even if the recipe calls for more.

Never exceed the amount of cure called for in the recipe. Be sure to measure carefully. A teaspoonful is always measured level, not heaping. *Always* keep nitrates and nitrites out of the hands (and mouths) of children and away from pets.

In some recipes for cured sausage, ascorbic acid (vitamin C) is added to help with color retention. It does not prevent spoilage and does not substitute for curing salts. Buy pure crystalline ascorbic acid at a pharmacy (vitamin C tablets contain binders and other ingredients that you would not want in your sausage).

CHAPTER 3

Making and Cooking Sausages:
The Essential Techniques

Sausage links and patties are easy to make
at home, and when you grind and season
your own, you know exactly what you've got —
good, fresh meat.

— Julia Child, *The Way to Cook*

ONCE YOU HAVE MASTERED THE BASIC STEPS in sausage making, you will be able to follow any recipe in this book with ease. In this chapter, you'll learn to make fresh sausage; the best ways to cook and store your homemade sausage; and how to dry, cure, or smoke your sausage.

The recipe here and most others in the book call for stuffing the sausage into casings. For most fresh sausage recipes, you have the option to leave the sausage in its bulk form or shape it into patties, as you wish.

(for detailed instructions, see pages 28 to 33)

1. Prepare natural casing by rinsing, flushing, and soaking.

2. Make the sausage stuffing by cutting the meat and fat into 1-inch cubes (freeze before grinding), measuring all seasonings, and kneading together the meat, fat, and seasonings.

3. Grind the meat, using your preferred method. With a hand grinder, grind the sausage ingredients together twice, adding the seasonings after the first grinding. Fry up a small amount of the mixture and taste to see if you want to adjust any seasonings.

4. Stuff the casing. Gather the sausage casing over the funnel and feed the ground mixture through the funnel until it reaches the opening. Tie the end of the casing into a knot and begin feeding small amounts of meat mixture through the funnel, filling the entire length of casing as you go. Maintain an even thickness of meat throughout the length of the casing.

5. Inspect the sausage for air bubbles and prick any you find with a pin or sausage perforator.

6. Twist off the sausage links, beginning at the tied end. Grasp about 3 inches of sausage and give it two or three twists to form a link. When the entire casing is done, cut the links apart with a sharp knife.

7. Refrigerate the sausages for a couple of hours or overnight to meld the flavors and firm the texture.

8. Cook the sausage thoroughly. Enjoy!

Run cool water over the casing to rinse salt from the outside. (step 1)

Hold the casing open under the nozzle of the faucet and run water through it, gently at first. (step 2)

COUNTRY-STYLE BREAKFAST SAUSAGE

- 4 feet small (1½-inch diameter) hog or sheep casing
- 2½ pounds lean pork butt
- ½ pound pork fat
- 1½ teaspoons dried sage
- 1½ teaspoons kosher or coarse salt
- ¾ teaspoon freshly ground white or black pepper (fine grind)
- ¾ teaspoon sugar
- ½ teaspoon crushed red pepper
- ½ teaspoon dried thyme
- ¼ teaspoon dried summer savory

MAKING FRESH SAUSAGE

Working with the equipment and ingredients (including casings) described in the preceding pages, you will begin by making about 3 pounds of fresh Country-style Breakfast Sausage (see ingredient list below). It takes about 45 minutes to soak and flush the casing; during this time you can prepare the sausage stuffing. Filling the casing will take another 15 to 30 minutes. You can easily make, cook, and eat your sausage on the same day.

Preparation

We've already discussed the concept of *mise en place*, so we assume you've gotten everything ready for your first sausage-making adventure. All of your equipment and ingredients are on hand and ready for use.

Getting the Casing Ready

These instructions are for traditional natural casings (What can we say? We're old-fashioned.) packed in salt. If you are using a casing packed in brine or another type of casing, follow the supplier's directions for preparing it.

1. Snip off about 4 feet of casing and rinse it under cool running water to remove any salt. Place in a bowl of cool water to cover and let it soak for about half an hour.

2. Rinse the casing again under cool running water. Hold one end of the casing open under the faucet nozzle.

Holding the knife blade away from you, cut out a section of casing with a break in it from the length of casing. (step 2)

Holding the casing in place, turn on the cold water gently, then more forcefully, to flush out any salt in the casing and pinpoint any tears or breaks. (Should you find a tear or break, simply cut out that section.)

3. Soak the casing again. This time, add 1 tablespoon of white vinegar for each cup of cool water in the bowl. The vinegar softens the casing and makes it more transparent, which makes the finished sausage look better. Leave the casing in the vinegar/water solution until you are ready to stuff it, then rinse well and drain.

Making the Sausage Stuffing

4. Cut the meat and fat into 1-inch cubes and place in the freezer for about 30 minutes before grinding to firm up the texture.

5. Measure the seasonings (for our introductory recipe, the seasonings are the sage, salt, white pepper, sugar, crushed red pepper, thyme, and savory) and combine them in a small bowl. Set aside.

6. Grind the meat.

If you are using a *hand grinder*, put the meat and fat through the fine disk (¼ inch or smaller). Mix the seasonings into the meat with your hands, kneading the mixture well. Freeze the mixture again for about 30 minutes, then put it back through the fine disk a second time.

If you are using a *food processor*, process the meat and fat to a fine dice and mix in the seasonings by hand after the entire batch has been processed.

If you are using a *grinder attachment* on a heavy-duty mixer, grind the meat and fat first and then mix in the seasonings by hand after the entire batch has been processed.

If you are using an *electric grinder* with a sausage-stuffing attachment, you may sprinkle the seasonings over the meat and fat and toss the mixture with your hands before grinding, since the grinding and stuffing will be one continuous operation. But the texture of your sausage will be better if you combine the meat, fat, and seasonings by hand.

If you will be stuffing the mixture into a sausage casing, you will want it to be firm but not dry. When recipes suggest adding liquid as needed to achieve a good consistency for stuffing, be careful not to make the mixture too wet.

Push the meat and fat through a hand grinder, allowing it to fall onto a plate. (step 6)

Electric mixer: Use the pusher to move meat through the grinder attachment with an electric mixer. (step 6)

Mixing by hand: When mixing in the seasonings by hand, as when you've ground meat in a food processor, mix thoroughly to distribute all of the seasonings through the meat mixture. (step 6)

7. Test the sausage. At this point, you can quickly fry up a small amount of the sausage mixture and taste the cooked sausage to see if you want to adjust seasonings. Mix any additional seasonings evenly into the raw mixture. (For recipes for cured or smoked sausages, you may omit this step. The additional processing will affect the flavor, making it difficult to adjust the seasonings at this early stage.)

Stuffing the Sausage

8. Stuff the casing.

If you are using a *sausage funnel* or the *hand grinder's sausage funnel*, coat the funnel well with water or grease it, then draw the sausage casing over the funnel so that the entire length is gathered onto the funnel and the end of the casing is even with the funnel opening.

Push the ground meat mixture through the funnel or feed spout with your fingers or meat pusher until it reaches the lip of the funnel opening. Pull about 2 inches of casing off the end of the funnel and tie it into a knot.

> ### UNSTICKY FINGERS
>
> When you are mixing sausage with your hands, place a bowl of cold water nearby. Rinse your hands frequently in the cold water so that the fat won't stick to your fingers.

Feeding small amounts of meat through the funnel at a time, continue stuffing the entire casing. Pack the casing firmly but not to the bursting point, maintaining an even thickness throughout the length of the casing. When all the meat has been used, slide any leftover casing off the funnel. Proceed to step 9 (pricking the sausages).

If you are using the *stuffing attachment on a heavy-duty mixer*, grease the stuffer and slide 3 to 4 feet of the casing onto the stuffer. Tie off the end of the casing (see illustration at right).

Turn the mixer on. Slowly feed the ground meat into the hopper using the pusher. Hold the tied end of the casing in one hand and guide the meat mixture as it fills the casing. It may be necessary to repack the stuffer with casing to use all of the meat mixture.

If you are using an *electric grinder*, turn it on. Feed the seasoned meat and fat cubes into the hopper. When the ground meat is flush with the opening of the tube, turn off the grinder. Pull about 2 inches of casing off the end of the tube and tie it into a knot.

Feeding small amounts of meat through the funnel or tube at a time, continue stuffing the entire casing with the electric stuffer. Pack the casing firmly but not to the bursting point, maintaining an even thickness throughout the length of the casing.

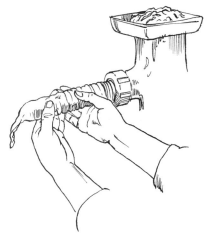

Slide the full length of the casing onto the funnel. Here, that is demonstrated on the stuffing attachment on an electric grinder. (step 8)

Tie off the end of the casing when you begin stuffing sausage. (step 8)

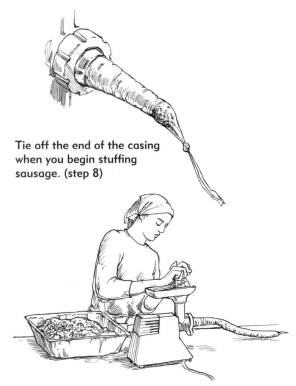

Electric grinder: Feed small amounts of meat at a time through the stuffing attachment. It helps to have an assistant holding the casing.

Crank stuffer: It helps to have two people when using a medium- to large-capacity stuffer. One person operates the crank as another eases the casing off the stuffing tube, being careful not to cause friction that will make the casing hang up and burst. (step 8)

Water stuffer: With a water-powered stuffer, one person can easily fill the casings. (step 8)

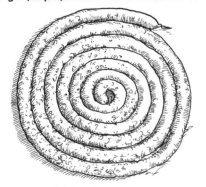

The finished length of sausage-filled casing is now ready to be twisted into links. (step 8)

When all the meat has been used, slide any leftover casing off the funnel. Proceed to step 9 (pricking the sausages).

If you are using a *sausage stuffer*, generally the steps will be filling the spout or cylinder, fitting the casing over the nozzle, then pushing the meat mixture evenly through the device into the casing. There are so many types and models of stuffers — from push to crank to electric — you will have to rely on the instructions that came with your model for specifics. Proceed to step 9 (pricking the sausages).

9. Prick the sausages. Inspect the length of the filled casings, looking for any air bubbles or pockets. Prick the bubbles with a pin or a sausage perforator. Air pockets can fill with fat during cooking; in dried sausage, they can allow mold to grow.

10. Twist off the links. Beginning at the tied end of the stuffed casing, grasp about 3 inches of sausage and gently give it two or three twists in one direction to form a link.

Continue twisting off links until the entire casing is done. (Some sausage makers alternate the direction in which they twist the links, but this is not essential.) With a very sharp knife, cut the links apart and cut off any empty casing at the end. The casing will fit the sausage mixture like a glove and the meat will not squeeze out.

Meld Flavors

11. To allow the flavors to meld together and penetrate the meat, arrange the links in a single layer on a platter, cover with plastic wrap, and refrigerate for at least a couple of hours, preferably overnight. Do not mature them outside of the refrigerator unless you have a spot (cold porch or cellar) that will not go over 40°F (4°C). Use a thermometer to be sure.

If you are not going to eat the sausage within 2 days, wrap the links individually in plastic wrap, pack them into a plastic freezer bag, and freeze. Frozen sausages will hold their flavor for 2 to 3 months. Thaw them completely before cooking (see page 36).

SAUSAGE SAFETY

No one wants to eat spoiled food. It often tastes rotten (literally), and it makes us sick. Spoilage is caused by the action of microorganisms on food. These organisms include molds, yeasts, and bacteria.

Bacteria are the main problem for the home sausage maker. When some bacteria are allowed to reproduce in an uncontrolled environment, they can cause illness and even death.

The five bacteria responsible for most foodborne illness are: *Salmonella*, *Clostridium perfringens*, *Staphylococcus aureus*, *Campylobacter*, and *Clostridium botulinum*. All are found

Gently twist the stuffed casing two or three times in one direction; gentleness is especially important with natural casing, as it breaks more easily than other types. (step 10)

Holding a sausage link in your hand, cut the links apart at the twists. (step 10)

Fresh sausages benefit from a brief aging period in the refrigerator; it allows the flavors to meld and penetrate the meat. (step 11)

CLEAN, COLD, AND COVERED, FOR SAFETY'S SAKE

Anyone who has ever been felled by food poisoning might put cleanliness *ahead* of godliness as a virtue. Even a mild case of food poisoning is no picnic in the park, and, at its worst, can be fatal.

When you make sausage at home, you take on the responsibility of providing food that is both safe and delicious. Here are the basic rules.

Ingredients. Starting at the grocery store, be sure that raw meat and poultry are packaged securely and kept separate from any foods that will be eaten without further cooking. To avoid cross contamination, take extra care that meat juices do not drip onto other food or onto countertops or utensils. (If they do, wash food in soap and hot water and rinse thoroughly or discard; disinfect countertops and utensils.) Refrigerate anything that can spoil. Keep it cold right up to the moment you start preparing the sausage. Never let meat warm to more than 40°F (4°C). Keep it as close to the freezing point as possible to bring bacterial action to a standstill. Chilling the meat also makes it easier to grind.

Your Kitchen. Scrub with hot water and detergent all surfaces that will be in contact with the meat. Be particularly careful of your cutting board. Disinfect wooden boards and countertops with a solution of 1 tablespoon of chlorine bleach in 1 gallon of water. Rinse everything thoroughly and allow to air-dry. Be sure the room is cool — under 70°F (21°C) — when you are making sausage.

Utensils. Pour boiling water over all utensils and your grinder — anything that will come into contact with the meat. Allow everything to cool completely before proceeding so that the residual heat does not warm up the meat and encourage the growth of bacteria.

Your Person. Remove rings and wash your hands carefully, scrubbing under your fingernails with a nail brush. Wash your hands again if you are called away from your sausage making to answer the phone, put the cat out, or any other activity. Put on a clean apron.

You are ready to begin.

throughout our environment and in most foods. All can cause illness and even death when they are allowed to multiply at will.

Salmonella bacteria are the most common source of food poisoning in humans. These bacteria can survive in frozen and dried foods, but do not reproduce at temperatures below 40°F (4°C) or above 140°F (60°C). They are destroyed if food is held above 140°F (60°C) for 10 minutes.

Clostridium perfringens can also strike if food is held at improper (too warm) temperatures for an extended period of time.

Staphylococcus aureus, like *Clostridium perfringens*, is inactive at temperatures below 40°F (4°C) and above 140°F (60°C). Staph germs that are allowed to multiply form a toxin that cannot be boiled, baked, or otherwise cooked away.

Campylobacter grows best at 108°F (42°C) to 113°F (45°C) and is the most common bacterial cause of diarrheal illness in the United States. Most cases of illness from this bug are associated with handling raw poultry or eating raw or undercooked poultry meat. Even one drop of juice from raw chicken meat can infect a person. Freezing reduces the number of bacteria on raw meat, and they are killed by thorough cooking to 170°F or 77°C for breast meat; 180°F or 82°C for thigh meat.

Clostridium botulinum organisms, though rare, are the biggest villains in the arsenal. They love room temperature and moisture, and they are anaerobic, meaning that they thrive and produce toxin in the absence of air. Under certain conditions, the bacteria produce spores; when the spores reproduce, they give off a powerful, deadly toxin. Two cups of the toxin could kill every human being in the city of Chicago. The toxin itself can be killed by 10 to 20 minutes of boiling, but the spores require 6 *hours* of boiling to stop them from reproducing. One of the main reasons nitrates and nitrites are used in making cured sausages is that those agents are effective against *Clostridium botulinum*.

How to Prevent Spoilage

To prevent bacteria from setting up shop in our homemade sausage, be sure to follow the cleanliness procedures described in "Clean, Cold, and Covered," (see previous page). This includes sterilizing all utensils and equipment, avoiding cross contamination, keeping your kitchen clean, and washing your hands thoroughly and often. (Bacteria absolutely *thrive* at body temperature.) Keep meat cool at all times, and work quickly so it doesn't have a chance to warm up.

A number of other factors inhibit the growth of bacteria in food, and sausage making has evolved to take advantage of all of these inhibiting factors to ensure the safety and edibility of the finished product.

The factors inhibiting bacterial growth are:

- Temperatures below 40°F (4°C) and above 140°F (60°C), which is why we stress keeping everything cold, then cooking it to well above 140°F (60°C).
- An acidic environment.
- High sugar content, though most sausage recipes don't call for enough to count.
- A lack of moisture (no known form of earthly life, even bacteria, can thrive without water), as when sausages are dried.
- Alcohol (to some extent), which is added to flavor some sausages.
- Garlic, cayenne, and certain other spices with antibiotic properties (to some extent) .
- Thoroughly cooking sausage by frying, grilling, or other means kills germs. Hot-smoking sausage produces enough heat to cook the sausage and kill the germs, though cold-smoking alone does not.
- Some chemical additives, including the nitrates and nitrites and ascorbic acid.

COOKING AND STORING SAUSAGE

When you've invested time and effort — especially if you hand-cranked to grind or stuff your links — to make delicious sausage, you'll want to be sure to cook it and store it to preserve the quality and flavor.

How to Cook Your Sausage

Fresh sausage should be cooked slowly and thoroughly until its internal temperature, as measured with an instant-read thermometer, reaches the following temperatures recommended by USDA and the Food and Drug Administration:

Beef, lamb, pork, fish, or game sausage: 160°F (71°C)

Poultry sausage: 165°F (74°C)

A cooked fresh sausage link will be firm to the touch and hot all the way through.

One good rule of thumb is to cook sausage links made from pork or beef for about 20 minutes for a 1-inch-diameter link. Sausage that is pan-fried or grilled should be browned evenly. (Sausage that is poached will not show the same color change.) For fatter sausages, cook another 5 to 10 minutes, then measure the internal temperature or cut off a slice and check to be sure the sausage is cooked through. Because wild game is usually quite lean, sausage made from it can be on the dry side. Treat it as you would any fresh sausage, but do not overcook.

Fresh sausage links made from poultry or seafood will cook more quickly: Ten to 15 minutes usually will suffice. Sausage that is panfried or grilled should be browned evenly. (Sausage that is poached will not show the same color change.) Measure the internal temperature or cut

TEMPERATURES RELATED TO SAFE HANDLING AND CONSUMPTION OF MEAT

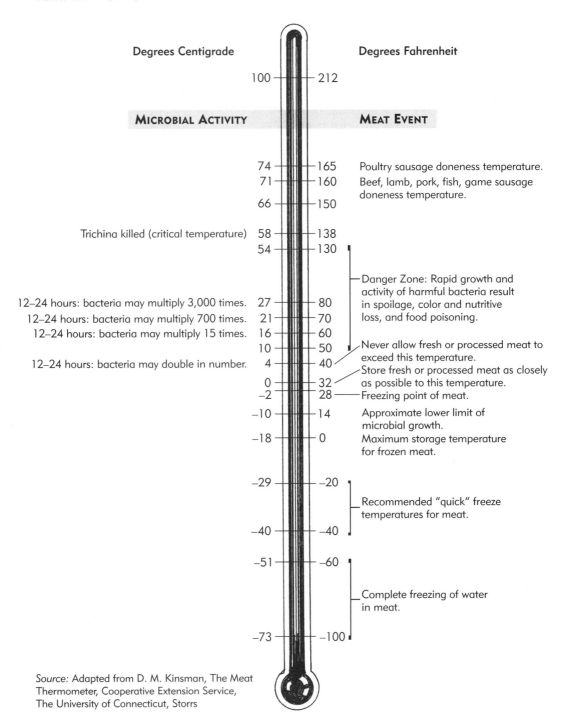

Degrees Centigrade

Degrees Fahrenheit

100 — 212

MICROBIAL ACTIVITY

MEAT EVENT

74 — 165   Poultry sausage doneness temperature.
71 — 160   Beef, lamb, pork, fish, game sausage
66 — 150   doneness temperature.

Trichina killed (critical temperature)   58 — 138
54 — 130

Danger Zone: Rapid growth and
activity of harmful bacteria result
12–24 hours: bacteria may multiply 3,000 times.   27 — 80   in spoilage, color and nutritive
12–24 hours: bacteria may multiply 700 times.   21 — 70   loss, and food poisoning.
12–24 hours: bacteria may multiply 15 times.   16 — 60
10 — 50   Never allow fresh or processed meat to
12–24 hours: bacteria may double in number.   4 — 40   exceed this temperature.
Store fresh or processed meat as closely
0 — 32   as possible to this temperature.
−2 — 28   Freezing point of meat.

−10 — 14   Approximate lower limit of
microbial growth.
−18 — 0   Maximum storage temperature
for frozen meat.

−29 — −20

Recommended "quick" freeze
temperatures for meat.

−40 — −40

−51 — −60

Complete freezing of water
in meat.

−73 — −100

Source: Adapted from D. M. Kinsman, The Meat
Thermometer, Cooperative Extension Service,
The University of Connecticut, Storrs

off a slice and check to be sure the sausage is cooked through.

Vegetarian sausage cooks quickly, and may be treated the same way as poultry and seafood sausage.

Always handle sausage links with tongs rather than spearing them with a fork or knife, because spearing allows flavorful juices to escape.

To Panfry Links. (Best for thick fresh sausages.) Starting the sausages in water helps to soften the casings and keep them from bursting; it also allows fat to be drained off. Place uncooked sausage in a covered, cold skillet with ½ cup of water. Bring to a boil, then reduce to a simmer. Cook until the sausages are almost done, about 10 minutes, depending on the size of the links. Drain thoroughly, then cook over medium-high heat, turning often with tongs or by shaking the pan, until the links are browned evenly, about 5 to 10 minutes longer.

To Pan-Broil Links. (Best for delicately seasoned fresh sausage and low-fat sausages, such as seafood. Also a good technique for most smoked or precooked sausages.) Heat a large heavy skillet over medium heat, then add 1 to 2 teaspoons of oil and the sausages. Cover and cook, turning the sausages often with tongs, until evenly browned. Fresh sausages will take 10 to 15 minutes to cook, depending on the type. Test for doneness with an instant-read thermometer. Precooked sausages will

Simmering sausages in water helps to soften casings and keep them from bursting.

need only about 5 minutes to brown and heat through.

To Poach Links. Gently cook sausages in simmering liquid (water, wine, beer, or other mixture) over low heat for about 20 minutes for 1-inch-diameter sausages. The liquid should just cover the sausages. Allow more or less time for larger or smaller sausages. Check for doneness by inserting an instant-read thermometer. You can eat poached sausages hot or refrigerate them for later use. Once cooked, they can be eaten cold or fried, microwaved, or grilled to rewarm.

To Bake Links. Sausages may be baked in a preheated 350°F (177°C) oven for 10 minutes. Increase the temperature to 425°F (218°C) and cook for 10 to 15 minutes longer, or until they test done.

To Grill Links. Poach the sausages (simmer very slowly over low heat) for 10 minutes in water or other liquid to cover. Beer is good for most pork sausages; white wine goes well with sweet or hot Italian sausage. Allow more or less time for larger or smaller sausages.

For *indoor grilling*, place the sausages on a grill pan over medium heat and cook for 10 minutes for 1-inch sausages, turning frequently, until browned.

For *outdoor grilling*, do not prick sausages before grilling, or you will lose a lot of flavor and moisture along with the fat and juices in the sausage. Grill over medium-hot coals and keep turning the sausages so they brown evenly. They should be cooked in 7 to 10 minutes on the grill. Extremely hot coals will burn the sausages.

To Broil Links. Precook the sausages by poaching them as for grilled sausages. Preheat the broiler to high. Broil the sausages for about 5 minutes, turning with tongs so they brown evenly.

Cooking Sausage Patties. Sausage patties may be pan-fried over medium-low heat, grilled, or broiled as you would hamburgers. Their cooking time will vary considerably depending on the type of meat or vegetarian ingredients they are made of, as well as their thickness. They should be hot all the way through, their juices should run clear, and meat sausages should no longer be pink in the center. Turn them once during the cooking time.

Cooking Bulk Sausage. To cook bulk sausage for use in soup, stew, lasagna, and other dishes, sauté it in a skillet, breaking it up with a wooden spoon or the back of a fork, and cook until the meat is no longer pink. Shake the pan frequently so the sausage moves around and is evenly browned.

Storing Your Homemade Sausage

Fresh sausage should be kept in the refrigerator. If you are not going to cook and eat it in 2 to 3 days, wrap each link or sausage patty individually in plastic wrap, place the links or patties in a plastic freezer bag, and freeze them. To freeze bulk sausage, wrap in plastic wrap or freezer paper, then place the links in a plastic freezer bag. Homemade frozen sausage will hold its flavor and texture for up to 3 months if your freezer is set at –15°F (–26°C).

Because of its high salt and fat content, sausage is not the best candidate for long-term freezing. Salt lowers the freezing point of water, so it shortens freezer life; fat does not freeze as well as protein and carbohydrates do, so it also decreases freezer life. Frozen sausage won't spoil after 3 months, but it will begin to decline in taste and quality.

Hot dogs and other cooked sausages may be refrigerated for up to 2 weeks and frozen for up to 3 months.

Dry sausage will keep indefinitely in the refrigerator until it is sliced

THE TRICHINOSIS PROBLEM

Several cases of trichinosis are reported in the United States every year. The disease is caused by a parasitic roundworm, *Trichinella spiralis*, or trichina. The worm or its larvae can be found in some pork, deer, and bear meat in certain areas of the world, including North America. The number of cases is small because of increased public awareness and the general adoption of precautionary measures, but the risk is still there.

If you eat infected meat, the larvae travel from your intestines to your muscles, where they can lodge and form cysts, causing fever, pain, and (in extreme cases) death.

Trichinosis, however, need not be a problem for the home sausage maker. Cooking meat to an internal temperature of 137°F (58°C) kills the larvae. However, in the case of fresh pork, bear, or venison, USDA recommends that consumers cook the meat to an internal temperature of 160°F (71°C). Although this is considerably higher than temperatures at which trichinae are killed, it kills other bacteria and allows for different methods of cooking that do not always result in even distribution of temperature throughout the meat.

Pork, bear, or venison that will eventually be consumed raw, as in a dried uncooked sausage, can be made safe by pre-freezing it at –20°F (–29°C) for 6 to 12 days; –10°F (–23°C) for 10 to 20 days; or 5°F (–15°C) for 20 to 30 days. If you do this, an accurate freezer thermometer is a must! When you are ready to make sausage, partially thaw the meat, then cut and grind it as the recipe directs. (It's easier to cut and grind very cold, firm meat.)

These conditions have been set by the USDA for commercial packers and are perfectly safe for the home sausage maker as long as you follow them faithfully. Never taste raw pork, bear, or venison and never sample sausage if it contains raw pork, bear, or venison that hasn't been treated as described above. When handling raw bear or venison, be sure to wear rubber gloves, especially if you have any cuts or scratches on your hands.

The exception would be if you are eating sausage in a part of the world known to be free of trichinosis. In Southeast Asia and parts of Europe (Italy, for example, famous for its prosciutto from Parma), raw pork is eaten without dire health consequences.

open. A perfectly cured and dried sausage can theoretically be hung in the open air for weeks without spoiling. If you live where it is cool and dry, this will extend the open-air life of your cured sausage. Once you cut into a sausage, however, it is best to refrigerate it and consume it within 3 weeks.

Sausage may also be canned. As a low-acid food, it must be canned using the pressure canning process. Information about pressure canning and instructions for canning sausage may be obtained from USDA or your local Cooperative Extension Service. See Resources (page 272) for contact information for USDA and for Agriculture and Agri-Food Canada.

HOW TO DRY SAUSAGE

If you have all the equipment necessary to make fresh sausage, you need only one more thing to make dried sausage: a cold place in which to dry your sausage and let it hang for a few weeks. (You may also want to invest in a smoker, which we'll describe in a few pages.) Choose a place that is convenient and not needed for other purposes while the sausage is drying.

Dried and semidried sausages were born of the desire to preserve meat for eating long after an animal was hunted. The first sausage maker was already accustomed to packing meat in salt to preserve it. Perhaps he noticed that salt from a certain source seemed to give meat a more appealing red color and a heartier taste than other salted meats. Perhaps she was a village woman known for her skillful use of herbs and her ingenuity in using up all parts of a slaughtered animal, including the stomach and the intestines. Perhaps they pooled their talents and added special curing salts (saltpeter, a naturally occurring source of nitrate) to their meat mixture and stuffed it into the cleaned-out entrails of the beast they had just slaughtered. If they decided to hang the whole business to dry in the heat and smoke of a campfire, you could say that they had just invented the first cured smoked sausage.

The idea that one could butcher an animal in the fall and still eat the meat the following spring must have been revolutionary. From these early experiments in meat preservation came all the types of historic, locally famous, unique cured sausage we enjoy today.

One of our favorite pastimes is prowling around in ethnic grocery stores — the "mom-and-pop" type — because so many of them preserve the old-country tradition of making or preparing much of what they sell. Walk into a store in one neighborhood we know on a Thursday afternoon, and you will invariably find the proprietor mixing up a batch of Italian sausage for the weekend trade. Hanging from a wire stretched above the meat case are dozens of links of salami and pepperoni along with balls of aged provolone cheese. Lining one of the walls are barrels of oil-cured olives and baskets of dried codfish — *baccalà* — and bags of homemade pasta. The aromas bring on herculean hunger pangs.

The proprietor won't part with his secret recipes, but he takes pride in making his sausages in full view of anyone present. Not every sausage today is extruded from a huge machine and packaged in plastic. Some of the best things in life are still made by hand.

Types of Dried Sausage

Dried sausages are categorized in two ways based on how they are processed. Dried sausages, which may or may not be fermented, are essentially preserved by a long, air-drying process. They are made by mixing curing ingredients, such as salt and

DRY SAUSAGE SAFETY

Dry sausages — such as pepperoni and summer sausage — that are preserved but never cooked have had a good safety record for hundreds if not thousands of years. But during the 1990s, some children and adults became ill from the *Escherichia coli (E. coli)* bacteria after eating dry cured salamis from a sausage plant. Somehow, the bug survived all of the processing, even in a carefully controlled commercial atmosphere.

USDA's Food Safety and Inspection Service had not, as of this writing, changed recommendations for consumer handling of dried sausage products, but the agency has required commercial producers to use new protocols in making dried, uncooked sausages.

What's a home sausage maker to do? The safest thing is to cook or smoke sausages to an internal temperature of 160°F (71°C) — 165°F (74°C) for poultry sausage — at some point before consuming them to ensure that all potentially harmful bacteria are killed.

Home-dried sausages will be free from trichinae if you've prefrozen the meat (see page 40). But you can't be certain that other potentially harmful bacteria have been killed.

If you do choose to make dry sausages that are not cooked, you should follow USDA's recommendation that people at risk (the elderly, very young children, pregnant women, and those with weakened immune systems) avoid eating them.

sodium nitrite, with ground or chopped meat, stuffing the mixture into casings, and then drying the sausage. What the early sausage makers learned was that the acid produced during the drying process and the lack of moisture in the finished meat killed the bacteria that allowed meat to spoil.

In essence, these hard, dried sausages, including pepperoni and most salamis, are never cooked. For that reason, they may pose some health risks and you should read the box on the previous page before you make or serve them.

Semidry sausages are usually smoked to fully cook and partially dry them. These sausages, including summer sausage, are semisoft. They keep well because of the way they are processed.

Where to Dry Sausage

People who live in northern climates traditionally make their dried sausages in the winter and hang them in the attic.

The Attic. If you use your attic, make sure of the following:

- The temperature must remain below 40°F (4°C) for the drying time indicated in the recipes. The temperature in the attic should not fall *below* freezing (32°F or 0°C) for extended periods of time. You don't want to freeze the sausage; you want to dry it. A humidity

level of 75 percent to 80 percent is ideal so that the sausage dries out evenly and not too quickly.

The amount of moisture in the air can be measured using a hygrometer, available at most hardware stores. However, a hygrometer is not always accurate; mechanical hygrometers may be in error by more than 20 percent. The North Dakota State University Extension Service reports that you can calibrate your hygrometer by sealing it in a plastic bag along with a cup containing ½ cup water and ¼ cup table salt. Let it sit for about 12 hours at room temperature. The meter should read about 75 percent relative humidity. If it does not, calculate the difference between the reading and 75 and make the adjustment whenever you use the meter for a reading.

Electronic meters tend to be more accurate, but they should also be calibrated, NDSU advises.

- Be certain that no birds, bats, or rodents can find their way into the attic. It would be disconcerting to find a squirrel swinging from your salami.
- The attic must be clean. Sweep away — or vacuum up — dust and dirt several days before you plan to hang the sausage. What the broom or vacuum cleaner doesn't pick up will have a chance to settle before the sausage is hung. Avoid stirring up dust while the sausage dries.

- For hanging the sausages, pound 4-inch nails, spaced 12 inches apart, halfway into a rafter. If the rafters are covered, you can construct a simple frame from 2 × 4s (see the illustration below).
- Attics are particularly effective for drying sausage if they are vented on the gable ends to provide an exchange of air and speed the drying process. Be sure the vents are covered with screening so critters can't find their way in.

A Refrigerator. If you have a second refrigerator or can obtain one cheaply, using it can be as practical as using the attic, and you can make sausage at any time of year. This is your best option if you live in a warm climate.

Remove all shelves except the top one. Tie your sausages to hang from the top rack.

Use a thermometer to make sure that the temperature remains constantly in the 38 to 40°F range (3 to 4°C). If the refrigerator has a fan (most modern ones do), it must be adjusted so it doesn't blow constantly; consult the manufacturer's instructions. Too much air movement will cause the sausage to dry on the outside before the inside has a chance to mature.

Use the refrigerator in your kitchen only as a last resort. You will be tying up the space for a long time, and the inconvenience will become a nuisance.

Other Alternatives. Use your imagination. An unheated part of the

A sausage-drying frame

house is a possibility in the winter in a cold climate. An unheated cellar might work also, but in either case, be sure the temperature and humidity are steady and there is enough ventilation.

If none of these locations works for you, investigate renting space in a local commercial meat-locker plant. Cooling rooms, used for aging meat, are usually kept at a constant temperature. This alternative may be the safest, too, because the conditions are so carefully controlled.

Drying Agents in Sausage

Dried sausages rely on three factors for preservation: alcohol, salt (and commercial curing agents), and temperature.

Alcohol begins the preservation process. In addition to being an excellent flavor enhancer, it has proven antibacterial properties. While it would be wasteful to use expensive wines and brandies from vintage years, the cheapest jug wines or brown-bag brandies are also poor choices. Cheaper wines and spirits contain agents that, when concentrated in a dried sausage, can lend an off flavor. The cardinal rule in using alcohol in food is, "If you wouldn't drink it, don't cook with it."

The alcohol evaporates, however, and so other agents are needed to continue the work.

Salt draws the moisture out of the meat, creating an environment that is hostile to the growth of molds and bacteria.

Curing agents help prevent spoilage, give sausage an appealing rosy color, and contribute flavor of their own. We recommend that you used premixed curing agents in the quantity listed on the package. See pages 21 to 24 for a discussion about the reasons why.

Temperature is almost as important as salt. The nasty little microbes that cause spoilage can't multiply at low temperatures.

The drying process intensifies and concentrates flavors, and this is what gives dried sausages their "spicy" reputation. Use only the purest and freshest herbs and spices.

HOW TO SMOKE SAUSAGE

The smoking process is done with one of two methods: a "cold smoke" or a "hot smoke."

Smoking meat at temperatures above 175°F (80°C) is called hot smoking. It cooks the meat while imparting a pleasant smoky flavor. The cooking temperatures are hot enough to stop unwanted bacteria and other organisms from multiplying. The combination of smoke and heat fixes the color and makes protein move to the surface of the sausage so it will hold its shape when the casing is removed. Hot-smoked sausage is as perishable as any roasted meat.

Smoking meat at temperatures below 175°F (80°C) is called cold smoking: It is basically a flavoring process. Meat that is cold-smoked is still essentially raw (unless it was pre-cooked or preserved in another manner) and must be treated as such. Usually, cold-smoked sausage has been cured with sodium nitrite or other curing agents. Cold-smoked sausage has a more intense smoke flavor than hot-smoked sausage, because uncooked sausage can absorb flavors better than cooked sausage.

Some of the recipes in this book call for both cold and hot smoking. The cold smoking contributes flavor; the hot smoking cooks the sausage.

Smoking is a technique, the basics of which can be taught. It is also an art. One learns, through practice, the "feel" of the method and the best way to turn out a consistently good product.

Smoking sausage improves its appearance and gives it a characteristic flavor and aroma. Careful attention must be paid to preventing spoilage. USDA has set forth principles and procedures for safely smoking sausage. The guidelines below are based closely on USDA recommendations.

Guidelines for Smoking Sausage

- Smoke only meat that is dry on the surface. A wet surface prevents meat from gaining a uniform smoked color.
- Hang sausages so they do not touch each other or the smokehouse wall. The entire surface of the meat must be exposed to ensure an even color.
- For your fire, burn hardwood, such as hickory, oak, apple, cherry, pear, peach, beech, chestnut, pecan, or maple. Mesquite, a hardwood shrub from the Southwest, is popular for its unique aroma. Dry corncobs may also be used. Many sausage smokers like to use damp sawdust because it produces a good smudge — that is, a fire that produces a lot of smoke with relatively little heat and is easy to control. You can also buy hardwood "briquettes" that are specially formulated so they don't flare up. Some

suppliers also sell chips from old oak wine barrels; wine-saturated oak gives the sausage a rich, unique taste.

- Never burn softwoods, such as pine, cedar, spruce, hemlock, fir, and cypress. They create oily, sooty smoke that turns the sausage dark and bitter.

Smokers

Your smokehouse can be simple or elaborate in design.

If you are a "weekend smoker" with a relatively small amount of sausage, a simple covered charcoal grill is sufficient. You can even rig up a makeshift smoker by hanging sausage beneath a heavy tarp and building a smoky fire underneath. You can convert the shell of an old refrigerator to serve as a smoker.

Here are some of the more common options, from the cheapest to the most deluxe.

Covered Charcoal Grill. For a small amount of hot-smoked sausage, use a covered charcoal grill. You will need an oven thermometer to monitor the temperature.

Prepare it by burning about 50 briquettes on the heat grate until they are covered with gray ash. Push the briquettes into two low piles on the sides, and center a pan of water between them. (You may also wish to include some soaked hardwood, for flavor.) The water will catch any dripping fat from the sausages and will create steam that helps destroy harmful bacteria. Place the sausages on the grill over the water pan. Close the lid and keep the air vents open.

A FEW DO'S AND DON'TS FOR SMOKING

DO frequently check the temperature inside your smoker. This is critical for hot smoking. Place an oven-safe thermometer inside the smoker; the air temperature in the smoker or grill should stay between 225 and 300°F (107.2 and 148.9°C) throughout the hot-smoking process.

DON'T buy a smoker that does not have a built-in thermometer.

DO use an instant-read thermometer to check the sausage temperature.

DON'T use gasoline or other accelerants to start the fire in your smoker, for the fumes and residues will contaminate your sausage. Use only approved fire starters.

DO check local building and fire codes if you are considering the construction of a permanent smokehouse.

To hot-smoke sausage, add about 10 new briquettes every hour, checking the temperature frequently to maintain the heat between 225 and 300°F (107 and 149°C) throughout the process. Follow recipe directions for times and temperatures.

Water Smoker. A vertical water smoker has a fire pan in the bottom to hold charcoal briquettes and two cooking racks near the top. A water pan above the coals adds moisture and helps regulate the temperature. A model with adjustable vents will enable you to regulate the heat and maintain an even temperature.

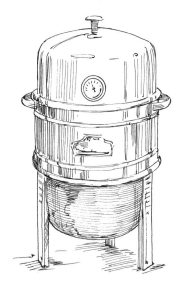

vertical water smoker

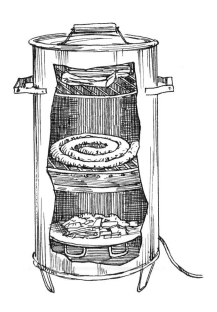

electric smoker

wood-burning smoker

Vertical water smokers similar to the one at top left use charcoal briquettes; look for a good heat-regulation system. An electric smoker, top right, is temperature-controlled and may require less attention during smoking. Wood-burning smokers, such as the one at left, accommodate large quantities of meat.

Barrel Smoker. You can build a temporary smokehouse with a drum or barrel connected by a stovepipe or covered trench to a fire pit. Cut both ends off the barrel and set it on top of the upper end of a 10- to 12-foot stovepipe that slopes downward toward the fire pit. Control the heat in the pit by covering it with sheet metal and mounding dirt around the edges to cut off the draft. You want a lot of smoke and not much flame. Fasten cleats to the top of the barrel lid and rest it on pieces of broomstick that support the hanging sausage. Hang a thermometer from a hole bored in the lid or from one of the broomsticks. Drape a piece of clean muslin or burlap over the top to protect the meat from insects. Inside the drum, set a water pan on two bricks.

Electric smokers. An electric smoker can usually handle about 40 pounds of sausage at a time and is easy to use because you don't have to maintain a fire or worry about regulating the temperature, as long as you follow manufacturer's directions. Premoistened wood chips create the

A Simple Smokehouse

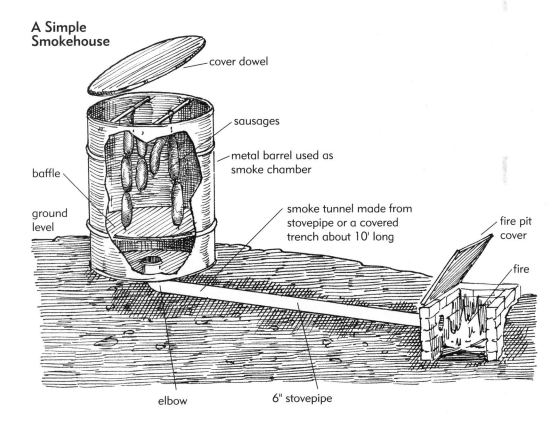

cover dowel

sausages

metal barrel used as smoke chamber

baffle

ground level

smoke tunnel made from stovepipe or a covered trench about 10' long

fire pit cover

fire

elbow

6" stovepipe

smoke. Electric smokers are not cheap, but once you get skilled at sausage making, a beautiful, shiny electric smoker may become a major temptation in your life.

Other commercial smokers. There are also gas-fired and charcoal- or wood-fired smokers on the market. If you are investing in a commercial smoker, choose one with a built-in thermometer.

For more information on sources for smokers, see our Resources list on page 272.

SKIP THE SALTPETER

In our recipes, we recommend that you use a commercial premixed cure in any recipe for cured sausage. Use the commercial premixed cure at the level recommended by the supplier. Premixed cures replace both the saltpeter and the salt in older recipes. See pages 21 to 24 for a complete discussion about why we advise using premixed cures.

Part Two

The
Sausages

CHAPTER 4

Pork Sausages

The autumn pig slaughter was until recently

the most important gastronomic event

on the European peasant calendar.

— Elisabeth Luard, *The Old World Kitchen*

PORK IS THE PERFECT SAUSAGE INGREDIENT because the pig is the perfect meat animal, able to pack on the most pounds from the least promising fodder. Nearly every last shred of the animal can be used, including the blood (for black pudding) and the bristles (for paintbrushes). Everything, as they say, but the squeal.

Over the centuries, France, Germany, Italy, and Spain developed the largest repertoires of pork sausages, from andouille to bratwurst to salami. Butchering was always done in the late fall to take advantage of cool weather, and a good store of sausages in the larder made the difference between hunger and satisfaction for the coming winter.

Because pork is a mild-tasting meat, you can season and spice it to create a number of different identities. Pork fat, smooth and bland, helps to bind together the ingredients well and creates a rich and juicy sausage.

Your homemade pork sausage will be just as satisfying to you as it has been to generations of home sausage makers. Review the instructions for sausage making in chapter 3 before starting.

Basic Breakfast Sausage

These country-style sausages are savory and versatile. Similar to the basic recipe in chapter 3 but spiced differently, they go beautifully with breakfast, brunch, or lunch, and they can be cooked and then reheated.

    4 feet small hog or sheep casing
  2½ pounds lean pork butt
   ½ pound pork fat
    1 tablespoon kosher or coarse salt
  1½ teaspoons dried sage
   ¾ teaspoon freshly ground white or black pepper (fine grind)
   ¾ teaspoon brown sugar
   ½ teaspoon dried thyme
   ¼ teaspoon dried marjoram
   ⅛ teaspoon ground cloves
   ⅛ teaspoon crushed red pepper

1. Prepare the casing (see page 28).

2. Cut the meat and fat into 1-inch cubes. Freeze the cubes for about 30 minutes to firm them up before grinding.

3. Grind the meat and fat together through the fine disk of a meat grinder.

4. In a large bowl, combine the meat, salt, sage, white pepper, sugar, thyme, marjoram, cloves, and crushed pepper. Mix well, using your hands. Freeze the mixture for 30 minutes.

5. Grind the seasoned mixture through the fine disk of the meat grinder.

6. Stuff the mixture into the prepared casing, prick air pockets, and twist off into 3-inch lengths. Cut the links apart with a sharp knife.

7. Place the links on a platter, cover, and refrigerate for a couple of hours or overnight to meld the flavors. Use within 2 to 3 days or freeze for up to 3 months.

8. Cook as directed on page 36 to an internal temperature of 160°F (71°C).

Makes 3 pounds

Maple Breakfast Sausage

The perfect accompaniment to pancakes or French toast, these sausages have the subtle sweetness of maple syrup accented with sage and mustard.

4 feet small hog or sheep casing

3 pounds lean pork butt or shoulder

1 small onion, chopped (about ½ cup)

1 tablespoon kosher or coarse salt

2 teaspoons dried sage

1 teaspoon dry mustard

¾ teaspoon freshly ground black pepper (fine grind)

¼ cup pure maple syrup

2 tablespoons milk

1. Prepare the casing (see page 28).

2. Cut the meat into 1-inch cubes. Freeze the cubes for about 30 minutes to firm them up before grinding.

3. Put the meat through the fine disk of a meat grinder. Add the onion and grind again.

4. In a large bowl, combine the meat mixture, salt, sage, mustard, and pepper. Mix well, using your hands. Stir in the maple syrup and milk, and toss lightly to blend. Do not overwork the meat mixture.

5. Stuff the mixture into the prepared casing, prick air pockets, and twist off into 3-inch lengths. Cut the links apart with a sharp knife. Or, shape into 16 patties.

6. Place the links or patties on a platter, cover, and refrigerate for a couple of hours or overnight to meld the flavors. Use within 2 to 3 days or freeze for up to 3 months.

7. Cook as directed on page 36 to an internal temperature of 160°F (71°C).

Makes 3 pounds

EASY SLICING

You can shape bulk fresh sausage into rolls (like icebox cookie dough), wrap them well in plastic wrap, and refrigerate until firm. It's easy to slice off circles the thickness you like to fry as patties.

Garlic Sausage

You may think, judging from its name, that this sausage has enough garlic in it to protect you from the plague (which it probably could do) and to keep your neighbors at a respectable distance. In fact, when garlic is cooked it loses much of its pungency, and the garlic in this recipe merely perfumes the meat. The sausage goes beautifully with potatoes.

5 feet medium hog casing

3½ pounds lean pork butt

½ pound pork fat

1 tablespoon plus 1 teaspoon kosher or coarse salt

2 teaspoons sugar

1 teaspoon freshly ground black pepper (fine grind)

¼ teaspoon ground allspice

¼ teaspoon ground cinnamon

¼ teaspoon freshly grated nutmeg

¼ teaspoon ground thyme

2 tablespoons minced garlic

1 teaspoon finely chopped fresh gingerroot

½ cup dry white wine or dry vermouth

1. Prepare the casing (see page 28).

2. Cut the meat and fat into 1-inch cubes. Freeze the cubes for about 30 minutes to firm them up before grinding.

3. Grind the meat and fat together through the fine disk of a meat grinder.

4. In a small bowl, combine the salt, sugar, pepper, allspice, cinnamon, nutmeg, thyme, garlic, gingerroot, and wine. In a large bowl, mix well the meat and spice mixtures, using your hands.

5. Stuff the mixture into the prepared casing, prick air pockets, and twist off into 4-inch links. Cut the links apart with a sharp knife.

6. Dry, uncovered, in the refrigerator for 1 to 2 days, turning the sausages frequently.

7. Freeze any sausages you don't want to cook. Prepare the rest by boiling them in water or chicken stock for about 25 minutes, until firm and cooked through, or until the sausage reaches 160°F (71°C) on an instant-read thermometer.

Makes 4 pounds

Cotechino

A specialty of the area around Reggio Emilia in northern Italy, cotechino is often twisted into links 8 or 9 inches long. The best cut of meat to use for cotechino is a fresh ham, because part of the flavor and delicate texture of this sausage is dependent on pork skin, with which this cut of meat is usually marketed. The sausages are usually boiled rather than fried, and they are a traditional part of the dish called bollito misto. *The next time fresh hams are on sale at your local grocery, try this recipe.*

2 to 3 feet small hog casing

2½ pounds lean fresh ham

½ pound pork skin with fat, cooked until lightly browned

2 tablespoons freshly grated Parmesan cheese

2 teaspoons freshly ground black pepper (medium grind)

1½ teaspoons kosher or coarse salt

1 teaspoon ground cinnamon

1 teaspoon freshly grated nutmeg

½ teaspoon cayenne pepper

½ teaspoon ground cloves

1. Prepare the casing (see page 28).

2. Cut the meat and skin into 1-inch cubes. Freeze the cubes for about 30 minutes to firm them up before grinding.

3. Put the cubes of meat and skin through the coarse disk of a meat grinder.

4. Toss together the meat mixture, Parmesan, black pepper, salt, cinnamon, nutmeg, cayenne, and cloves. Freeze for 30 minutes, then grind through the fine disk.

5. Stuff the mixture into the prepared casing, prick air pockets, and twist off into 8- to 9-inch lengths. Cut the links apart with a sharp knife.

6. Place the links on a platter, and allow them to dry, uncovered, in the refrigerator for 2 days. Turn them frequently so they dry evenly. To store cotechino, freeze for up to 3 months.

7. To serve, poach the sausages for 45 minutes.

Makes 3 pounds

Luganega

These ancient sausages were named by the Romans who first came across them in Basilicata, in southern Italy, which was then known as Lucania. Today, the sausage is made throughout Italy, with the very best said to be made in Lombardy. This is the quintessential sausage for using in risottos. Skinned and crumbled, it makes a delicious and authentic contribution to tomato sauces.

4 feet medium hog casing

3½ pounds lean pork butt

½ pound pork fat

1½ teaspoons kosher or coarse salt

1 teaspoon grated lemon zest

1 teaspoon grated orange zest

1 teaspoon freshly ground black pepper (medium grind)

½ teaspoon ground coriander

½ teaspoon freshly grated nutmeg

1 clove garlic, minced

½ cup dry vermouth

1 cup freshly grated Parmesan cheese

1. Prepare the casing (see page 28).

2. Cut the meat and fat into 1-inch cubes. Freeze the cubes for about 30 minutes to firm them up before grinding.

3. Grind the meat and fat with the fine disk of a meat grinder.

4. In a large bowl, combine the salt, lemon and orange zests, pepper, coriander, nutmeg, garlic, and vermouth. Add the meat mixture and Parmesan; mix well, using your hands.

5. Stuff the mixture into the prepared casing, prick air pockets, and twist off into 8- to 10-inch lengths. Cut the links apart with a sharp knife.

6. Place the links on a platter, and let them dry, uncovered, for 2 or 3 hours in the refrigerator. Use within 3 days, or freeze.

7. To cook, broil or poach the sausage for 20 to 25 minutes, or until firm and cooked through and the sausage reaches 160°F (71°C) on an instant-read thermometer.

Makes 4 pounds

Giorgio DeGianni's Italian Sausage

When Reno DeGianni asked his father, Giorgio, for this recipe, he was told it's the first time anyone ever wrote it down. It's a recipe to try when you are ready for a sausage-making challenge, as it makes a megabatch of sausage. The ingredients are measured by weight, so you should get out your kitchen scale when you begin preparations. You can read more about Reno and Giorgio on the following page.

85 yards small hog casings	32 ounces salt
1 liter red wine	10 ounces white sugar
6 cloves garlic, crushed	6 ounces ground black pepper
100 pounds trimmed and deboned pork butts, 85 percent lean	2 ounces ground nutmeg
	1 ounce cayenne

1. Prepare the casings (see page 28).

2. In a large bowl, mix the wine and garlic cloves and let stand at room temperature while you prepare the meat and seasonings.

3. Grind the pork through the coarse disk of a meat grinder. Freeze it for 30 minutes, then put it through the fine disk. When working with such a large quantity of meat, you should leave it in a cooler and grind small batches at a time.

4. Combine the salt, sugar, pepper, nutmeg, and cayenne. Sprinkle the salt mixture on top of the meat. Mix well, using your hands, until the meat becomes sticky.

5. Strain the garlic pulp from the wine and pour the wine over the seasoned meat. Mix until the wine is absorbed.

6. Stuff the mixture into the prepared casings, prick air pockets, and twist off to desired length. Freeze for up to 3 months. Cook as directed on page 36 to an internal temperature of 160°F (71°C).

Makes 100 pounds

RENO DeGIANNI AND BILL LEATHEM
SAUSAGE AS BUSINESS AND PLEASURE

Reno and Bill, with their colleague, Eunice, run Stuffers in Langley, British Columbia, which started out as (and still is) a natural-casing processor and distributor, and expanded into selling sausage-making supplies (see Resources, page 272).

"Local people would just show up at our door and ask about casings and other sausage supplies," says Bill, "so we set up a small retail store in the front of the building. That part of our business has grown a lot, along with sales to small butcher shops, and now we are selling on the Web, too."

Bill and Reno sample many of their customers' products, and when the workday is done, they go home and make sausage on their own. Bill's recent creations include turkey-cranberry sausage and apple-pork sausage, both in lamb casings.

For Reno, work and home are even more connected. His godfather built the Stuffers structure in the 1950s as a meat-cutting plant where his father, Giorgio, worked as a custom cutter and sausage maker. Reno worked part time when he was a teenager, curing hams and bacon. "I'm left-handed," he explains, "so I couldn't work at the cutting tables with other butchers without bumping into them."

Reno has always made Italian sausage and salami with his father, who was born near Milan. They still enjoy making sausage together on weekends. Reno is building a new house that will include a temperature- and humidity-controlled room for aging sausage and wine.

"I'm setting up at home so I can learn the science behind sausage making," Reno says. "I want to be able to explain it to the average person so they can be successful at making cured and dried sausages, which are more difficult."

Stuffers' customers in the Pacific Northwest are especially interested in making game sausage, Bill and Reno say. They also get a lot of inquiries about edible vegetarian casings, which have not yet been perfected. But as Reno says, "McDonald's has introduced a veggie burger, so you know that a change is coming."

Northern Italian-Style Hot or Sweet Sausage

This classic sausage is easy to make and delicious, too. You can roast or grill the sausages, or you can leave all or part of the meat as bulk sausage that can be sautéed and added to tomato sauce.

   3 feet medium hog casing

2½ pounds lean pork butt

   ½ pound pork fat

   1 tablespoon kosher or coarse salt

   2 teaspoons ground coriander

   2 teaspoons freshly ground black pepper (medium grind)

   1 teaspoon crushed red pepper (for medium-hot sausage; use more for very hot sausage. Omit for sweet sausage)

   2 cloves garlic, minced

1. Prepare the casing (see page 28).

2. Cut the meat and fat into 1-inch cubes. Freeze the cubes for about 30 minutes to firm them up before grinding.

3. Grind the meat and fat together through the coarse disk of a meat grinder.

4. In a large bowl, combine the meat mixture, salt, coriander, black pepper, crushed red pepper (if using), and garlic. Mix well, using your hands.

5. Stuff the mixture into the prepared casing, prick air pockets, and twist off into 3-inch lengths. Cut the links apart with a sharp knife.

6. Place the links on a platter, cover, and refrigerate for a couple of hours or overnight to meld the flavors. Use within 2 to 3 days or freeze for up to 3 months.

7. Cook as directed on page 36 to an internal temperature of 160°F (71°C).

Makes 3 pounds

Sicilian-Style Hot Sausage

The hot version of Sicilian-style sausage can be made as hot as you please by adding more crushed red pepper.

 5 feet medium hog casing

4½ pounds lean pork butt

 ½ pound pork fat

 2 tablespoons kosher or coarse salt

 1 tablespoon fennel seed

 1 tablespoon freshly ground black pepper (medium grind)

 Crushed red pepper to taste (about 2 teaspoons for medium-hot)

1. Prepare the casing (see page 28).

2. Cut the meat and fat into 1-inch cubes. Freeze the cubes for about 30 minutes to firm them up before grinding.

3. Grind the meat and fat together through the coarse disk of a meat grinder.

4. In a large bowl, combine the meat mixture, salt, fennel, black pepper, and crushed red pepper. Mix together, using your hands.

5. Stuff the mixture into the prepared casing, prick air pockets, and twist off into 3- or 4-inch lengths. Cut the links apart with a sharp knife.

6. Place the links on a platter, cover, and refrigerate for a couple of hours or overnight to meld the flavors. Use within 2 to 3 days or freeze for up to 3 months.

7. Cook as directed on page 36 to an internal temperature of 160°F (71°C).

Makes 5 pounds

Sicilian-Style Sweet Sausage

This sweeter Sicilian-style sausage is flavored with garlic and anise seed. Both fennel, used in the hot version, and anise contribute a sweet licorice flavor to the sausage.

    5 feet medium hog casing
   4½ pounds lean pork butt, cubed
    ½ pound pork fat, cubed
    2 tablespoons kosher or coarse salt
    1 tablespoon freshly ground black pepper (medium grind)
    1 teaspoon anise seed
    2 cloves garlic, minced

1. Prepare the casing (see page 28).

2. Cut the meat and fat into 1-inch cubes. Freeze the cubes for about 30 minutes to firm them up before grinding.

3. Grind the cubed meat and fat through the coarse disk of a meat grinder.

4. In a large bowl, combine the meat mixture, salt, pepper, anise seed, and garlic. Mix together, using your hands.

5. Stuff the mixture into the prepared casing, prick air pockets, and twist off into 3- or 4-inch lengths. Cut the links apart with a sharp knife.

6. Place the links on a platter, cover, and refrigerate for a couple of hours or overnight to meld the flavors. Use within 2 to 3 days or freeze for up to 3 months.

7. Cook as directed on page 36 to an internal temperature of 160°F (71°C).

Makes 5 pounds

Chorizo

In Spain and Mexico, you can find chorizos both fresh and dried. This fresh version is not the Mexican kind with an acidic side that crumbles readily when cooked. Either way, they are sure to satisfy a craving for something spicy (see page 78 for Spanish-Style Chorizo).

5 feet medium hog casing	1 teaspoon fennel seed
3½ pounds lean pork butt	1 teaspoon crushed red pepper
½ pound pork fat	4 cloves garlic, minced
1½ tablespoons kosher or coarse salt	¼ cup dry red wine
2 teaspoons freshly ground black pepper (medium grind)	2 tablespoons brandy
	1 tablespoon red wine vinegar

1. Prepare the casing (see page 28).

2. Cut the meat and fat into 1-inch cubes. Freeze the cubes for about 30 minutes to firm them up before grinding.

3. Grind the cubed meat and fat through the coarse disk of a meat grinder.

4. In a large pan with a cover, combine the meat mixture, salt, black pepper, fennel, red pepper, garlic, wine, brandy, and vinegar. Mix together, using your hands.

5. Refrigerate, covered, for 3 to 4 hours. This gives the wine and brandy a chance to extract maximum flavor from the herbs and spices, and for the meat to absorb some of the liquid.

6. Stuff the mixture into the prepared casing, prick air pockets, and twist off into 4-inch lengths. Cut the links apart with a sharp knife.

7. Place the links on a platter, cover, and refrigerate for a couple of hours or overnight to meld the flavors. Use within 2 to 3 days or freeze for up to 3 months.

8. Cook as directed on page 36 to an internal temperature of 160°F (71°C).

Makes 4 pounds

Pork and Apple Sausage

Pork, apple, leeks, and fresh rosemary combine to make a delectable moist sausage that tastes almost sweet, thanks to a splash of reduced apple cider.

2½ feet medium hog casing

2¾ pounds lean pork butt or shoulder

¼ pound pork fat

1 cup apple cider

1 tablespoon canola oil

2 small leeks, cleaned and chopped (white parts only)

1 Granny Smith apple, peeled, cored, and chopped

1 tablespoon kosher or coarse salt

½ teaspoon freshly ground black pepper (fine grind)

½ teaspoon grated lemon zest

2 tablespoons chopped fresh parsley

2 tablespoons chopped fresh rosemary

1. Prepare the casing (see page 28).

2. Cut the meat and fat into 1-inch cubes. Freeze the cubes for about 30 minutes to firm them up before grinding.

3. While the meat chills, simmer the cider in a saucepan, uncovered, until it reduces to ¼ cup of syrupy liquid, 20 minutes. Remove from heat; set aside.

4. Meanwhile, heat the oil in a medium-sized skillet over moderate heat. Add the leeks and apple; sauté for 3 to 5 minutes, until the apples are golden.

5. Put the cubes of meat through the fine disk of a meat grinder. Toss the ground meat with the salt, pepper, lemon zest, parsley, and rosemary, freeze for 30 minutes, and grind a second time.

6. In a large bowl, combine the meat mixture with the leeks and apple and the cooled reduced cider. Mix well, using your hands.

7. Stuff the mixture into the prepared casing, prick air pockets, and twist off into 4-inch lengths. Cut the links apart with a sharp knife. Place the links on a platter, cover, and refrigerate up to overnight to meld the flavors. Use within 2 to 3 days or freeze for up to 3 months.

8. Cook as directed on page 36 to an internal temperature of 160°F (71°C).

Makes 3 pounds

Pork and Pistachio Sausage

Toasted pistachios add texture, and nutmeg and black pepper perk up the taste of these pork sausages. Fry or grill to serve.

5 feet medium hog casing

3½ pounds lean pork butt or shoulder

½ pound pork fat

1 tablespoon freshly ground black pepper (fine grind)

1 tablespoon kosher or coarse salt

1 teaspoon freshly grated nutmeg

1 tablespoon chopped fresh rosemary, or 1 teaspoon dried

½ cup chopped, toasted unsalted pistachios

1. Prepare the casing (see page 28).

2. Cut the meat and fat into 1-inch cubes. Freeze the cubes for about 30 minutes to firm them up before grinding.

3. Put the meat and fat through the fine disk of a meat grinder.

4. In a large bowl, combine the meat mixture, pepper, salt, nutmeg, and rosemary. Mix well, using your hands. Freeze for 30 minutes.

5. Grind the seasoned mixture through the fine disk. Add the pistachios and mix well, using your hands.

6. Stuff the mixture into the prepared casing and twist off into 4-inch lengths. Cut the links apart with a sharp knife.

7. Place the links on a platter, cover, and refrigerate for a couple of hours or overnight to meld the flavors. Use within 2 to 3 days or freeze for up to 3 months.

8. Cook as directed on page 36 to an internal temperature of 160°F (71°C).

Makes 4 pounds

TOASTING NUTS

Toasting nuts before using them in a recipe intensifies their flavor. Nuts may be toasted in a single layer in a 350°F (175°C) oven. Toast them, stirring occasionally, for 10 to 15 minutes, or until they are golden brown. You can also toast nuts in an ungreased skillet over medium heat; stir frequently to prevent burning.

Southwestern Pork Sausage

Every fall, the aroma of roasting chile peppers perfumes the air in the Desert Southwest. Chiles, cumin, and coriander combine here to evoke those smells and tastes. These sausages are medium hot; adjust the crushed red pepper up or down to suit your own taste.

   5 feet medium hog casings

3½ pounds lean pork butt or shoulder

  ½ pound pork fat

  1 tablespoon plus 2 teaspoons kosher or coarse salt

  1 tablespoon freshly ground black pepper (fine grind)

  2 teaspoons crushed red pepper

  1 teaspoon ground coriander

  1 teaspoon ground cumin

  ½ teaspoon ancho chile powder

  4 cloves garlic, finely chopped

1. Prepare the casing (see page 28).

2. Cut the meat and fat into 1-inch cubes. Freeze the cubes for about 30 minutes to firm them up before grinding.

3. Put the meat and fat through the fine disk of a meat grinder.

4. In a large bowl, combine the meat mixture, salt, pepper, crushed red pepper, coriander, cumin, chile powder, and garlic, using your hands. Freeze for 30 minutes.

5. Grind the seasoned meat through the fine disk of a meat grinder.

6. Stuff the mixture into the prepared casing, prick air pockets, and twist off into 4-inch lengths. Cut the links apart with a sharp knife.

7. Place the links on a platter, cover, and refrigerate for a couple of hours or overnight to meld the flavors. Use within 2 to 3 days or freeze for up to 3 months.

8. Cook as directed on page 36 to an internal temperature of 160°F (71°C).

Makes 4 pounds

Polish Sausage

This is Bill St. Onge's first sausage. The home sausage maker now has 34 sausages in his repertoire. Read about Bill on page 127.

6 feet small hog casing

5 pounds ground pork butt (80 percent lean)

½ cup nonfat dry milk

2½ tablespoons kosher or coarse salt

1 teaspoon cayenne pepper

1 medium-sized onion, finely diced

1 large green pepper, diced fine

1 heaping tablespoon minced garlic

1½ cups chicken stock

1. Prepare the casing (see page 28).

2. In a large bowl, combine the pork, milk, salt, cayenne, onion, green pepper, garlic, and chicken stock. Mix well, using your hands.

3. Stuff the mixture into the prepared casing, prick air pockets, and twist off into 3- or 4-inch links. Cut the links apart with a sharp knife.

4. Cook as directed on page 36 to an internal temperature of 160°F (71°C). Use within 2 to 3 days or freeze for up to 3 months.

NOTE: Bill likes to cook his sausages in a preheated 400°F (200°C) oven for 20 minutes, turning them several times and not letting them touch while they cook.

Makes 5 pounds

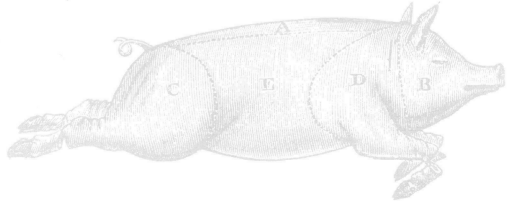

Liverwurst

This smooth, creamy sausage is one of the most popular of all the German wursts. A thick slice sandwiched between two slabs of homemade bread with a round of Bermuda or Vidalia onion is wickedly delicious. This recipe is different from those using natural casings, in that the liverwurst is stuffed into a large collagen or plastic casing, or a homemade muslin one (see illustration on the following page for instructions on making one). The sausage is cooked in hot water, then chilled before eating.

1 pound fresh pork liver

¾ pound lean pork butt

¼ pound pork fat

3 tablespoons nonfat dry milk

2 teaspoons sweet paprika

2 teaspoons kosher or coarse salt

1 teaspoon freshly ground white pepper

1 teaspoon sugar

½ teaspoon ground coriander

½ teaspoon dried marjoram

¼ teaspoon ground allspice

¼ teaspoon ground cardamom

¼ teaspoon ground mace

1 large sweet white onion, finely diced (makes about 1½ cups)

1 foot large (4-inch diameter) collagen, plastic, or muslin casing

1. Cut the meats and fat into 1-inch cubes. Refrigerate the cubes for about 30 minutes to firm them up before grinding.

2. Separately grind the cubes of liver, pork, and fat through the fine disk of a meat grinder. Then mix together and grind again.

3. Sprinkle the milk, paprika, salt, pepper, sugar, coriander, marjoram, all-spice, cardamom, mace, and onion over the ground meat. Mix well, using your hands.

4. Grind the mixture through the fine disk twice more, freezing the mixture for 30 minutes between grindings. (Or process in a food processor.)

5. Stuff the mixture into the casing. It helps to fold the open end of the casing down over itself to get things started. This makes it easier for the meat mixture to reach the bottom. Pack the meat as firmly as possible.

6. Stitch or tie the open end so it is firmly closed.

7. In a large kettle, bring enough water to a boil to cover the liverwurst by 2 to 3 inches.

8. Put the sausage in the boiling water and place a heavy plate on top of it to keep it submerged. When the water returns to a boil, reduce the heat so that the water maintains a temperature of 175°F (79°C). Cook, covered, for 3 hours.

9. Plunge the liverwurst into a bowl of ice water to cool quickly. Drain well, pat dry, and refrigerate, covered, overnight before removing the casing.

10. Store the liverwurst in the refrigerator and eat within 10 days.

Makes a 2-pound sausage

HOW TO MAKE A MUSLIN CASING

For a 2-pound liverwurst, you will need a piece of unbleached muslin about 12 inches long and 8 inches wide. Fold the muslin lengthwise. Using a small stitch, sew across one of the short ends in a half-circle pattern, as shown, and down the open side. Set aside until you are ready to stuff it.

12 inches

folded edge

8 inches

Shaker Scrapple

Ohio Shakers in the nineteenth century may have taken this recipe from their Pennsylvania cousins. The original called for hog jowls, feet, liver, and tongue, and noted that the cook should not be stingy with the marjoram. It's fine to use a combination of pork cuts, or even a leftover cooked roast.

2 pounds pork, fresh or cooked, cut into ½-inch pieces

4 quarts water

2 teaspoons kosher or coarse salt

1 teaspoon dried sage

½ teaspoon freshly ground black pepper (medium grind)

2 teaspoons chopped fresh marjoram (or 1 teaspoon dried)

2 cups cornmeal

2 cups whole wheat flour

Bacon grease or lard, for frying

1. In a large saucepan, bring to a boil the pork pieces and the water. Reduce the heat and simmer for 20 minutes; drain, reserving 3 quarts of the broth. Let the meat cool.

2. Chop the meat very finely or run it through the coarse disk of a meat grinder.

SCRAPPLE

If you connect scrapple with the Pennsylvania Dutch, you are correct, as most of our recipes for it originate from those thrifty German immigrants. (The "Dutch," you may recall, are actually *Deutsch*, or German.) As its name suggests, scrapple uses up scraps of meat in a hearty dish that is a combination of meat loaf and cornmeal mush.

Although it isn't stuffed into a sausage casing, scrapple is a fine way to preserve fresh or cooked pork. You can start with either leftover cooked pork, as in the Shaker recipe, or fresh pork. There are probably as many variations as there are Pennsylvania Dutch farmers. Scrapple was traditionally made in the fall, at butchering time.

3. Bring the reserved broth to a boil in a heavy pot and add the salt, sage, pepper, and marjoram.

4. Mix together the cornmeal and flour. Add this slowly to the boiling broth, stirring constantly.

5. Stir in the finely chopped meat and cook over low heat, stirring frequently, for about 30 minutes, until the mixture has thickened.

6. Pour the meat mixture into two 9- by 5-inch loaf pans. Shake the pans so that the mixture settles, cover, and refrigerate overnight.

7. To cook, cut the cold scrapple into slices ¼-inch thick. Heat the bacon grease until it is very hot and fry the slices until golden and crisp, about 5 minutes per side. Serve hot. Sliced, cold scrapple pieces may also be frozen for up to 3 months.

Makes two 4-pound loaves

Pennsylvania Scrapple

This version of scrapple uses a broader range of seasonings and is typical of recipes from the area around Lancaster, Pennsylvania.

½ pound pork liver

1½ pounds lean pork shoulder or butt

2 teaspoons kosher or coarse salt

¼ teaspoon black pepper (medium grind)

1 onion, chopped

Water

1¼ cups all-purpose flour

½ cup buckwheat or whole wheat flour

½ cup yellow cornmeal

1 teaspoon ground coriander

1 teaspoon ground mace

1 teaspoon ground thyme

1 teaspoon fresh marjoram, or ½ teaspoon dried

1. Pour boiling water to cover the liver and let stand for 5 minutes. Drain and rinse in cold water.

2. In a large pot, combine the liver, pork shoulder, salt, pepper, and onion. Cover with water and cook over medium heat, covered, for 2 hours, or until meat is fork tender. Remove the meat from the broth and set aside to let it cool.

3. Measure the broth and add water to make 4½ cups of liquid. In a large pot, bring the liquid to a boil.

THE PREFERRED WAY TO EAT SCRAPPLE

Properly prepared, scrapple has the flavor of a good pork sausage and the crispness of bacon. That's why it makes a perfect breakfast meat and accompaniment to fried eggs. Purists warn that you should *never* fry scrapple in anything but lard or bacon grease. Some people like to pour maple syrup over fried scrapple. Others like to sauté a few apple slices in the pan along with the meat, or serve the fried scrapple with fresh applesauce.

4. Whisk together the all-purpose flour, buckwheat flour, cornmeal, coriander, mace, thyme, and marjoram in a bowl. Gradually stir the mixture into the boiling liquid. Simmer over low heat, uncovered, for about 30 minutes, stirring frequently.

5. Put the meat through the coarse disk of a meat grinder or finely chop it. Add the ground meat to the flour mixture, stirring to combine. The mixture will be thick.

6. Pour the mixture into two 9- by 5-inch loaf pans, cover, and refrigerate overnight.

7. To cook, cut the cold scrapple into slices ¼-inch thick. In a large skillet, heat the bacon grease until very hot and fry the slices until golden and crisp, about 5 minutes per side. Serve hot. Sliced, cold scrapple pieces may also be frozen for up to 3 months.

Makes two 4-pound loaves

Estonian Christmas Barley Sausage

This sausage recipe is a favorite Christmas dish from Estonia, courtesy of Ella Aed, who was born there in 1920. It has become a family tradition for her daughter, Mare-Anne Jarvela, who lives in New Hampshire. Serve the sausage warm, with lingonberry or cranberry jelly.

8½ feet medium hog casing

2½ cups pearl barley

4 to 5 ounces salt pork, cubed

1 tablespoon caraway seed, or more as needed

1 tablespoon freshly ground black pepper (medium grind), or more as needed

2 teaspoons kosher or coarse salt

1 bay leaf

1 medium onion, chopped

8 cups water

1. Prepare the casing (see page 28).

2. In a large pot, combine the barley, salt pork, caraway seed, pepper, salt, bay leaf, onion, and water. Bring to a boil. Lower the heat and simmer for 1 hour, stirring frequently. Add a little water, if needed, to prevent scorching.

3. Taste the mixture and adjust the seasonings, if necessary. Remove from the heat and let the porridge cool.

4. Cut the casing into five pieces, each about 20 inches long. Stuff the porridge into the casings, being careful not to overstuff. Tie the casings on both ends.

5. Bring water to cover the sausages to a boil in a large pot. Cook the sausages in the boiling water for about 5 minutes. Remove the sausages from the pot and let cool.

6. Refrigerate the sausages for up to 3 days, or freeze.

7. To serve, preheat oven to 400°F (200°C). Place sausages in a large pan and bake them for about 1 hour, until the casings are brown and crisp.

Makes about five 20-inch sausages (about 4 pounds)

ELLA AND JOHANNES AED

ANCESTRAL SAUSAGE MAKES ITS WAY
TO SWEDEN, THEN NEW HAMPSHIRE

Ella Mandla and Johannes Aed were born in Estonia, she in 1920 and he in 1919. They became friends when they met at a folk-dance group. In 1944, the Russian army moved in to occupy Estonia, and Ella and Johannes joined about 250 other refugees aboard a leaky old sailboat attempting to cross the Baltic Sea to neutral Sweden. The boat had to sail at night without lights to avoid the Russian ships that prowled the waters.

After 36 hours, the refugees reached the island of Gotland, off the coast of Sweden. They were free. They also were nearly penniless. Each person had been able to bring just one small suitcase. Ella brought — in her head — her favorite Estonian recipes, including the Christmas barley sausage that her mother had taught her to make.

Ella and Johannes were married in 1946. With four months' pay, they were able to buy a bicycle. After five years, they had saved enough to buy a small house. Their daughter, Mare-Anne, was born in 1951. Every Christmas, the family made sausage together. Mare-Anne's grandmother, who also had immigrated to Sweden, carved tiny toothpicks to fasten the ends of the sausages. The Estonian holiday customs blended with those of Sweden, but the barley sausage was a constant.

Today, Ella and Johannes still make Christmas sausage at their home in Västervik, south of Stockholm. At the same time, in New Hampshire, Mare-Anne is making the ancestral sausage for her husband and sons. It wouldn't be Christmas without it.

Italian-Style Dry Sausage

This sausage is sometimes referred to as salamette *because the links resemble small salamis. It is simple to make and can be enjoyed about 6 weeks after it has been hung up to dry.*

8 pounds lean, prefrozen pork butt (see Notes)

2 pounds prefrozen pork fat (see Notes)

3 tablespoons plus 1 teaspoon kosher or coarse salt

2 tablespoons freshly ground black pepper (coarse grind)

1 tablespoon plus 2 teaspoons fennel seed

1 tablespoon sugar

2 teaspoons anise seed

½ teaspoon ascorbic acid

Curing salt (use supplier's recommended quantity for 10 pounds of meat; see Notes)

1 tablespoon finely minced garlic

1 cup dry red wine

6 feet medium (2-inch diameter) hog casing

1. Partially thaw the meat and fat, then cut them into 1-inch cubes.

2. While the meat and fat are still cold, grind them separately through the coarse disk of a meat grinder.

3. In a large bowl, combine the meat, fat, salt, pepper, fennel seed, sugar, anise seed, ascorbic acid, curing salt, garlic, and wine. Mix well, using your hands. Spread the mixture in a large shallow pan, cover loosely with wax paper, and cure it in the refrigerator for 24 hours.

4. Prepare the casing (see page 28).

5. Stuff the mixture into the prepared casing, prick air pockets, and twist off into 4-inch links. Tie off each link with butcher's twine. Do not separate the links.

6. Hang the links in a drying area for 6 to 8 weeks. Test the sausage after 6 weeks by cutting off one link and slicing through it. If the texture is firm enough to suit your taste, the remaining sausage can be cut down and wrapped tightly in plastic wrap for storage in the refrigerator. Prolonged drying will result in a sausage that has the texture of something like beef jerky, which must be gnawed on to be eaten.

NOTES:

- Prepare pork according to the instructions on page 40 to ensure that it is free from trichinosis. See "Dry Sausage Safety" on page 42.
- We recommend that you use a commercial premixed cure in any recipe for cured sausage. Premixed cures replace the saltpeter in older recipes.

Makes 10 pounds

BANNED IN ROME

In the fourth century, the Christian emperor Constantine the Great tried to ban sausages from the Roman Empire because they were consumed with great gusto at pagan orgies. (He wasn't too crazy about the orgies, either.)

By this time, however, every Italian village had developed its specialty sausage, and not even the scowls of the emperor could deter sausage lovers.

Spanish-Style Chorizo

This dried type of chorizo is the most common (for fresh chorizo, see page 63).

8 pounds lean, prefrozen pork butt (see Notes)

2 pounds prefrozen pork fat (see Notes)

3 tablespoons plus 1 teaspoon kosher or coarse salt

3 tablespoons cayenne pepper

2 tablespoons freshly ground black pepper (fine grind)

2 tablespoons sugar

1 tablespoon crushed red pepper

1 teaspoon cumin seed

1 teaspoon crushed dried oregano

1 teaspoon fennel seed

½ teaspoon ascorbic acid

Curing salt (use supplier's recommended quantity for 10 pounds meat; see Notes)

¾ cup brandy

¼ cup red wine vinegar

2 tablespoons minced garlic

6 feet medium hog casing

1. Partially thaw the meat and the fat, then cut them into 1-inch cubes.

2. While the meat and fat are still cold, grind them separately through the coarse disk of a meat grinder.

3. In a large bowl, sprinkle the salt, cayenne, black pepper, sugar, crushed red pepper, cumin, oregano, fennel, ascorbic acid, curing salt, brandy, vinegar, and garlic on the meat. Mix thoroughly, using your hands. Spread the mixture in a large, shallow pan, cover loosely with wax paper, and cure it in the refrigerator for 24 hours.

4. Prepare the casing (see page 28).

5. Stuff the mixture into the prepared casing, prick air pockets, and twist off into 4-inch links. Tie off each link with butcher's twine. Do not separate the links.

6. Hang the sausage to dry for about 8 weeks. Test the sausage after 8 weeks by cutting off one link and slicing through it. If the texture is firm enough to suit your taste, the remaining sausage can be cut down and wrapped tightly in plastic wrap for storage in the refrigerator. Prolonged drying will result in a sausage that has the texture of something like beef jerky, which must be gnawed on to be eaten.

Notes:

- Prepare the pork according to the instructions on page 40 to ensure that it is free from trichinosis. See "Dry Sausage Safety" on page 42.
- We recommend that you use a commercial premixed cure in any recipe for cured sausage. Premixed cures replace the saltpeter in older recipes.

Makes 10 pounds

RANDAL CHILD
"JUST DIVE IN WITH BOTH HANDS"

Randal bought an earlier edition of this book a few years ago and quickly became enthused about sausage making. "Cooking is a passion for me," he says, "and I love to make everything from scratch, including my own sausage. I know what's in it and can get precisely what I want."

Randal, who lives in West Haven, Utah, north of Salt Lake City, buys meat from a "marvelous meat shop" in Ogden. He has a KitchenAid mixer with a meat-grinder attachment and likes to buy a nice roast and grind it up for burgers and sausage. He buys his spice mixes from Penzey's in Wisconsin (see Resources on page 272 for more information) and so far has made Polish, Italian, and Russian sausage as well as bratwurst. He hasn't tried smoked or cured sausage yet, but they are out there on his culinary horizon.

Randal's advice for newcomers to sausage making? "Just dive in with both hands."

Braunschweiger

This smooth, creamy German sausage from the town of Braunschweig is made from pure pork, is mildly spiced, and has a distinctive smoky flavor. The pork liver and milk in the recipe are responsible for the unique flavor of the sausage. The curing and smoking distinguish the sausage from its cousin, Liverwurst (see page 68).

2½ pounds pork liver, trimmed

2½ pounds pork butt with fat

¼ cup nonfat dry milk

1 tablespoon plus 2 teaspoons kosher or coarse salt

1 tablespoon sugar

2 teaspoons freshly ground white pepper (fine grind)

1 teaspoon crushed mustard seed

½ teaspoon ground marjoram

¼ teaspoon ground allspice

¼ teaspoon ascorbic acid

Curing salt (use supplier's recommended quantity for 5 pounds of meat)

2 tablespoons finely minced onion

½ cup ice water

4 feet medium (2-inch diameter) hog casing

1. Cut the liver and pork butt into 1-inch cubes. Freeze the cubes for about 30 minutes before grinding.

2. Grind them separately through the fine disk of a meat grinder. Mix the meats together in a large bowl.

3. Add the milk, salt, sugar, pepper, mustard seed, marjoram, allspice, ascorbic acid, curing salt, onion, and water. Mix well, using your hands. Freeze the mixture for 30 minutes.

4. Regrind through the fine disk.

5. Prepare the casing (see page 28).

6. Stuff the mixture into the casing, prick air pockets, and tie off with butcher's twine into 6- to 8-inch links.

7. Simmer the sausage in a large kettle of water at 180 to 190°F (82 to 88°C) for 1 hour.

8. Remove the sausage from the water, dry thoroughly, and smoke at 150°F (66°C) for 2 hours, until it reaches an internal temperature of 160°F (71°C).

9. Place the braunschweiger in a large pot of cool water for 30 minutes, then remove and dry it. The sausage may be refrigerated for up to 2 weeks.

Makes 5 pounds

saltpeter

Literally "salt of rock," and also known as *niter*, saltpeter (potassium nitrate, KNO_3, is found in nature as a saltlike crust or efflorescence on rocks and stone walls. As sausage making developed over the centuries, people noticed that salt from certain areas — the stuff known as saltpeter — seemed to keep meat rosy in color and give it a hearty taste. It was much later that chemists determined it was the nitrates in the salt that had this effect. Saltpeter was traditionally used in sausage making to preserve color and to prevent botulism. (It was also used to make gunpowder.) A diuretic with a sharp, saline taste, saltpeter is still used in some old-time recipes, although most sources recommend the use of premixed cures containing sodium nitrate and/or sodium nitrite. (See page 22 for more information.)

Calabrese Salami

This sausage is called calabrese *after its origins in Calabria, the toe of the Italian "boot," a mostly mountainous land that faces Sicily. The Apennines are the central geographic feature and they dictate the way of life in the region. Although there is some tillable land, and Calabria is known for its excellent vegetables, the area is most famous for its porkers. If there is a region of Italy more proud of its sausages than any other, it has to be Calabria. (You would no doubt get an argument about that statement from a Sicilian.) If there is anything that rivals the importance of pork in Calabria, it is the fiery red peppers that the region also produces. Pork and lots of red pepper, that's Calabrese salami.*

7 pounds lean, prefrozen pork (see Notes)

3 pounds diced pork fat (see Notes)

3 tablespoons plus 1 teaspoon kosher or coarse salt

3 tablespoons crushed red pepper

1 tablespoon freshly ground white pepper (fine grind)

½ teaspoon ascorbic acid

Curing salt (use supplier's recommended quantity for 10 pounds of meat)

½ cup brandy

½ cup dry vermouth

2 teaspoons pure anise extract (or ¼ cup anisette liqueur)

6 feet medium (2-inch diameter) hog casing

1. Partially thaw the pork and fat, then cut into 1-inch cubes.

2. While the pork is still cold, grind it through the coarse disk of a meat grinder.

3. Grind the fat, still cold, through the fine disk of the meat grinder.

4. In a large bowl, mix together the meat and fat. Add the salt, crushed red pepper, white pepper, ascorbic acid, curing salt, brandy, vermouth, and anise. Mix well, using your hands.

5. Prepare the casing (see page 28).

6. Stuff the mixture into the prepared casing, prick air pockets, and twist off into 8-inch links. Tie off each link with butcher's twine; do not separate the links. Hang to dry for 8 weeks.

7. Wrap the sausage in plastic wrap and refrigerate.

NOTES:

- Prepare the pork according to the instructions on page 40 to ensure that it is free from trichinosis. See "Dry Sausage Safety" on page 42.
- We recommend that you use a commercial premixed cure in any recipe for cured sausage. Premixed cures replace the saltpeter in older recipes.

Makes 10 pounds

Garlic Sausage

The French have a surefire cure for the problem of garlic breath: Everyone eats garlic sausage, and then no one can smell the garlic on anyone else.

7 pounds prefrozen pork (preferably fresh, not cured, ham); see Notes

3 pounds pork fat (see Notes)

3 tablespoons plus 1 teaspoon kosher or coarse salt

3 tablespoons finely minced garlic

1 cup brandy

2 tablespoons sugar

1 tablespoon sweet paprika

1 tablespoon freshly ground white pepper (fine grind)

1 teaspoon crushed bay leaf

½ teaspoon ascorbic acid

½ teaspoon dried basil

½ teaspoon ground cinnamon

½ teaspoon ground cloves

½ teaspoon ground mace

½ teaspoon dried oregano

½ teaspoon ground sage

½ teaspoon dried thyme

¼ teaspoon cayenne pepper

¼ teaspoon dried summer savory

Curing salt (use supplier's recommended quantity for 10 pounds of meat)

4 feet large beef casing (about 4 inches)

1. Partially thaw the meat and fat, then cut them into 1-inch cubes.

2. While the meat is still cold, grind it through the coarse disk of a meat grinder. Then grind the fat, still cold, through the coarse disk.

3. Mix together the meat and fat, and freeze the mixture for 30 minutes.

4. Grind the meat mixture through the fine disk of the meat grinder.

5. Mix in the salt, garlic, and brandy.

6. In a food processor or blender, process the sugar, paprika, white pepper, bay leaf, ascorbic acid, basil, cinnamon, cloves, mace, oregano, sage, thyme, cayenne, and summer savory until you have a fine powder.

7. Mix the powdered herbs and spices into the meat with your hands, blending thoroughly.

8. Spread the meat mixture in a large pan, cover loosely with wax paper, and cure in the refrigerator for 24 hours.

9. Prepare the casing (see page 28).

10. Stuff the mixture into the prepared casing, prick air pockets, and twist off into 6- to 7-inch links. Tie off each link with butcher's twine; do not separate the links. (See Notes.) Hang the sausage to dry for 8 to 12 weeks, or until it is firm. Test the sausage after 8 weeks by cutting off one link and slicing through it. If the texture is firm enough to suit your taste, the remaining sausage can be cut down and wrapped tightly in plastic wrap for storage in the refrigerator.

NOTES:

- Prepare pork according to the instructions on page 40 to ensure that it is free from trichinosis. See "Dry Sausage Safety" on page 42.
- We recommend that you use a commercial premixed cure in any recipe for cured sausage. Premixed cures replace the saltpeter in older recipes.
- Depending on the beef casing, it may be easier to cut the casing into 6- to 7-inch lengths, tie each length at one end, stuff the casing, then tie the other end.

Makes 10 pounds

GARLIC'S GOODNESS

Garlic has been shown to have antibiotic properties, and it is also a traditional remedy for high blood pressure. Shakespeare, for practical reasons, no doubt, cautioned his actors about eating too much of it. But Egyptian slaves wouldn't work without it, and Aristophanes claimed that it was an aphrodisiac. The ancient blind poet Homer credited garlic with saving Ulysses from Circe's pork barrel.

So, you are in famous company the next time you open your mouth after enjoying some garlic sausage.

Andouille

This heavily spiced, smoky sausage is associated with Louisiana's rich Cajun cuisine and often plays an important role in gumbo and jambalaya. It's also grilled and sliced as an appetizer, sure to perk up anyone's palate. In Louisiana, the sausage is smoked over pecan wood and sugarcane, which imparts a delectable flavor. This recipe calls for hot smoking and the sausage is ready to eat after smoking. See Notes for information about cold smoking.

6 feet beef middle casing
(2 to 3 inches in diameter)

5 pounds pork butt (see Notes)

1 pound pork fat (see Notes)

½ cup chopped garlic

¼ cup cracked black pepper

4 tablespoons kosher or coarse salt

2 tablespoons cayenne

1 tablespoon thyme

1. Prepare the casing (see page 28).

2. Cut the pork and fat into 1-inch cubes. Freeze the cubes for about 30 minutes to firm them up before grinding.

3. Grind the meat and fat through the fine disk of a meat grinder.

4. In a large bowl, combine the meat mixture, garlic, pepper, salt, cayenne, and thyme. Mix well, using your hands.

5. Stuff the mixture into the prepared casing, prick air pockets, and twist into 12-inch links. Tie off each link with butcher's twine; do not separate the links. Air-dry for a few hours.

6. Hot-smoke at 175°F (79°C) to 200°F (93°C) for 4 to 5 hours, using pecan or hickory wood if possible. The sausage should be firm and should reach an internal temperature of 160°F (71°C). Store in the refrigerator for 5 to 7 days, or freeze and use as needed.

NOTE: If you want to cold-smoke the sausage, prepare the pork and fat according to the instructions on page 40 to ensure that it is free from trichinosis. Then, reduce the salt to 2 tablespoons and add a premixed cure at the level recommended by the supplier. To cold-smoke, dry the sausage overnight in the refrigerator, then cold-smoke at 70 to 90°F (21 to 32°C) for at least 12 hours, until the sausage firms up. Cook before eating.

Makes 6 pounds

Linguiça

Linguiça is the basic spicy country sausage beloved in Portugal; it is a close cousin to andouille and other smoked country sausages. This recipe calls for hot smoking and the sausage is ready to eat after smoking. See the Note with the Andouille recipe on the preceding page for information about cold smoking.

4 pounds boneless pork butt with up to 25 percent fat

2 tablespoons sweet paprika

1 tablespoon plus 2 teaspoons kosher or coarse salt

1 tablespoon ground coriander

1 teaspoon crushed red pepper

½ teaspoon allspice

½ teaspoon ground cinnamon

½ teaspoon ground cloves

7 cloves garlic, minced

½ cup cold water

¼ cup red wine vinegar

4 feet medium hog casings

1. Cut the pork into 1-inch cubes. Freeze the cubes for about 30 minutes to firm them up before grinding.

2. Grind the meat through the coarse disk of a meat grinder.

3. In a large bowl, combine the meat with the paprika, salt, coriander, crushed red pepper, allspice, cinnamon, cloves, garlic, water, and vinegar. Mix well, using your hands.

4. Cover the mixture and refrigerate overnight.

5. Prepare the casing (see page 28).

6. Stuff the mixture into the prepared casing, prick air pockets, and twist into 10-inch links. Tie off each link with butcher's twine; do not separate the links. Let the sausage air-dry in the refrigerator for a few hours.

7. Hot-smoke at 175°F (79°C) to 200°F (93°C) for 4 to 5 hours. The sausage should be firm and should reach an internal temperature of 160°F (71°C). Store in the refrigerator for 5 to 7 days, or freeze and use as needed.

Makes 4 pounds

Chinese Sausage

The thin pork sausages (lop chong or laap ch'eung) *you find in Chinatowns or Chinese groceries are spicy, slightly sweet, and delicious in stir-fries and other dishes. If desired, you can smoke the cooked sausages over aromatic wood for extra flavor.*

3 pounds pork shoulder

½ pound pork fat

3 tablespoons brown sugar

1 tablespoon kosher or coarse salt

2 teaspoons five-spice powder

2 teaspoons crushed red pepper

1 teaspoon grated orange zest

2 tablespoons soy sauce

8 feet small sheep or lamb casing

1. Cut the pork and fat into 1-inch cubes. Freeze the cubes for about 30 minutes to firm them up before grinding.

2. Grind the pork and fat through the coarse disk of a meat grinder.

3. In a large bowl, combine the meat, sugar, salt, five-spice powder, crushed red pepper, orange zest, and soy sauce. Mix well, using your hands.

4. Place the bowl, covered with wax paper, in the refrigerator to chill for at least 2 hours or overnight.

5. Prepare the casing (see page 28).

6. Stuff the mixture into the prepared casing, prick air pockets, and twist off into 6-inch lengths. Tie off each link with butcher's twine; do not separate the links.

7. Dry the sausages in the refrigerator overnight.

8. Preheat the oven to 200°F (93°C).

9. Place the sausages on a rack over a roasting pan. Bake for about 5 hours, until the sausages are firm and nearly dry to the touch. Turn off the oven, but let the sausages stay in it for 2 hours longer.

10. Discard the fat in the roasting pan. Eat sausages warm, or refrigerate for up to a week, until ready to use. These sausages will keep for 2 months in the freezer.

Makes about 3 pounds

CHAPTER 5

Beef, Lamb, and Veal Sausages

A cook turns a sausage, big with blood and fat,

over a scorching blaze without a pause,

to broil it quick.

— Homer, the *Odyssey*

WE DON'T KNOW EXACTLY WHAT KIND OF SAUSAGES Ulysses and his cohorts were eating, but we can practically smell the smoke and hear the sizzle as the fat drips into the flames. Grilling sausages outdoors, whether in the backyard or over a campfire, still brings out the adventurer in all of us. The beef, lamb, and veal sausages in this chapter come to us from all over the world — Homer's Mediterranean isles, Central Europe's farms, English pubs, and our own American Midwest.

Although pork is the meat thought of most often for sausage, many delicious and distinctive sausages traditionally are made from beef, lamb, and veal. Beef chuck is usually an economical and tasty cut to use for sausage making; leaner cuts may require the addition of extra fat to keep the sausage juicy. Lamb and veal sausages are naturally tender and palatable, and amenable to a variety of seasonings.

Experience your own sausage "odyssey" as you try out the recipes that follow.

Country-Style Beef Breakfast Sausage

For fullest flavor, refrigerate these links overnight and cook them up in the morning. But for those who are into instant gratification at breakfast time, buy the beef already ground, mix the meat and seasonings when you get up, shape the mixture into patties, and fry them in a skillet until browned on both sides. A teaspoon of cayenne sparks up the flavor if you like yours hot.

4 feet small sheep or hog casing

2½ pounds blade-cut beef chuck

½ pound beef fat

1 tablespoon plus ½ teaspoon kosher or coarse salt

2 teaspoons crumbled or ground dried sage

1½ teaspoons freshly ground black pepper (medium grind)

1 teaspoon cayenne pepper (optional)

1 teaspoon dried thyme

1. Prepare the casing (see page 28).

2. Cut the meat and fat into 1-inch cubes. Freeze the cubes for about 30 minutes to firm them up before grinding.

3. Grind the meat and fat through the fine disk of a meat grinder. Add the salt, sage, black pepper, cayenne (if using), and thyme. Mix well, using your hands.

4. Stuff the mixture into the prepared casing, prick air pockets, and twist off into 4-inch lengths. Cut the links apart with a sharp knife.

5. Place the links on a platter, cover, and refrigerate for a couple of hours or overnight to meld the flavors. Use within 2 to 3 days or freeze for up to 3 months.

6. Cook as directed on page 36 to an internal temperature of 160°F (71°C).

Makes 3 pounds

FRESH FOR FLAVOR

To substitute chopped fresh herbs for the dried sage and thyme in this recipe, or to use fresh herbs in just about any recipe calling for dried, increase the amount of fresh herbs. Generally, the rule of thumb is 1 tablespoon fresh for 1 teaspoon dried herbs.

Romanian Jewish Beef Sausage

The intense seasoning in this sausage — garlic, coriander, allspice, mustard, pepper, and other flavors — creates a savory and remarkable blend.

5 to 6 feet small lamb casing

4 pounds beef chuck

½ pound beef shoulder or other fatty cut of beef

¼ pound beef suet

2 tablespoons kosher or coarse salt

2 tablespoons whole mustard seed

1 tablespoon freshly ground black pepper (medium grind)

2 teaspoons brown sugar

2 teaspoons ground coriander

1 teaspoon dry mustard

½ teaspoon ground allspice

½ teaspoon ground bay leaf

¼ teaspoon ground cloves

2 tablespoons chopped garlic

Water (optional)

1. Prepare the casing (see page 28).

2. Cut the meat and suet into 1-inch cubes. Freeze the cubes for about 30 minutes to firm them up before grinding.

3. Grind the meat and suet through the coarse disk of a meat grinder. In a large bowl, combine the meat mixture, salt, mustard seed, pepper, sugar, coriander, dry mustard, allspice, bay leaf, cloves, and garlic. Mix well, using your hands. Freeze the mixture for about 30 minutes.

4. Grind the seasoned meat through the coarse disk of the meat grinder. Add up to ½ cup water, if necessary, to moisten the mixture enough to stuff it into the casing.

5. Stuff the mixture into the prepared casing, prick air pockets, and twist off into 5-inch lengths. Cut the links apart with a sharp knife.

6. Place the links on a platter, cover, and refrigerate for a couple of hours or overnight, to meld the flavors.

7. Cook as directed on page 36 to an internal temperature of 160°F (71°C).

Makes about 5 pounds

Beefy Pub Bangers

Bangers is British slang for the popular sausages made of meat — tradition-ally pork — and breadcrumbs and served in pubs all over the British Isles. Serve them grilled or fried.

6 feet small hog casing

2 pounds blade-cut beef chuck, well marbled

2 cups fresh breadcrumbs

2¼ teaspoons kosher or coarse salt

1 teaspoon freshly ground black pepper (medium grind)

½ teaspoon ground mace

½ teaspoon dried thyme

¼ teaspoon ground coriander

¼ teaspoon freshly grated nutmeg

2 egg yolks, beaten

1. Prepare the casing (see page 28).

2. Cut the meat into 1-inch cubes. Freeze the cubes for about 30 minutes to firm them up before grinding.

3. Grind the meat through the fine disk of a meat grinder.

4. In a large bowl, combine the meat, breadcrumbs, salt, pepper, mace, thyme, coriander, nutmeg, and egg yolks. Mix well, using your hands. Freeze for about 30 minutes.

5. Grind the seasoned meat a second time through the fine disk.

6. Stuff the mixture into the prepared casing, prick air pockets, and twist off into 4-inch lengths. Cut the links apart with a sharp knife.

7. Arrange the links on a platter and refrigerate, covered, for a couple of hours or overnight, to meld the flavors.

8. Cook as directed on page 36 to an internal tempera-ture of 160°F (71°C).

Makes 2 pounds

SKINLESS BANGERS

Some pubs skip the casing and serve skin-less bangers (which sounds racier than they are). To make this variation, shape the meat mixture into logs, roll each log in beaten egg and then in dry breadcrumbs, and chill on a baking sheet until firm. Panfry the skinless sausages until golden, about 15 minutes.

Kishke

Kishke (or kishka) are Jewish sausages often served with or in cholent, a hearty, slow-cooking stew traditionally served on the Sabbath.

    3 feet medium beef casing

    2 pounds ground chuck

    2 small onions, finely chopped

    2 teaspoons kosher or coarse salt

    1 teaspoon freshly ground black pepper (medium grind)

    2 egg yolks

⅓ to ½ cup matzo meal

1. Prepare the casing (see page 28). Cut the casing into 8-inch lengths and sew one end of each length with cotton thread.

2. In a large bowl, mix the beef, onions, salt, pepper, and egg yolks. Sprinkle with ⅓ cup matzo meal and work all the ingredients together, adding matzo meal to a total of ½ cup to make it the consistency of meatloaf.

3. Stuff the mixture into the prepared casing, allowing room for expansion. Sew closed the open end of each sausage.

4. Bring a large pot of water to a boil; cook the sausages, uncovered, in the boiling water for 5 minutes. Drain.

5. Preheat the oven to 350°F (175°C).

6. Roast the sausages in a pan in the oven, basting frequently with the pan juices, for about 1½ hours, until well browned. After cooking, they may be sliced and served warm or added in chunks to cholent. Remove the thread before serving.

Makes 2 pounds

Mustardy Beef Sausage

Coarsely textured, this sausage gets its memorable flavor from a combination of mustard, rosemary, and garlic. Be sure to use fresh rosemary, if you can. This sausage tastes best the second day, grilled or roasted.

4 feet medium hog casing

2 pounds blade-cut boneless chuck with
   25 percent fat

4 cloves garlic, minced

2 teaspoons whole yellow mustard seeds

2 teaspoons minced fresh rosemary leaves, or
   1 teaspoon dried rosemary, crushed

2 teaspoons kosher or coarse salt

1 teaspoon freshly ground black pepper (medium grind)

1 teaspoon sugar

½ teaspoon crushed red pepper (optional)

1 tablespoon Dijon mustard

1. Prepare the casing (see page 28).

2. Cut the meat into 1-inch cubes. Freeze the cubes for about 30 minutes to firm them up before grinding.

3. Grind the meat with the garlic, mustard seed, and rosemary through the coarse disk of a meat grinder.

4. In a large bowl, combine the meat mixture, salt, black pepper, sugar, crushed red pepper (if using), and mustard. Mix well, using your hands.

5. Stuff the mixture into the prepared casing, prick air pockets, and twist off into 4-inch lengths. Cut the links apart with a sharp knife.

6. Place the links on a platter, cover, and refrigerate overnight to meld the flavors. Use within 2 to 3 days or freeze for up to 3 months.

7. Cook as directed on page 36 to an internal temperature of 160°F (71°C).

Makes 2 pounds

Lamb, Rosemary, and Pine Nut Sausage

The delicate flavor of spring lamb can make a delicious sausage, especially with these characteristic Mediterranean flavors.

      4 feet sheep or small hog casing
  2½ pounds lean spring lamb
      ½ pound lamb fat
      2 tablespoons pine nuts, toasted
      1 tablespoon minced fresh rosemary leaves, or
          1½ teaspoons dried rosemary, crushed
      1 teaspoon freshly ground black pepper (medium grind)
      1 teaspoon kosher or coarse salt
      2 cloves garlic, minced

1. Prepare the casing (see page 28).
2. Cut the meat into 1-inch cubes. Freeze the cubes for about 30 minutes to firm them up before grinding.
3. In a large bowl, combine the meat, fat, pine nuts, rosemary, pepper, salt, and garlic. Mix well, using your hands.
4. Grind the mixture through the fine disk of a meat grinder.
5. Stuff the mixture into the prepared casing, prick air pockets, and twist off into 3-inch links. Cut the links apart with a sharp knife.
6. Refrigerate and use within 3 days, or freeze for up to 2 months. Cook as directed on page 36 to an internal temperature of 160°F (71°C).

Makes 3 pounds

Minted Lamb Sausage

If you like the classic pairing of roast lamb and mint jelly, you'll like this sausage. Of course, you can experiment with different varieties of mint to suit your taste. Consider lemon, pineapple, or apple mint instead of the usual spearmint. Whenever possible, use fresh mint leaves rather than dried.

4 feet sheep or small hog casing	1 tablespoon kosher or coarse salt
2½ pounds lean lamb, cubed	
½ pound lamb fat, cubed	1 teaspoon freshly ground black pepper (medium grind)
2 tablespoons chopped fresh mint leaves	½ tablespoon grated lemon zest

1. Prepare the casing (see page 28).

2. Cut the meat into 1-inch cubes. Freeze the cubes for about 30 minutes to firm them up before grinding.

3. In a large bowl, combine the meat, fat, mint, salt, pepper, and lemon zest. Mix well, using your hands. Freeze the mixture for about 30 minutes.

4. Grind the mixture through the fine disk of a meat grinder.

5. Stuff the mixture into the prepared casing, prick air pockets, and twist off into 3-inch links. Cut the links apart with a sharp knife.

6. Refrigerate and use within 3 days, or freeze for up to 2 months. Cook as directed on page 36 to an internal temperature of 160°F (71°C).

Makes 3 pounds

Lamb, Ginger, and Fruit Sausage

This unusual variation on lamb sausage gets its zest from crystallized ginger and dried apricots.

4 feet sheep or small hog casing

2½ pounds lean lamb, cubed

½ pound lamb fat, cubed

1 tablespoon kosher or coarse salt

1 teaspoon freshly ground black pepper (medium grind)

2 tablespoons finely chopped dried apricots

1 tablespoon finely chopped crystallized ginger

2 tablespoons lemon juice or white wine

1. Prepare the casing (see page 28).

2. Cut the meat into 1-inch cubes. Freeze the cubes for about 30 minutes to firm them up before grinding.

3. In a large bowl, combine the meat and fat cubes with the salt, pepper, apricots, ginger, and lemon juice. Mix well, using your hands. Freeze the mixture for about 30 minutes.

4. Grind the mixture through the fine disk of a meat grinder.

5. Stuff the mixture into the casing, prick air pockets, and twist off into 3-inch lengths. Cut the links apart with a sharp knife.

6. Refrigerate and use within 3 days, or freeze for up to 2 months. Cook as directed on page 36 to an internal temperature of 160°F (71°C).

Makes 3 pounds

EATING HAGGIS ON NEW YEAR'S EVE

If you are ever in Scotland on New Year's Eve, known there as Hogmanay, the most traditional thing you can do is to eat haggis. The word *haggis* is thought to be derived from the French word *hachis*, meaning "to chop." What you will be served is a large round sausage encased in a sheep stomach. It is most properly served to the sound of a kilted Highlander playing the bagpipes. It is customary to have a sip of neat whiskey between mouthfuls.

CHRISTOPHER KOETKE
TEACHING CHEFS-IN-TRAINING ALL ABOUT SAUSAGE

Christopher is a chef-instructor in the School of Culinary Arts at Kendall College in Evanston, Illinois. All of the culinary students learn basic sausage making, and some go on to take Chef Koetke's elective in the finer points of the art.

This elective course is an intensive, four-day session, a total immersion in sausage making that results in about 25 varieties of sausage, perhaps 500 pounds in all. At the end of the four days, Christopher will have passed along not only his expertise but his passion for sausage as well.

"Sausage is universal! It's a worldwide experience — Chinese, Thai, Mexican, Polish, Spanish, Cajun, even good old American hot dogs," Chris explains. "It's like making bread, a hands-on, tactile experience, and once people do it, they love it."

Chris has been eating and enjoying sausage "forever," as he says. He first started working under a French chef when he was 13, and went on to train in France, where he got involved with charcuterie and learned to make dry cured sausages as well as fresh. Back in Illinois, he was able to draw on the rich ethnic mix in Chicago to discover even more sausage varieties.

"Some people worry about using nitrites in cured sausage," he says, "but you can't get around it. Not only are nitrites a tradition, but they help keep the color and you need them as a preservative. Alcohol is another ingredient that adds flavor and, if used in high enough concentrations, can kill bacteria."

Christopher tells his culinary students, "Go out there and be creative. You'll blow people's minds with all the varieties of sausage." His enthusiasm is contagious, too. His students often seek out unusual sausages and bring them to him to taste and analyze. "I learn something in every class," the teacher says.

Merguez

Christopher Koetke, a chef-instructor in the School of Culinary Arts at Kendall College, shared this recipe for merguez, a spicy African lamb sausage commonly found in Algeria, Tunisia, and Morocco and used to garnish couscous. Merguez is often seasoned with red chiles, but here, paprika and ground sumac are used. You can find ground sumac wherever Middle Eastern foods are sold. Learn more about Chris's sausage passion on the preceding page.

6 feet sheep casing

3½ pounds lamb meat, trimmed of most fat

1 pound lamb fat

3½ tablespoons Hungarian sweet paprika

1 tablespoon plus 2 teaspoons kosher or coarse salt

1½ tablespoons ground sumac

1 tablespoon ground cumin

1 tablespoon cayenne pepper

1 teaspoon ground anise seed

1 teaspoon dried oregano

½ teaspoon freshly ground black pepper (medium grind)

½ teaspoon quatre épices

1 clove garlic, finely minced

¾ cup cold water

1. Prepare the casing (see page 28).

2. Cut the meat and fat into 1-inch cubes. Freeze the cubes for about 30 minutes to firm them up before grinding.

3. Grind the meat and fat through the fine disk of a meat grinder.

4. Combine the salt, sumac, cumin, cayenne, anise seed, oregano, black pepper, quatre épices, paprika, garlic, and water in a small bowl. Combine this spice slurry with the meat in a large bowl and mix well with your hands until the meat becomes slightly elastic.

5. Stuff the mixture into the prepared casing, prick air pockets, and twist off into 8- to 10-inch links. Do not separate the links.

6. Hang for 1 day in a cooler or refrigerator.

7. Use in the next 2 days, or freeze for up to 2 months. Cook as directed on page 36 to an internal temperature of 160°F (71°C).

NOTE: Sumac is a shrub native to Turkey. Its fleshy petals and berries are dried and pulverized to make a purple-red, sharp-tasting spice.

Makes 4½ pounds

Bockwurst

Traditionally seasoned with parsley and chives, this mild-flavored veal sausage tastes best poached and eaten hot.

2 feet small (1½ inches diameter) hog casing

1¾ pounds veal

¼ pound pork fat

1 teaspoon kosher or coarse salt

¾ teaspoon ground cloves

½ teaspoon freshly ground white pepper (medium grind)

¼ cup finely minced onion

2 teaspoons finely chopped flat-leaf parsley

2 teaspoons minced chives

1 cup milk

1 egg, beaten

1. Prepare the casing (see page 28).

2. Cut the meat and fat into 1-inch cubes. Freeze the cubes for about 30 minutes to firm them up before grinding.

3. Grind the veal and the pork fat separately through the fine disk of a meat grinder.

4. In large bowl, combine the veal, fat, salt, cloves, pepper, onion, parsley, chives, milk, and egg. Mix well, using your hands. Freeze for 30 minutes.

5. Grind the seasoned mixture through the fine disk of the meat grinder.

6. Stuff the mixture into the prepared casing, prick air pockets, and twist off into 3- to 4-inch lengths. Cut the links apart with a sharp knife.

7. Cook immediately or store, covered, in the refrigerator for up to 2 days.

8. To cook, poach in simmering water for 25 to 30 minutes.

Makes 2 pounds

WHAT'S IN A NAME?

bockwurst

Bock means "buck" or "he-goat" in German, perhaps the original meat in this mild-flavored veal sausage. *Wurst*, of course, means "sausage." In Germany, bockwurst is often served in the spring, washed down with full-bodied, hoppy bock beer.

Midwestern Potato Sausage

The Swedish immigrants who settled the upper Midwest and northern Plains states in the nineteenth century brought a strong tradition of sausage making to this country. These sausages are poached after they are stuffed, then refrigerated. This blend of meat and vegetables is a meal in itself!

4 feet medium hog casing

3 pounds blade-cut beef chuck

2 pounds potatoes, peeled and diced

1 small onion, chopped

½ cup nonfat dry milk

2 tablespoons kosher or coarse salt

2 teaspoons caraway seed

1 teaspoon ground allspice

1 teaspoon freshly ground black pepper (medium grind)

Water

1. Prepare the casing (see page 28).

2. Cut the meat into 1-inch cubes. Freeze the cubes for about 30 minutes to firm them up before grinding.

3. Grind the meat, potatoes, and onion through the coarse disk of a meat grinder.

4. In a large bowl, combine the meat mixture, dry milk, salt, caraway seed, allspice, and pepper. Mix well, using your hands.

5. Add water as needed (up to ½ cup) to moisten the mixture enough to hold it together. Freeze for 30 minutes.

6. Grind the seasoned mixture through the coarse disk of the meat grinder.

7. Stuff the mixture into the prepared casing, prick air pockets, and twist off into 5-inch lengths. Do not separate the links.

8. Bring a large pot of lightly salted water to a boil. Add the sausages, reduce the heat, and poach the sausages in the simmering water for 40 minutes.

9. Drain the sausages, pat dry, and cut the links apart with a sharp knife. Refrigerate them, covered, for up to 3 days. To serve, sauté gently in a heavy skillet until golden brown.

Makes about 5 pounds

Castle Street Veal Sausage

Chef Michael Ballon of Castle Street Café in Great Barrington, Massachusetts, developed this elegant, rich veal sausage. It is a bit complicated to make, requiring two grindings of the meat and the preparation of a mousse to enrich the mixture — but well worth it!

4 pounds veal shoulder, cubed

2 tablespoons kosher or coarse salt

1 teaspoon dried basil

1 teaspoon freshly ground black pepper (medium grind)

1 teaspoon dried thyme

2 bunches fresh parsley, coarsely chopped

4 eggs

¾ cup cornstarch

¾ cup (6 ounces) heavy cream

3 cups grated Parmesan cheese

6 feet medium hog casing

1. Combine the veal, salt, basil, pepper, and thyme in a large bowl. Add the parsley and mix well, using your hands.

2. Grind the mixture through the coarse disk of a meat grinder.

3. Combine the eggs, cornstarch, and cream and beat well with a whisk or an electric mixer until the cornstarch is dissolved. For best results, work quickly to keep the mixture cold.

4. In a food processor, process one-quarter of the cold veal mixture and the egg mixture until smooth. Transfer the mixture to a large mixing bowl and combine with the remaining veal mixture. Add the Parmesan and mix well. Refrigerate, covered, for at least 2 hours.

5. While the mixture chills, prepare the casing (see page 28).

6. Grind the chilled meat mixture through the fine disk of the meat grinder.

7. Stuff the mixture into the prepared casing, prick air pockets, and twist off into 6-inch lengths.

8. Bring a large pot of water to a boil. Add the sausages, reduce the heat, and poach the sausages in the simmering water for 20 minutes.

9. Drain the sausages, pat dry, and cut the links apart with a sharp knife. Refrigerate them, covered, for up to 2 days. Cook as directed on page 36 for cooked sausages.

Makes 4 pounds of sausage

MICHAEL BALLON,
CASTLE STREET CAFÉ,
GREAT BARRINGTON, MASSACHUSETTS

Chef Ballon is mostly self-trained, but he did formally study pâté and sausage making at the New York Restaurant School.

He gets the meat he serves at his restaurant (as well as hog casings for his sausage) from a butcher on 14th Street in New York City, legendary heart of the meat-packing area. "Most markets today get their meat already broken down, but if you can find a genuine butcher — a dying art, I'm afraid — you can get the finest hanging and dry-aged meat," he says.

Chef Ballon usually buys a whole loin of veal, using most for chops and the rest for this memorable sausage. Veal shoulder works well for the sausage, too. He also makes a country-style pork sausage that he uses in cassoulet.

Veal Saltimbocca Sausage

Saltimbocca literally means "leap into the mouth," a reference to the Roman specialty of thinly sliced veal layered with fresh sage leaves and prosciutto that is sautéed in butter and simmered in white wine. That's enough to make anyone want the dish to leap into the mouth! This sausage mimics many of those flavors.

4 feet small hog casing

2 pounds veal shoulder

2 tablespoons butter

4 ounces white mushrooms, minced

12 fresh sage leaves, chopped

2 teaspoons kosher or coarse salt

½ teaspoon ground white pepper (medium grind)

½ cup dry white wine

1. Prepare the casing (see page 28).

2. Cut the meat into 1-inch cubes. Freeze the cubes for about 30 minutes to firm them up before grinding.

3. Grind the veal through the fine disk of a meat grinder. Refrigerate.

4. In a medium-sized skillet, melt the butter over low to medium heat. When the butter foams, add the mushrooms and sauté, stirring the mushrooms occasionally, until all the liquid evaporates and the mushrooms brown, 5 to 7 minutes. Refrigerate the mixture for 30 minutes.

5. In a large bowl, combine the ground veal, mushroom mixture, sage, salt, pepper, and wine in a large bowl. Mix well, using your hands.

6. Grind the meat mixture through the fine disk of the meat grinder.

7. Stuff the mixture into the prepared casing, prick air pockets, and twist off into 5-inch links.

8. Bring a large pot of water to a boil. Add the sausages, reduce the heat, and poach the sausages in the simmering water for 20 minutes.

9. Drain the sausages, pat dry, and cut the links apart with a sharp knife. Refrigerate for up to 2 days or freeze for up to 2 months. To serve, reheat gently until warmed through.

Makes 2 pounds

All-Beef Summer Sausage

This easy-to-make sausage uses two shortcuts: You buy meat that is already ground and you use liquid smoke and oven baking rather than hot-smoking the sausage. Purists can make the sausage the traditional way: Grind your own meat and hot-smoke the sausages (omit liquid smoke) until they reach an internal temperature of 160°F (71°C). Summer sausage makes an excellent snack or hors d'oeuvre sliced and served with thinly sliced rye bread.

3 feet large beef casing

3 pounds ground chuck with 25 percent fat

4 cloves garlic, minced

1 tablespoon kosher or coarse salt

2 teaspoons brown sugar

1 teaspoon whole mustard seed

1 teaspoon freshly ground black pepper (medium grind)

Curing salt (use supplier's recommended quantity for 3 pounds of meat)

1 cup water

¾ teaspoon liquid smoke

1. Prepare the casing (see page 28).

2. In a large bowl, combine the ground meat and the garlic. Mix well, using your hands.

3. In a smaller bowl, combine the salt, sugar, mustard seed, pepper, curing salt, water, and liquid smoke. Stir until blended. Add the water mixture to the meat mixture. Mix well, using your hands.

4. Stuff the mixture into the prepared casing, prick air pockets, and twist off into 6-inch lengths. Cut the links apart with a sharp knife. Place the links on a platter, cover, and refrigerate overnight to meld the flavors.

5. Preheat the oven to 200°F (93°C).

6. Arrange the links on a broiler pan and bake for 4 hours, or until the internal temperature reaches 160°F (71°C) on an instant-read thermometer. The meat will remain bright red even when fully cooked. (Alternatively, the links can be smoked in a smoker following manufacturer's instructions.)

7. Cool the sausages. Eat immediately or refrigerate for up to 3 weeks.

Makes 3 pounds

Kosher Salami

This recipe makes real kosher salami if you have access to kosher-butchered beef. If not, then, just like kosher dill pickles, it's the flavor that counts. Since this is an all-beef recipe, use blade-cut chuck, which has about the right proportion of lean to fat. Trim away all fat when cubing the meat and precisely measure the amounts. Before you jump into this recipe, check on the smokehouse or dig out the instructions to the electric smoker, because you will be needing it soon.

8 pounds lean beef chuck

2 pounds beef fat

3 tablespoons plus 1 teaspoon kosher or coarse salt

1½ tablespoons sugar

1 tablespoon coarsely ground coriander seed

1 tablespoon freshly ground white pepper (fine grind)

1½ teaspoons coarsely crushed white pepper

½ teaspoon ascorbic acid

Curing salt (use supplier's recommended quantity for 10 pounds of meat; see Notes)

1 cup dry white wine

1½ teaspoons finely minced garlic

4 feet large beef casing

1. Cut the meat and fat into 1-inch cubes. Refrigerate the cubes for about 30 minutes to firm them up before grinding.

2. Grind the beef through the fine disk of a meat grinder into a large bowl.

3. Grind the fat through the coarse disk of a meat grinder into the bowl with the meat.

4. Mix together the salt, sugar, coriander, finely and coarsely ground white pepper, ascorbic acid, curing salt, wine, and garlic and pour the mixture over the meat and fat. Mix well, using your hands.

5. Spread the mixture in a large pan and cure in the refrigerator for 24 to 48 hours.

6. Prepare the casing (see page 28).

7. Stuff the mixture into the prepared casing and twist off into 8- or 9-inch links. Tie off each link with butcher's twine; do not separate the links.

8. Hang the sausage in a cold place to dry for 1 week.

9. Wipe the sausage dry and smoke at 120°F (49°C) for 8 hours.

10. Increase the smoking temperature to 150 to 160°F (66 71°C) and smoke for an additional 4 hours.

11. Because the smoking aids in the drying process, the salami should be ready to eat after about 3 weeks of additional drying in a cold place. (See Notes.) When dried, cut the links apart with a sharp knife, wrap the salami in plastic, and refrigerate.

NOTES:

- We recommend that you use a commercial premixed cure in any recipe for cured sausage. Premixed cures replace the saltpeter in older recipes.
- The processing in this recipe may not fully cook the beef. See "Dry Sausage Safety" on page 42.

Makes 10 pounds

GRINDING SPICES

The simplest way to grind whole spices, which is the most flavorful way to go, is with an old-fashioned mortar and pestle. The pestle does the pounding and rubbing for you. Choose a ceramic or marble mortar and pestle, because wooden sets absorb food odors easily.

If you want to keep elbow grease to a minimum, you might take the lead from some sausage makers, who keep around a spare electric coffee grinder for grinding spices. There are also hand-operated grinders available. Just twist the top, and the ground spices fall into the jar below.

Mennonite Smoked Beef Sausage

This recipe, adapted from one in an old Mennonite cookbook, makes a sweet, smoky, beefy treat.

6 feet large beef casing

10 pounds beef chuck, including fat

1½ cups brown sugar

3 tablespoons plus 1 teaspoon kosher or coarse salt

2 tablespoons freshly ground black pepper (medium grind)

½ teaspoon ascorbic acid

Curing salt (use supplier's recommended quantity for 10 pounds meat; see Note), dissolved in 1 cup water

1. Prepare the casings (see page 28).

2. Cut the meat into 1-inch cubes. Freeze the cubes for about 30 minutes to firm them up before grinding.

3. Grind the beef through the coarse disk of a meat grinder.

4. In a large bowl, combine the meat, sugar, salt, pepper, ascorbic acid, and dissolved curing salt. Mix well, using your hands.

5. Stuff the sausage into the prepared casing, prick air pockets, and tie off into 10-inch links with butcher's twine; do not separate the links.

6. Hang in a cold spot to dry for 24 hours.

7. Cold-smoke for about 12 hours at 90°F (32°C) and then increase the smokehouse temperature to about 120°F (49°C) and smoke for 4 or 5 hours longer, until the sausage is firm.

8. Hang the sausage in a cool place to dry for at least 2 more weeks before eating. When dried, cut the links apart with a sharp knife, wrap the sausage in plastic, and refrigerate. Peel away the casing before eating.

NOTES:

- We recommend that you use a commercial premixed cure in any recipe for cured sausage. Premixed cures replace the saltpeter in older recipes.
- The processing in this recipe may not fully cook the beef. See "Dry Sausage Safety" on page 42.

Makes 10 pounds

JOE BRANDEL
THE ADVANCED BEGINNER

"I call myself an advanced beginner," Joe Brandel says cheerfully. "Sausage making is a great hobby." Joe grew up near a Polish delicatessen and always loved sausage. He "dabbled" in smoking, but never tried making his own sausage until recently, when his family gave him a grinder and stuffer for Christmas. "It took about 15 minutes to master the stuffer, and I quickly learned not to overstuff the links," he says.

Joe used knowledge gained from years of working in the refrigeration and air-conditioning business in New Hampshire to make a temperature-controlled smoker from an old refrigerator. "I make sausage on Saturday, smoke it on Sunday. So far, nothing has had to go to the dog — everything has turned out well," he says. "I made some smoked jerky, starting with about 10 pounds of meat and ending up with 3½ pounds of jerky. It sure didn't last long with my family and friends."

So far, Joe has made hot Italian sausage (his son's favorite), breakfast sausages, and kielbasa in addition to the jerky. He'd like to try smoking bacon, too. He is pleased to pass along a few tips to new sausage makers:

- Get as much information as you can, especially if you are going to make cured sausage.
- Experiment, and don't get discouraged. Be patient with the process.
- Try working with about 10 pounds of meat at a time to start.
- Be serious about cleanliness at all times.

Thuringer Sausage

This wurst is a German invention that is more often than not marketed as a fresh sausage. It is smoked slightly, and therefore will keep longer than fresh sausage, but since it is not completely dried, it should be consumed within a couple of weeks.

1 pound prefrozen pork fat (see Notes)

4 pounds lean beef

2 tablespoons plus 1 teaspoon kosher or coarse salt

1 tablespoon freshly ground white pepper (fine grind)

1 tablespoon sugar

2 teaspoons sweet paprika

½ teaspoon pulverized caraway seed

½ teaspoon ground celery seed

½ teaspoon crushed coriander

½ teaspoon ground mace

½ teaspoon crushed mustard seed

¼ teaspoon ascorbic acid

¼ teaspoon freshly ground nutmeg (fine grind)

Curing salt (use supplier's recommendation for 5 pounds of meat; see Notes)

4 feet medium (1-inch-diameter) hog casing

1. Partially thaw the pork fat and cut it into 1-inch cubes. Cut the beef into 1-inch cubes, then freeze the cubes for about 30 minutes to firm them up before grinding.

2. Grind the fat and meat separately through the fine disk of a meat grinder.

3. In a large bowl, combine the fat and meat, salt, pepper, sugar, paprika, caraway seed, celery seed, coriander, mace, mustard seed, ascorbic acid, nutmeg, and curing salt. Mix well, using your hands.

4. Spread the mixture in a large, shallow pan, cover loosely with wax paper, and cure it in the refrigerator for 24 hours.

5. Prepare the casing (see page 28).

6. Stuff the mixture into the prepared casing, prick air pockets, and twist off into 4- to 6-inch links. With butcher's twine, tie two separate knots between *every other* link, and one knot at the beginning and another at

the end of the stuffed casing. Cut the pairs apart from each other with a sharp knife.

7. Hang up the sausage to dry in a cool place, or store, uncovered, in the refrigerator for 2 days.

8. Bring the sausage to room temperature, then cold-smoke at 90°F (32°C) for 12 hours.

9. Hang to dry for another day or two before eating. Make sure the sausage is kept cool.

NOTES:

- Prepare pork according to the instructions on page 40 to ensure that it is free from trichinosis.
- The processing in this recipe may not fully cook the beef. See "Dry Sausage Safety" on page 42.
- We recommend that you use a commercial premixed cure in any recipe for cured sausage. Use the commercial premixed cure at the level recommended by the supplier. Premixed cures replace the saltpeter in older recipes.

Makes 5 pounds

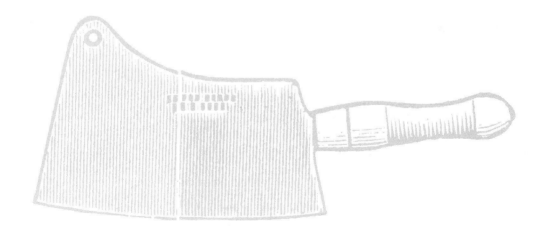

CHAPTER 6

Combination Sausages

Sausage usually carries the label of its birthplace

even when it is imitated in foreign countries

which have forgotten that the frankfurter was

invented in Frankfort and boloney in Bologna.

— Waverley Root, *The Food of France*

SOME OF OUR FAVORITE TRADITIONAL SAUSAGES are artful combinations of pork, beef, veal, lamb, and even surprising ingredients, such as potatoes. Sausage originated with people using up the scraps of what they had at butchering time, making something tasty, nourishing, and versatile out of some pretty unpromising raw material.

In Europe, innovations in sausage making centered on some of the important areas of salt deposits — the mountains of eastern France; the area around Salzburg (literally, "Salt Town"), Austria; the Alsace-Lorraine; and several regions within Eastern Europe and Poland. The domestic animals of each area found their way, in the end (for them), into sausages that reflected local foodways and crops.

Frankfurters, Vienna sausages, Genoa salami, Bavarian summer sausage — all of these and their many cousins are commonplace sights in our supermarkets today, far from their points of origin. When we make our own, going back to the original recipes, we also make a connection to our sausage-making forebears.

Fresh Polish Kielbasa

The ingredients and even the pronunciation of kielbasa are as variable as the vagaries of spring weather, the time of year when kielbasa is traditionally made. What passes for kielbasa in one area might be regarded as inauthentic in another. This version uses pork, beef, and veal. These sausages are excellent grilled over a charcoal fire and eaten in a hard roll lathered with spicy brown mustard.

6 feet large hog casing

3 pounds lean pork butt

1 pound lean beef chuck

½ pound veal shoulder

½ pound pork fat

2 tablespoons sweet paprika

1 tablespoon freshly ground black pepper (medium grind)

2½ teaspoons kosher or coarse salt

2 teaspoons dried marjoram

2 teaspoons dried summer savory

½ teaspoon ground allspice

3 cloves garlic, minced

1. Prepare the casing (see page 28).

2. Cut the pork, beef, veal, and fat into 1-inch cubes. Freeze the cubes for about 30 minutes to firm them up before grinding.

3. Grind the meats and fat together through the coarse disk of a meat grinder.

4. In a large bowl, combine the meat mixture, paprika, pepper, salt, marjoram, summer savory, allspice, and garlic. Mix well, using your hands.

5. Stuff the mixture into the prepared casing, prick air pockets, and twist the sausage into long links. Lengths of 18 to 24 inches are traditional.

6. Coil the links and allow them to dry in a cool place for 4 hours or refrigerate for 24 hours, uncovered.

7. Cut the links apart with a sharp knife and refrigerate for 2 to 3 days or freeze for up to 2 months. Cook by roasting in a 425°F (220°C) oven for 45 minutes to an internal temperature of 160°F (71°C).

Makes 5 pounds

THE REAL WAY TO EAT BRATWURST, SHEBOYGAN-STYLE

In Sheboygan, Wisconsin, the self-styled Bratwurst Capital of the World, bratwurst making, cooking, and eating is serious business.

Each of the meat markets in town has its own recipe for bratwurst (mace is rumored to be one of the secret ingredients). In order to put on a "brat fry," as it's called, true bratwurst lovers make a pilgrimage to their favorite meat market for "brats" (rhymes with "trots") and to a bakery for crusty "hard rolls," the traditional holder for the cooked meat.

Bratwurst is always grilled slowly over a charcoal fire that is not too hot (coals should be covered with gray ash, not glowing). However, this is never referred to as "grilling." It is called "frying out," and the grill itself is called a "fryer," as is the person who is doing the frying. The bratwurst is never pricked during grilling, lest any of the precious juices and flavors leak out. It takes about 20 minutes, with lots of turning, to produce a perfectly cooked brat. (It's traditional for the fryer to drink a beer during this process.)

After the brats are done, some Sheboyganites simmer them briefly (5 to 10 minutes) in a mixture of beer, melted butter, and raw onions, but this is optional. If you want to try it, combine two cans of beer, half a stick of butter, and one peeled and sliced onion, and bring to a simmer. (In the city of Milwaukee, 1 hour to the south of Sheboygan, some prefer to simmer the bratwurst in this mixture *before* frying, but this is not done in Sheboygan.)

Bratwurst is always served hot with brown mustard, a dab of ketchup, dill pickles, and raw onions ("the works") piled into a buttered hard roll. Two brats to a roll is called a double. Single brats are for wimps.

Wash it all down with another cold beer or two.

Bratwurst

When German immigrants settled in the Midwest in the mid-nineteenth century, they brought their lust for sausage with them. Bratwurst, usually made with both pork and veal, tastes best grilled over charcoal until golden brown on all sides.

3 feet small hog casing

1½ pounds lean pork butt

1 pound veal shoulder

½ pound pork fat

1 teaspoon freshly ground white pepper (medium grind)

1 teaspoon kosher or coarse salt

½ teaspoon crushed caraway seed

½ teaspoon dried marjoram

¼ teaspoon ground allspice

1. Prepare the casing (see page 28).

2. Cut the pork, veal, and pork fat into 1-inch cubes. Freeze the cubes for about 30 minutes to firm them up before grinding.

3. Grind the pork, veal, and pork fat separately through the fine blade of a meat grinder. Mix the ground meats and fat together, freeze for 30 minutes, and grind again.

4. In a large bowl, combine the meat mixture, salt, caraway seed, marjoram, and allspice. Mix well, using your hands.

5. Stuff the mixture into the prepared casing, prick air pockets, and twist off into 4- to 5-inch lengths. Cut the links apart with a sharp knife.

6. Refrigerate for up to 2 days. The bratwurst can be panfried or grilled over charcoal until golden and cooked to an internal temperature of 160°F (71°C), about 20 minutes.

Makes 3 pounds

CHUCK MIESFELD
THE BEST BRATS IN WISCONSIN
(AND THE RECIPE IS A SECRET, SO DON'T ASK)

Chuck Miesfeld's last name is a household word in Sheboygan, Wisconsin, the town on Lake Michigan that prides itself on its bratwurst and other memorable German sausages. Miesfeld's Triangle Market is one of several small, family-owned businesses that specialize in handmade sausages and hand-cut meats.

It's not unusual for a Sheboyganite to do a week's grocery shopping at one of the big-box supermarkets in town and then make separate trips to Miesfeld's for bratwurst and to City Bakery for the hard rolls that make the perfect foil for the spicy sausage. If Miesfeld's runs out of brats, it's a major crisis.

Chuck is a third-generation sausage maker whose grandfather started making brats, summer sausage, and other favorites in the 1940s. Chuck and his employees still use the same recipe and make bratwurst fresh nearly every day, especially in the summer. They pride themselves on quality and freshness, and it pays off in customer loyalty and awards for Wisconsin's Best Bratwurst.

About that recipe: Chuck will tell you that Miesfeld's uses pork shoulder, 80 percent lean, and seasons the meat with salt, pepper, and nutmeg. Contrary to rumor, Miesfeld's does not add mace. The rest is a secret known only to him and to one of his best friends, a spice wholesaler who lives in Little Chute, Wisconsin, and hand-mixes the brat seasoning blend. (The handwritten recipe is kept under lock and key, and the friend isn't talking.)

He may not give you his secret brat recipe, but Chuck will tell you what he considers Miesfeld's secret to success:

- Always abide by the rules of cleanliness. Keep the meat under 40°F (4°C) at all times.
- Use the very freshest spices and herbs you can find.
- Take pride in your work.

Loukanika

These spicy Greek sausages — fragrant with coriander, orange zest, and classic retsina wine — make you think you are eating at a table overlooking the blue Aegean Sea rather than your own backyard.

6 feet medium hog casing

2 pounds lean pork

1 pound boneless lamb leg or shoulder

½ pound pork fat

1 large onion, chopped

4 cloves garlic, chopped

2 tablespoons olive oil

1 tablespoon ground coriander

1 tablespoon kosher or coarse salt

1 teaspoon ground cumin

1 teaspoon freshly ground black pepper

2 teaspoons chopped fresh thyme, or 1 teaspoon dried

Grated zest from 1 orange (about 2 tablespoons)

½ cup retsina or Metaxa (Greek brandy)

1. Prepare the casing (see page 28).

2. Cut the pork, lamb, and fat into 1-inch cubes. Refrigerate the cubes for about 30 minutes to firm them up before grinding.

3. Sauté the onion and garlic in the olive oil over low heat until softened, about 5 minutes. Do not let the garlic burn. Refrigerate the mixture for 30 minutes.

4. In a large bowl, combine the onion mixture with the pork, lamb, pork fat, coriander, salt, cumin, pepper, thyme, and orange zest. Mix well, using your hands.

5. Grind the mixture through the fine disk of a meat grinder.

6. Add the wine to moisten the mixture and knead well, using your hands.

7. Stuff the mixture into the prepared casing, prick air pockets, and twist off the sausage into 6-inch links. Cut the links apart with a sharp knife.

8. Refrigerate for up to 3 days, or freeze for up to 2 months.

9. Cook as directed on page 36 to an internal temperature of 160°F (71°C).

Makes about 4 pounds

Asian Duck and Pork Sausage

The pork and the duck leg meat are mixed with the savory signatures of the East — garlic, scallions, ginger, and sweet five-spice powder — in this unusual sausage.

    4 feet small hog or sheep casing
    2 pounds pork butt
   10 duck legs, skinned, boned, and diced
      (about 1 pound of meat)
    2 teaspoons kosher or coarse salt
    1 teaspoon five-spice powder
    ½ teaspoon freshly ground black pepper
      (medium grind)
    2 tablespoons chopped scallions
    2 teaspoons minced garlic
    2 teaspoons grated fresh gingerroot
    ¼ cup rice wine or dry white wine

1. Prepare the casing (see page 28).

2. Cut the pork into 1-inch cubes. Freeze the cubes for about 30 minutes to firm them up before grinding.

3. Grind the pork and duck through the fine disk of a meat grinder.

4. In a large bowl, combine the pork, duck, salt, five-spice powder, pepper, scallions, garlic, and gingerroot. Mix well, using your hands. Add the rice wine and mix well.

5. Stuff the mixture into the prepared casing, prick air pockets, and twist off into 5-inch links. Cut the links apart with a sharp knife.

6. Place the links on a platter, cover, and refrigerate for 24 hours so flavors meld and sausage firms up. Use within 2 to 3 days or freeze for up to 3 months.

7. To cook, grill, turning frequently, for about 20 minutes, until golden brown and cooked to an internal temperature of 165°F (74°C).

Makes about 3 pounds

Feta Links

A more recent creation of home sausage maker Bill St. Onge, this sausage has Greek flavors very different from those in his first sausage, a Polish inspiration. Read about Bill on page 127.

    4 feet small hog casings
 2½ pounds ground beef with 25 percent fat
 2½ pounds ground lamb with 25 percent fat
    ½ cup nonfat dry milk
    1 tablespoon kosher or coarse salt
    1 tablespoon dried basil
    1 tablespoon dried oregano
    1 teaspoon onion powder
    1 cup chopped fresh spinach
    8 ounces feta cheese with liquid
    1 large red bell pepper, finely diced
    1 heaping tablespoon minced garlic
    1 tablespoon lemon juice
 1½ cups chicken stock

1. Prepare the casing (see page 28).

2. In a large bowl, combine the beef, lamb, dry milk, salt, basil, onion powder, oregano, spinach, feta, garlic, lemon juice, and chicken stock. Mix well, using your hands.

3. Stuff the mixture into the prepared casing, prick air pockets, and twist off into 4-inch links.

4. Cook as directed on page 36 to an internal temperature of 160°F (71°C). Use within 2 to 3 days or freeze for up to 3 months.

Makes 5 pounds

Spicy Pizza Sausage

A bold and zesty sausage, this is not stuffed into a casing; it can be divided into single-pizza portions and frozen until needed. You can buy the meat already ground, or buy boneless cuts and grind them (finely) yourself. The mixture also makes tasty meatballs to add to spaghetti sauce.

1 pound ground pork

1 pound ground turkey

2 teaspoons fennel seed

2 teaspoons kosher or coarse salt

1½ teaspoons crushed red pepper

½ teaspoon dried basil, or 1 teaspoon chopped fresh

½ teaspoon dried oregano, or 1 teaspoon chopped fresh

½ teaspoon freshly ground black pepper (medium grind)

¼ cup chopped fresh parsley

3 garlic cloves, minced

2 tablespoons grated Parmesan or Asiago cheese

½ cup dry red wine

1 teaspoon olive oil

1. In a large bowl, combine the ground meats and mix well. Add the fennel seed, salt, crushed red pepper, basil, oregano, black pepper, parsley, garlic, and Parmesan. Mix well, using your hands. Add the wine; mix well.

2. In a large skillet, heat the olive oil over medium heat, then sauté the sausage, stirring to help the sausage crumble, for 10 minutes, until the meat is evenly browned. Use on top of pizza; freeze any leftovers in usable portions. Or, divide the raw mixture into four or five portions and freeze them separately in resealable plastic bags for up to 2 months.

Makes 2 pounds

RICK AND KATHIE BROWN
MAKING SAUSAGE THEIR BUSINESS

Rick Brown has been making sausage since he was a little boy at his grandmother's side. "I loved making sausage with my grandmother," he remembers. "She had learned to make it from her own parents, my great-grandparents, who came here from Austria in the late 1800s and always raised and slaughtered their own animals." Rick and his grandmother made hot and sweet Italian sausage, Polish sausage, and many other kinds.

Rick worked in the restaurant-supply business but always hoped to make sausage a vocation and not just a hobby. His chance came after his grandmother died. She left him her sausage stuffer and something else: a little seed money for a new business. In August of 2001, Rick and his wife, Kathie, opened The Sausage Source in a small storefront in Hillsboro, New Hampshire.

At first Rick and Kathie both kept their day jobs and worked in the store at night and on weekends. Sausage aficionados and curious passersby stopped in to check out the seasoning mixes, shiny new grinders and stuffers, refrigerator cases full of hog casings, brightly labeled bottles of hot sauce, kits for making sausage and jerky, and many other items. Their Web site brought more customers to the store (see Resources on page 272 for more information), and after about nine months, Rick cautiously reduced his day job to part time and expanded his hours at Sausage Source. He also built a little kitchen with a walk-up window where people can buy sausage subs and grinders, made on-site and cooked fresh every day.

Kathie, meanwhile, took over all of the bookkeeping tasks, maintains the mailing lists, and processes Web orders. They ship hog casings, their own seasoning mixes, and many other items as far as Europe and Australia. Rick explains the appeal of his business: "Most people want good sausage that's already made. I help them learn to make it themselves. Customers who come here can try our own sausages, which we make with our own mixes, and then they can branch out on their own."

Frankfurters

The humble hot dog is the most widely consumed sausage in the world. Most of the hot dogs you buy in the supermarket are nutritional nightmares, with more than 50 percent of their weight coming from fat, water, and salt. This is not your only choice, as the following recipe demonstrates.

3 feet sheep or small hog casing

1 pound lean pork

¾ pound lean beef

¼ pound pork fat

1 teaspoon ground coriander

1 teaspoon sweet paprika

½ teaspoon ground mustard seed

¼ teaspoon ground mace

¼ teaspoon dried marjoram

¼ cup finely minced onion

1 small clove garlic, minced

1½ teaspoons sugar

1 tablespoon kosher or coarse salt

1 teaspoon freshly ground white pepper (medium grind)

1 egg white

¼ cup milk

1. Prepare the casing (see page 28).

2. Cut the pork, beef, and fat into 1-inch cubes. Freeze the cubes for about 30 minutes to firm them up before grinding.

3. Meanwhile, in a food processor or blender, combine the coriander, paprika, mustard seed, mace, marjoram, onion, and garlic. Purée until smooth. Add the sugar, salt, pepper, egg white, and milk. Mix thoroughly.

4. Grind the pork, beef, and fat cubes separately through the fine disk of a meat grinder. Mix together, then freeze for 30 minutes, and grind again.

ORDERING A HOT DOG WHEN YOU TRAVEL

Here's what to say to order a hot dog when you are away from home. Do as they do.

Spain: *Perrito caliente*
Italy: *Caldo cane*
France: *Chien chaud*
Germany: *Heisser Hund* or *Wurst*
Portugal: *Cachorro quento*
Sweden: *Korv* or *varmkorv*
Norway: *Grillposer*
Czech Republic: *Park v rohliku*
Netherlands: *Worstjes*
Finland: *Makkarat*

5. In a large bowl, combine the meat and onion mixtures. Mixing tends to be a sticky procedure, so wet your hands with cold water, then mix the ingredients with your hands.

6. Freeze the mixture for 30 minutes, then grind it through the fine disk of the grinder once more.

7. Stuff the mixture into the prepared casing, prick air pockets, and twist off into 6-inch links. Do not separate them.

8. Bring a large pot of water to a gentle simmer; add the links and parboil in the *gently* simmering water for 20 minutes.

9. Drain the franks, then dunk them into ice water to chill thoroughly.

10. Remove the franks from the water, pat dry, and refrigerate. Because they are precooked, the frankfurters can be refrigerated for up to 1 week, or they may be frozen for up to 2 months. Reheat until warmed through.

Makes 2 pounds

hot dog

According to the American Meat Institute, the all-American hot dog may have originated with a popular sausage known as a "dachshund" or "little dog" sausage created in the late 1600s by Johann Georghehner, a butcher in Coburg, Germany. (This is vehemently disputed by the city of Frankfurt, Germany, which claims that the frankfurter developed there in 1484, and by Vienna (Wien), Austria, which points to the "wiener" sausage as the ancestor of the hot dog.)

What is most likely is that butchers of several European nationalities immigrated to the United States in the nineteenth century and started making a common European sausage that was eaten with bread. One report says a German immigrant sold the "dachshund" sausage tucked into a roll with sauerkraut in New York City's Bowery in the 1860s. Another German butcher opened the first hot dog stand on Coney Island in 1871. The German habit of eating bread and sausage together made the hot dog a portable feast, and it didn't take long before a sausage tucked into a bun was standard fare at ballparks, fairs, and other public events.

Those who doubt the dachshund/ little-dog etymology think the name was a sarcastic comment on the provenance of the sausages sold at Yale University dorms in the 1890s.

Swedish Potato Sausage

This sausage is popular in Sweden, where it is called Potatis Korv, *and among U.S. descendants of the Swedish immigrants who settled the upper Midwest.*

4 feet medium hog casing

1 pound very lean beef

½ pound lean pork butt

½ pound pork fat

5 large potatoes

1 large onion, peeled and coarsely chopped

2 teaspoons kosher or coarse salt

½ teaspoon freshly ground black pepper (medium grind)

½ teaspoon freshly ground white pepper (medium grind)

¼ teaspoon ground allspice

¼ teaspoon ground mace

¼ teaspoon freshly grated nutmeg

1 clove garlic, minced

Chicken broth for cooking sausage

1. Prepare the casing (see page 28).

2. Cut the beef, pork, and pork fat into 1-inch cubes. Freeze the cubes for about 30 minutes to firm them up before grinding.

3. Grind the meats and fat separately through the fine disk of a meat grinder. Freeze until you are ready for Step 6.

4. Peel and boil the potatoes in lightly salted water for 10 minutes. They will be quite firm in the center. Allow them to cool before proceeding.

5. Cube the cooled potatoes and mix with the onion. Put the mixture through the fine disk of the grinder.

6. In a large bowl, combine the ground meats and fat and the potato mixture. Add the salt, black pepper, white pepper, allspice, mace, nutmeg, and garlic. The mixture will be sticky, so dip your hands in cold water, then mix well, using your hands.

7. Stuff the mixture into the prepared casing, prick air pockets, and twist off into 12-inch links. With butcher's twine, tie two separate knots between each link and one knot at each end. Separate the links by cut-

ting between the two knots, then bring the ends of each link together and tie to form a ring.

8. Poach the rings in chicken broth to cover for 45 minutes. Serve warm or refrigerate and serve cool. The sausages may be refrigerated for up to 3 days or frozen for up to 2 months.

Makes 5 pounds

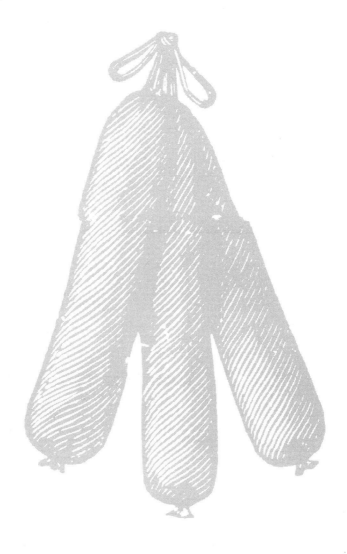

Vienna Sausage

You may have encountered Vienna sausages on the end of a toothpick at a 1950s-style cocktail party. In the store, they come in little cans and look like short hot dogs. Actually, the name is a clue: In Austria, these are called wiener würstchen, *or little wiener sausages,* Wien *being the Austrian spelling for Vienna. This version is infinitely better than the canned ones.*

3 feet sheep or small hog casing

1 pound lean beef

1 pound lean pork

½ pound veal shoulder

½ pound pork fat

¼ cup plus 1 tablespoon all-purpose flour

1½ teaspoons ground coriander

1½ teaspoons kosher or coarse salt

1 teaspoon sweet paprika

1 teaspoon sugar

½ teaspoon cayenne pepper

½ teaspoon ground mace

2 tablespoons finely minced onion

½ cup cold milk

½ cup cold ice water

1. Prepare the casing (see page 28).

2. Cut the beef, pork, veal, and pork fat into 1-inch cubes. Freeze the cubes for about 30 minutes to firm them up before grinding.

3. Grind the beef, pork, veal, and pork fat separately through the fine blade of a meat grinder, then mix the meat and fat in a large bowl. Add the flour, coriander, salt, paprika, sugar, cayenne, mace, onion, milk, and water to the meat. Mix well, using your hands. Freeze for 30 minutes.

4. Put the mixture through the fine disk of the meat grinder.

5. Stuff the mixture into the prepared casing, prick air pockets, and twist off into 4-inch lengths. Do not separate the links.

6. Place the links in a large pot and cover with water. Bring to a boil, reduce the heat, and barely simmer for 45 minutes.

7. Remove the links, immerse in cold water, pat dry, and refrigerate. Vienna sausages are excellent grilled over a fire, or they can be reheated in simmering water for 10 minutes. Use within a week or freeze for up to 2 months.

Makes 3 pounds

BILL ST. ONGE
34 DIFFERENT VARIETIES AND COUNTING

Bill St. Onge was 7 years old when he started helping his grandfather make sausage. A few years later, he complained to his grandfather that the sausage was too greasy, and his grandfather said, "Fine. You make the sausage." And Bill did, starting with a fresh Polish sausage made from a recipe he got from a Polish neighbor.

"When my daughter was 6, I taught her how to make the Polish sausage. And now I'm teaching my grandchildren," Bill says with delight. He draws on his French heritage to make *gorton* (a pork spread), his New England upbringing to make maple links, and his interest in worldwide sausages to make everything from Portuguese linguiça and English bangers ("one of the best things to come out of England") to Chinese sweet sausage and Yiddish *karnatzlach* ("easier to eat than to say") — 34 varieties in all. He usually buys his meat already ground and mixes in the seasonings with his hands. He does not like an emulsified sausage, so he usually does not regrind the meat and seasonings.

A self-confessed "sausage-aholic," Bill has this advice for novices:

- Start simple, and always buy the best-quality meat. No pig noses.
- I use a Tupperware burger maker to make sausage patties.
- If you like your sausage lean, you can replace some of the fat with chicken stock for moistness and dry skim milk or bread-crumbs as a binder.
- It's hard to fail making a new sausage, once you know the basic formula.
- I like to grill sausage over briquettes and oak for best flavor.
- If your sausage seems to lack a certain "something," try adding red wine — it does wonderful things to sausage.

Cajun Boudin Blanc

This spicy concoction is a religion unto itself in southwestern Louisiana, settled centuries ago by Cajun (Acadian) families. It's made in long, droopy links, and it is usually cooked by steaming, preferably with a Cajun fiddler or accordion player in the background. This is not a sausage that is eaten fastidiously with a knife and fork. The right way to do it is to squeeze the greasy, hot, delicious contents directly into your mouth. Toss the casings when you are done.

3 pounds boneless pork butt, cut into 2-inch chunks (include some fat)

1 tablespoon kosher or coarse salt

1 teaspoon freshly ground black pepper (medium grind)

½ teaspoon dried thyme or 1 teaspoon fresh

2 bay leaves

2 tablespoons butter

1½ cups long-grain white rice

1 large onion, finely chopped

½ cup finely chopped scallions

9 feet small hog casing

½ cup finely chopped fresh parsley

2 teaspoons cayenne pepper

1 teaspoon crushed red pepper

1. Bring a large kettle of water to a boil. In a large saucepan, combine the pork, 1 teaspoon of the salt, the black pepper, thyme, and bay leaves, cover with the boiling water, and simmer for about 2 hours, until the pork falls apart.

2. With a slotted spoon, remove the meat and refrigerate it. Strain and reserve the broth.

3. In a heavy saucepan, melt the butter, add the rice, onion, and scallions, and sauté for about 5 minutes, until the rice looks translucent. Add 2½ cups of the reserved broth and cook the rice, covered, over low heat until it is tender, about 15 minutes. (Reserve any leftover broth.)

4. Prepare the casing (see page 28).

5. Grind the pork through the coarse disk of a meat grinder into a large bowl.

6. Mix the pork with the cooked rice mixture, the remaining 2 teaspoons of salt, and the parsley, cayenne, and crushed red pepper. If the mixture seems dry, add enough reserved broth or water to make it very moist.

7. Stuff the mixture into the prepared casing and prick air pockets. Twist off into 20-inch links or leave as one long rope. Refrigerate, covered, for up to 3 days if you are not ready to cook them.

8. To cook, heat links in simmering water for 15 minutes, or coil them into the basket of a steamer and steam, covered, for 15 minutes. Cut the links apart with a sharp knife and serve hot.

Makes about 4 pounds

Boudin Blanc

To most of the world, boudin blanc (French for "white pudding") is a delicate sausage similar to a quenelle — a mild, finely textured, almost creamy little treat. It bears little resemblance to the boudin blanc of Louisiana's Cajun country, a sturdy construction of pork, rice, onions, and red pepper noted for its darker color and its heat. This is the traditional French preparation.

1 pound boneless, skinless chicken breast, cubed

1 pound veal shoulder, cubed

4 feet medium hog casing

½ pound pork fat, cubed

3 large onions, sliced

1 cup milk

¾ cup dried breadcrumbs

1 teaspoon kosher or coarse salt

¼ teaspoon allspice

¼ teaspoon freshly ground nutmeg

¼ teaspoon freshly ground white pepper (medium grind)

1 tablespoon chopped fresh chives

1 tablespoon chopped fresh parsley

2 large eggs

2 large egg whites

1 cup heavy cream

Milk

Water

1. Put the cubed chicken and veal in the freezer to firm up before grinding. Prepare the casing (see page 28).

2. Grind the pork fat through the fine disk of a meat grinder.

3. In a large skillet over medium heat, slowly melt half of the ground fat to render it.

4. Add the onions to the rendered fat and cook slowly, covered, for 15 to 20 minutes, until the onions are translucent. Let cool.

5. In a medium-sized saucepan, bring the milk to a boil and add the breadcrumbs. Cook, stirring constantly, until the mixture thickens enough to stick to the spoon, about 5 minutes. Let cool.

6. Grind the chicken and veal together through the fine disk of the grinder.

7. Combine the ground meats in a large bowl. Add the onions, the remaining ground fat, salt, allspice, nutmeg, pepper, chives, and parsley. Mix well, using your hands. Freeze the mixture for 30 minutes.

8. Grind the mixture through the fine disk.

9. Using an electric mixer or a food processor, beat the mixture until it is thoroughly blended. With the motor running, add the eggs and egg whites. Beat for a couple minutes more, then add the breadcrumb mixture. Continue beating and add the cream, a little at a time.

10. Stuff the mixture into the prepared casing and twist off into 4-inch links. Do not separate the links. Refrigerate, covered, for 1 or 2 days.

11. Prick the casing with a needle and place the sausages in a large pot. Cover them with a mixture of half milk and half water. Bring the liquid to a simmer and cook gently for 30 minutes, until cooked to an internal temperature of 160°F (71°C).

12. Drain the links and let cool. Cut them apart with a sharp knife. Pat dry, then refrigerate, covered, for up to 3 days. Cook by grilling or frying until just heated through.

Makes about 4 pounds

Genoa Salami

This salami is large, robust, and flavored with brandy instead of the red wine found in many Genoas. We also use beef and pork, but pork with veal is delicious too.

5 pounds lean beef from chuck, round, or shank

3 pounds prefrozen pork butt (see Notes)

2 pounds prefrozen pork fat (see Notes)

3 tablespoons plus 1 teaspoon kosher or coarse salt

2 tablespoons whole pepper-corns

1½ tablespoons sugar

1 tablespoon freshly ground white pepper (medium grind)

1 teaspoon ground cardamom

1 teaspoon ground coriander

½ teaspoon ascorbic acid

Curing salt (use supplier's rec-ommended quantity for 10 pounds of meat; see Notes)

2 teaspoons garlic, minced

1 cup good-quality brandy

4 feet large beef casing

1. Cut the beef, pork, and fat into 1-inch cubes. Refrigerate the cubes for about 30 minutes to firm them up before grinding.

2. Grind the meats and fat separately through the coarse disk of a meat grinder.

3. Mix the beef, pork, and fat together and freeze for about 30 minutes.

4. Grind the mixture through the fine disk of the meat grinder.

5. In a large bowl, combine the meat mixture, salt, peppercorns, sugar, pepper, cardamom, coriander, ascorbic acid, curing salt, garlic, and brandy.

6. Cover the mixture and cure in the refrigerator for 24 hours.

7. Prepare the casing (see page 28).

8. Stuff the mixture into the prepared casing and tie off into 12-inch links with butcher's twine. Do not separate the links. Hang the links to dry in a cold place. Since the salami is very thick, 8 weeks is the minimum time you should allow for drying before you sample. Test the sausage after

8 weeks by cutting off one link and slicing through it. If the texture is firm enough to suit your taste, the remaining sausage can be cut down and wrapped tightly in plastic for storage in the refrigerator. Depending upon your specific drying conditions, 12 weeks is about the optimum drying time.

NOTES:

- Prepare pork according to the instructions on page 40 to ensure that it is free from trichinosis.

- The meat is not cooked; please see "Dry Sausage Safety" on page 42.

- We recommend that you use a commercial premixed cure in any recipe for cured sausage. Premixed cures replace the saltpeter in older recipes.

Makes 10 pounds

SALAMI

Of all the various kinds of dried sausages, probably more are labeled "salami" than anything else. The term encompasses many different sizes and shapes of highly spiced dried sausages. Some are short and fat; others, quite long. Some have a distinctive smoky flavor while in others, wine is the dominant flavor. Whether you prefer it sliced thin and piled high in a submarine sandwich or cubed and sautéed with onions as a base for a rich tomato sauce, you will agree that the culinary world is a much more exciting place, thanks to salami.

Italian Salami

A peppery salami, this is speckled with bits of fat and is traditionally made in a short, stubby shape. It is sometimes made using all pork.

5 pounds prefrozen pork shoulder (see Note)

3 pounds lean beef

2 pounds prefrozen pork fat (see Note)

3 tablespoons plus 1 teaspoon kosher or coarse salt

1 tablespoon freshly ground black pepper (fine grind)

2 teaspoons freshly ground white pepper (fine grind)

2 teaspoons sugar

1 teaspoon ground coriander

½ teaspoon ascorbic acid

Curing salt (use supplier's recommended quantity for 10 pounds of meat)

1 teaspoon minced garlic

1 cup dry white wine

4 feet large beef casings

1. Partially thaw the pork, beef, and fat and cut them into 1-inch cubes.

2. Grind the beef, pork, and fat separately through the coarse disk and then mix together in a large pan. Add the salt, black pepper, white pepper, sugar, coriander, ascorbic acid, curing salt, garlic, and wine to the meat mixture and mix well, using your hands.

3. Cover and cure in the refrigerator for 24 hours.

4. Prepare the casing (see page 28).

5. Stuff the mixture into the prepared casing, prick air pockets, and tie off into 6- or 7-inch links with butcher's twine. Do not separate the links.

6. Hang the sausage to dry in a cold place for 8 to 12 weeks. Test the sausage after 8 weeks by cutting off one link and slicing through it. If the texture is firm enough to suit your taste, the remaining sausage can be cut down and wrapped tightly in plastic for refrigeration up to 3 weeks.

NOTE: Prepare the pork according to the instructions on page 40 to ensure that it is free from trichinosis. The meat is not cooked; please see "Dry Sausage Safety" on page 42.

Makes 10 pounds

Veal Salami

The seasonings in this salami, made with veal and pork, are both spicy and sweet and accented by brandy and vermouth.

5 pounds lean veal

3 pounds prefrozen pork (see Note, preceding page)

2 pounds prefrozen pork fat (see Note, preceding page)

3 tablespoons plus 1 teaspoon kosher or coarse salt

2 tablespoons sugar

1 tablespoon freshly ground black pepper (medium grind)

1 tablespoon freshly ground white pepper (medium grind)

1 teaspoon crushed anise seed

½ teaspoon ascorbic acid

½ teaspoon freshly grated nutmeg

Curing salt (use supplier's recommended quantity for 10 pounds of meat)

½ cup brandy

½ cup dry vermouth

4 feet large beef casing

1. Cut the veal, pork, and pork fat into 1-inch cubes. Refrigerate the cubes for about 30 minutes to firm them up before grinding.

2. Grind the veal, pork, and fat separately through the coarse disk of a meat grinder. Mix the veal and fat and freeze the mixture, along with the pork, for 30 minutes. Grind the veal mixture using the fine disk of the grinder.

3. In a large pan, combine the veal/fat mixture with the ground pork. Add the salt, sugar, black pepper, white pepper, anise seed, ascorbic acid, nutmeg, curing salt, brandy, and vermouth. Mix well, using your hands. Loosely cover the pan and cure the mixture in the refrigerator for 24 hours.

4. Prepare the casing (see page 28).

5. Stuff the mixture into the prepared casing, prick air pockets, and tie off into 6- or 7-inch lengths with butcher's twine. Do not separate the links.

6. Hang the salami to dry in a cool place for 8 to 12 weeks. Test the sausage after 8 weeks by cutting off one link and slicing through it. If the texture is firm enough to suit your taste, the remaining sausage can be cut down and wrapped tightly in plastic for refrigeration for up to 3 weeks.

Makes 10 pounds

Pepperoni

Pepperoni sausage is sometimes referred to as a "stick" of pepperoni because that's just about what it resembles. Most of the red color in commercial pepperoni is from paprika. Indeed, if it were from cayenne pepper, you would need a fire extinguisher nearby when eating it. There are many different varieties of pepperoni, some decidedly hotter than others, but most if not all rely on a beef and pork combination. All are quite pungent. Pepperoni come in different sizes, the most common being about an inch in diameter. Some commercial packers put up what they call "pizza pepperoni," which is about twice the diameter of regular pepperoni and is not as dry. This type is better able to withstand the high temperature of a baking pizza without becoming a crispy critter. If you intend to use your pepperoni primarily as a topping for pizza, you might want to experiment with the drying time for best results.

7 pounds prefrozen pork butt, including fat

3 pounds lean beef chuck, round or shank

3 tablespoons plus 1 teaspoon kosher or coarse salt

3 tablespoons sweet paprika

2 tablespoons cayenne pepper

1 tablespoon crushed anise seed

1 tablespoon sugar

½ teaspoon ascorbic acid

Curing salt (use supplier's recommended quantity for 10 pounds of meat; see Notes)

1 teaspoon very finely minced garlic

1 cup dry red wine

6 feet small hog casing

1. Cut the pork and beef into 1-inch cubes. Freeze the cubes for about 30 minutes to firm them up before grinding.

2. Grind the pork and beef separately through the coarse disk of a meat grinder.

3. In a large pan, combine the meats, salt, paprika, cayenne, anise seed, sugar, ascorbic acid, curing salt, garlic, and wine. Mix well, using your hands.

4. Cure the mixture, covered loosely with waxed paper, in the refrigerator for 24 hours.

5. Prepare the casing (see page 28).

6. Stuff the mixture into the prepared casing, prick air pockets, and twist off into 10-inch links. With butcher's twine, tie two separate knots between *every other* link, and one knot at the beginning and another at the end of the stuffed casing. Cut between the double knots. This results in pairs of 10-inch links. Hang the pepperoni by a string tied to the center of each pair.

7. Hang the pepperoni to dry for 6 to 8 weeks. Test the sausage after 6 weeks by cutting off one link and slicing through it. If the texture is firm enough to suit your taste, the remaining sausage can be cut down and wrapped tightly in plastic for storage in the refrigerator for several months.

NOTES:

- Prepare the pork according to the instructions on page 40 to ensure that it is free from trichinosis.

- The meat is not cooked; please see "Dry Sausage Safety" on page 42.

- We recommend that you use a commercial premixed cure in any recipe for cured sausage. Premixed cures replace the saltpeter in older recipes.

Makes 10 pounds

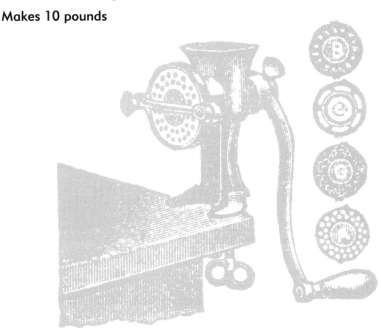

Smoked Country-Style Sausage

Sometimes you will see something similar to this sausage in the fresh meat case at the grocery, labeled "smoked country links." It is delicious both as a breakfast sausage or as part of an hors d'oeuvres selection.

4 feet small hog casing

3 pounds pork butt, about 25 percent fat

2 pounds beef chuck, about 25 percent fat

¼ cup nonfat dry milk

1 tablespoon plus 1 teaspoon kosher or coarse salt

1 tablespoon paprika

1 tablespoon sugar

2 teaspoons mustard seed

2 teaspoons freshly ground white pepper (fine grind)

¼ teaspoon ascorbic acid

Curing salt (use supplier's recommended quantity for 5 pounds of meat)

½ cup ice water

1. Prepare the casing (see page 28).

2. Cut the pork and beef into 1-inch cubes. Freeze the cubes for about 30 minutes to firm them up before grinding.

3. Grind the pork through the fine disk of a meat grinder. Grind the beef through the coarse disk of the grinder.

4. In a large bowl, combine the meats. Add the dry milk, salt, paprika, sugar, mustard seed, white pepper, ascorbic acid, curing salt, and water. Mix well, using your hands.

5. Stuff the mixture into the prepared casing, prick air pockets, and twist off into 2- to 3-inch links. Tie off each link with butcher's twine. Do not separate the links.

6. Smoke for 2 hours at 180 to 190°F (83 to 88°C).

7. Bring a large pot of water to a boil. Add the sausages and reduce the heat to maintain a water temperature of 180 to 190°F (83° to 88°C). Simmer the sausages for 30 minutes, to an internal temperature on an instant-read thermometer of 160°F (71°C).

8. Place the sausages in a bowl of cold water for 30 minutes. Drain, dry thoroughly, and store in the refrigerator for up to 2 weeks.

Makes 5 pounds

Mettwurst

This delicious German sausage is smoked and precooked but, like ring bologna, it must be kept refrigerated. It can be stored for up to 2 weeks.

4 feet medium hog casing

3 pounds lean beef chuck

2 pounds pork butt with fat

1 tablespoon plus 1 teaspoon kosher or coarse salt

1 teaspoon freshly ground white pepper (medium grind)

½ teaspoon ground allspice

½ teaspoon ground celery seed

½ teaspoon grated nutmeg

¼ teaspoon ground marjoram

¼ teaspoon ascorbic acid

Curing salt (use supplier's recommended quantity for 5 pounds of meat)

½ teaspoon freshly grated gingerroot

1. Prepare the casing (see page 28).

2. Cut the beef and pork into 1-inch cubes. Freeze the cubes for about 30 minutes to firm them up before grinding.

3. Grind the beef and pork separately through the fine disk of a meat grinder, and then mix them together in a large bowl. Add the salt, pepper, allspice, celery seed, nutmeg, marjoram, ascorbic acid, curing salt, and gingerroot. Mix well, using your hands.

4. Stuff the mixture into the prepared casing, prick air pockets, and twist off into 6-inch links. Tie off each link with butcher's twine. Do not separate the links. Cure in the refrigerator for 24 hours.

5. Smoke at about 110 to 120°F (44 to 49°C) for 2 hours, and then raise the temperature to 150°F (66°C) and smoke for 2 hours longer.

6. Bring a large pot of water to a boil. Add the sausages and reduce the heat to maintain a water temperature of 180 to 190°F (83° to 88°C). Simmer the sausages for 30 minutes. The sausages should rise to the top when they are done and the internal temperature on an instant-read thermometer should be 160°F (71°C).

7. Place the Mettwurst in a bowl of cold water for 30 minutes, remove, dry thoroughly, and refrigerate for up to 2 weeks.

Makes 5 pounds

Bavarian Summer Sausage

In one sense, this is not a true summer sausage, since it is not as dry as other sausages that claim the name. It must be refrigerated for longer storage, even when the casing is still intact. In another sense, though, it is as summery a sausage as you can find, because it goes so beautifully with a stein of ice-cold German lager, a loaf of rye bread, and a shady tree on a sultry afternoon.

4 pounds beef chuck with fat

1 pound pork butt with fat

2 tablespoons sugar

1 tablespoon plus 1 teaspoon kosher or coarse salt

1 tablespoon whole mustard seed

2 teaspoons freshly ground white pepper (medium grind)

¼ teaspoon ascorbic acid

Curing salt (use supplier's recommended quantity for 5 pounds of meat)

4 feet medium hog casing

1. Prepare the casing (see page 28).

2. Cut the beef and pork into 1-inch cubes. Freeze the cubes for about 30 minutes to firm them up before grinding.

3. Grind the beef and pork separately through the fine disk of a meat grinder.

4. In a large bowl, combine the meats, sugar, salt, mustard seed, pepper, ascorbic acid, and curing salt. Mix well, using your hands.

5. Stuff the mixture into the prepared casing, prick air pockets, and twist off into 4-inch links. Tie off each link with butcher's twine. Do not separate the links.

6. Smoke at 140°F (60°C) for 4 hours, or until the sausage is firm to the touch. Increase the temperature to 180 to 190°F (83 to 88°C) and continue smoking for 2 hours longer, to an internal temperature of 160°F (71°C) on an instant-read thermometer.

7. Let cool and refrigerate, wrapped in plastic, for up to 1 week.

Makes 5 pounds

Smoked Kielbasa

A smoked version of kielbasa (see our recipe for fresh on page 113) is closer to what you will find in the grocer's meat case. It goes well with bock beer and rye bread, with some good brown mustard.

4 feet medium hog casing

3 pounds pork butt with fat

2 pounds beef chuck, trimmed

¼ cup nonfat dry milk

1 tablespoon plus 1 teaspoon kosher or coarse salt

1 tablespoon sweet paprika

1 tablespoon sugar

2 teaspoons freshly ground white pepper (medium grind)

½ teaspoon ground celery seed

½ teaspoon ground coriander

½ teaspoon dried marjoram

½ teaspoon freshly grated nutmeg

½ teaspoon dried thyme

¼ teaspoon ascorbic acid

Curing salt (use supplier's recommended quantity for 5 pounds of meat)

1 tablespoon minced garlic

½ cup ice water

1. Prepare the casing (see page 28).

2. Cut the pork and beef into 1-inch cubes. Freeze the cubes for about 30 minutes to firm them up before grinding.

3. Grind the pork through the coarse disk of a meat grinder. Grind the beef through the fine disk.

4. Mix the meats together in a large bowl. Add the dry milk, salt, paprika, sugar, pepper, celery seed, coriander, marjoram, nutmeg, thyme, ascorbic acid, curing salt, garlic, and water. Mix well, using your hands.

5. Stuff the mixture into the prepared casing, prick air pockets, and twist off into 8- to 10-inch links. Tie off each link with butcher's twine. Do not separate the links. Cure, covered, in the refrigerator for 24 hours.

6. Smoke at 180 to 190°F (83° to 88°C) for 2 hours, or until the internal temperature is 160°F (71°C).

7. Place the links in a large bowl of cool water for 30 minutes, then dry thoroughly and store in the refrigerator for up to 2 weeks.

Makes 5 pounds

Garlic Ring Bologna

Garlic Ring Bologna is not a fully cured sausage. It is smoked, but must be kept under refrigeration until it is eaten.

2 pounds pork

1 or 2 veal hearts (about 1 pound total)

2 pounds pork fat

1 tablespoon plus 1 teaspoon kosher or coarse salt

2 teaspoons crushed mustard seed

2 teaspoons freshly ground white pepper (fine grind)

1 teaspoon ground allspice

1 teaspoon dried marjoram

¼ teaspoon ascorbic acid

Curing salt (use supplier's recommended quantity for 5 pounds of meat; see Note)

4 cloves garlic, very finely minced

4 feet medium hog casing

1. Cut the pork, veal hearts, and fat into 1-inch cubes. Freeze the cubes for about 30 minutes to firm them up before grinding.

2. Grind the pork, veal heart, and fat separately through the fine disk of a meat grinder.

3. In a large bowl, combine the meats, fat, salt, mustard seed, pepper, allspice, marjoram, ascorbic acid, curing salt, and garlic. Mix well, using your hands.

4. Freeze the mixture for 30 minutes.

5. Prepare the casing (see page 28).

6. Grind the seasoned meat mixture through the fine disk of the grinder.

7. Stuff the mixture into the prepared casing, prick air pockets, and twist off into 18-inch links. Be careful not to overstuff, or when you form the rings, the casing may burst. Tie double knots between the links with butcher's twine, then cut the links between the knots. Bring the tied ends of each link together and tie securely, forming a ring.

8. Hang the sausage in a cool drying area for 24 hours or refrigerate for 8 to 10 hours, uncovered.

9. Smoke at 110 to 120°F (44 to 49°C) for 2 hours.

10. Bring a large pot of water to a boil. Add the sausages and reduce the heat to maintain a water temperature of 180 to190°F (83 to 88°C). Simmer the rings for 20 to 30 minutes. The sausages should rise to the top when they are done and reach an internal temperature of 160°F (71°C) on an instant-read thermometer.

11. Drain, let cool, dry thoroughly, and wrap in plastic. Refrigerate for up to 2 weeks.

NOTE: We recommend that you use a commercial premixed cure in any recipe for cured sausage. Premixed cures replace the saltpeter in older recipes.

Makes 5 pounds

Smoked Italian Sausage

These sausages have a decidedly different flavor from other Italian-style sausages. The simplicity of the recipe is deceptive: The thyme and rosemary combine with the complex herbal base of the sweet vermouth and smoky flavor to produce an aromatic and seductive sausage that is hard to stop eating once you've started. A loaf of fresh, crusty bread and a dry red wine are excellent foils to the meat.

4 feet medium hog casing

3 pounds pork butt, with fat

2 pounds beef chuck, fat included

3 tablespoons sweet paprika

1 tablespoon plus 1 teaspoon kosher or coarse salt

1 teaspoon freshly grated nutmeg

¼ teaspoon ascorbic acid

Curing salt (use supplier's recommended quantity for 5 pounds of meat; see Note)

2 teaspoons chopped fresh rosemary

2 teaspoons chopped fresh thyme

½ cup sweet vermouth

1. Prepare the casing (see page 28).

2. Cut the pork and beef into 1-inch cubes. Freeze the cubes for 30 minutes to firm them up before grinding.

3. Grind the pork through the coarse disk of a meat grinder. Grind the beef through the fine disk.

4. In a large bowl, combine the pork, beef, paprika, salt, nutmeg, ascorbic acid, curing salt, rosemary, thyme, and vermouth. Mix well, using your hands.

5. Stuff the mixture into the prepared casing and twist off into 4- or 5-inch links. Tie off each link with butcher's twine. Do not separate the links.

6. Smoke for about 2 hours at 180 to 190°F (83 to 88°F), or until the internal temperature is 160°F (71°C).

7. Let the sausages cool, then refrigerate for up to 2 weeks.

NOTE: We recommend that you use a commercial premixed cure in any recipe for cured sausage. Premixed cures replace the saltpeter in older recipes.

Makes 5 pounds

CHAPTER 7

Game Sausages

After going 12 miles we were fortunate enough

to find a few willows, which enabled us

to cook a dinner of jerked elk.

— journals of Meriwether Lewis and William Clark

I**T IS PROBABLY SAFE TO SAY** that the vast majority of people alive today in the so-called civilized world have never tasted even one of the many species of wild game available to the hunter. In fact, one need not even be a hunter to sample some of nature's delicacies, since many species of game are raised on licensed ranches and preserves, and their meat is available for sale to restaurants, butcher shops, and the general public. Don't be deterred by the fact that the local supermarket stocks only domestic fowl and red meat. Search out the various game meats that are available. Make friends with a hunter (especially if he or she is a good shot). It should not be hard to find one; a U.S. government study says more than 13 million people, 16 years old and older, spent an average of 17 days hunting in 2001. Check with your local butcher, the classified ads in cooking magazines, and the Resources listed on page 272.

GENERAL THOUGHTS ON GAME COOKERY

Historically, game cookery is the foundation of our culinary landscape. Our earliest immigrant forefathers (and mothers) could not have survived had they not hunted for their food. Before they arrived, Native Americans lived and migrated according to the availability of game, and perfected the art of using up every last scrap of a carcass.

Many people today wouldn't know where to begin if they had to track, kill, dress, and prepare their own meat. But even those with no prowess as hunters welcome a new dish, a different taste, or a unique recipe to stave off the boredom that can ensue from eating the same old things, day after day. If you are interested in the challenge and excitement of trying something different, here are a few basic rules for cooking with game.

"Young is tender, old is tougher." This adage is true whether we are talking about domestic animals or about the bear you bagged yesterday. Certainly steaks, chops, and roasts are most people's first choices. But an

HOW TO TRANSFORM PORK INTO BOAR

You'll need a large roasting pan and space in the refrigerator to hold it to make pork into something close to wild boar. Don't start this just before a hunting trip; you have to turn the meat twice a day during the transformation process.

> 5 pounds fresh ham (not cured or smoked), boned and skinned, with fat
> 4 cups (or enough to cover) ruby port wine
> 1 tablespoon whole juniper berries
> 1 tablespoon whole black peppercorns
> 3 bay leaves
> 3 or 4 whole fresh sage leaves
> 3 or 4 sprigs fresh thyme

Lay the fresh ham flat in a roasting pan just large enough to accommodate it. Pour the wine over the meat, then sprinkle over all the juniper berries, peppercorns, bay leaves, sage, and thyme. Marinate, covered, in the refrigerator for 4 days. Turn the meat twice a day. At the end of 4 days, pat the meat dry, remove any spices clinging to it, and use as you would fresh boar meat.

animal has a fixed number of those prized parts. The rest — especially in a muscular older animal — is sausage material. A corollary to this rule is that the older the meat, the more developed the flavor. In other words, game gets gamier with age.

"The best-dressed game is the best-tasting game." We're not talking high fashion here. If you hunt for your own meat, be sure to field-dress it properly. The size and species of the animal, as well as weather conditions (especially temperature), all play a role in determining the proper procedures to follow. If you are inexperienced or unsure of the right way to go about it, be sure to consult one of the many books and magazines that deal with hunting and butchering game, or contact your local Cooperative Extension Service.

"The essence is in the fat." In big game, especially, the strongest flavor is found in the fat of the animal. Unless you really relish the strongest of gamy flavors, it is best to trim the fat from the game animal and replace it in a recipe with pork or beef fat, both of which tend to be mild-tasting.

Because wild animals are active and develop their muscles, their meat is usually quite lean. To make sausage, you will definitely need to add fat.

"Some wild game animals bring home more than the bacon." Bear and boar can be carriers of trichinosis. Wild rabbits can carry tularemia. Any time that you handle raw game meat, wear rubber gloves for safety, and be sure to maintain a scrupulously clean kitchen to avoid any cross contamination. See page 34 for a refresher course on the importance of cleanliness.

"By the tail hangs a tale." Just as domestic beef is aged or "hung," so, too, must game be aged to improve flavor, texture, and tenderness. If you are in doubt about proper procedures, consult a reliable source on game meats.

GAME MEAT CHARACTERISTICS

Each species' meat has its own distinct characteristics. Most people can tell the difference between chicken and beef even if they are blindfolded — not necessarily so much by the taste (which can be deceptive) as by the texture. *Mouth feel* is the term food researchers use to describe how the texture of something feels in the mouth. We usually can tell immediately by mouth feel whether something we are chewing on is familiar or strange.

Although food scientists have their own vocabulary for describing flavors, most of us would be hard pressed to describe what chicken tastes like or how a freshly caught brook trout is different from one that has spent 3 months in the freezer. That is the problem of trying to describe what rabbit or elk meat tastes like to someone who has never eaten it.

The following chart is a rough guide to some of the more common game species. It can serve as a starting point when you are trying to determine which herbs and spices might go well with a particular meat.

Game	Characteristic Flavor
Bear	Lean, dark meat
Bison (buffalo)	Similar to beef but often leaner
Boar	Lean meat, gamy flavor, similar to pork
Deer (whitetail)	Like beef, but with a richer flavor
Dove	Like chicken dark meat, tender and rich
Duck	Dark, tender meat, strong flavor
Elk	Dark meat, tastes like mild, almost sweet beef; hint of venison flavor
Goose	Dark, lean meat, very flavorful
Moose	Darker and stronger than beef, similar to elk
Partridge or Pheasant	Somewhere between chicken and duck
Rabbit (cottontail)	Light meat, similar to chicken
Squirrel	Pink meat, can be sweet or gamy
Turkey	Lean, dark meat, very flavorful
Woodchuck	Rich, red flesh with a distinctive gamy flavor

Bear Sausage

If you actually bag a bear, you will want to triple or quadruple this recipe. The seasonings go well with bear meat, and the dried cranberries comple-ment the richness of the meat and look good in the sausage.

5 feet medium hog casing

4 pounds bear meat, trimmed of all fat

1 pound pork fat

2 tablespoons kosher or coarse salt

2 teaspoons freshly ground black pepper (medium grind)

1 teaspoon celery seed

½ teaspoon dried savory

½ teaspoon dried thyme leaves

1 cup dried cranberries

½ cup dry red wine

1. Prepare the casing (see page 28).

2. Cut the bear and pork fat into 1-inch cubes. Freeze the cubes for about 30 minutes to firm them up before grinding.

3. In a large bowl, combine the meat, fat, salt, pepper, celery seed, savory, thyme, cranberries, and red wine. Mix well, using your hands.

4. Grind the mixture through the coarse disk of a meat grinder. Grind the mixture through the fine disk.

5. Stuff the sausage into the prepared casing, prick air pockets, and twist off into 3-inch links. Cut the links apart with a sharp knife.

6. Arrange the links on a platter, cover, and refrigerate to age for 2 days.

7. Cook as directed for fresh pork sausage on page 36, being sure to cook the sausages to at least 160°F (71°C).

Makes 5 pounds

Italian-Style Boar Sausage

Not everyone (in fact, only people in 23 U.S. states) has access to wild boar meat. If you don't, use the trick in the box on page 146 to make ordinary pork taste almost like the real thing. But plan ahead — converting pork to "boar" takes 4 days.

5 feet medium hog casing

4 pounds boar (see Note)

1 pound pork fat

2 tablespoons kosher or coarse salt

2 teaspoons crushed fennel seed

2 teaspoons freshly ground black pepper (medium grind)

1 to 2 teaspoons crushed red pepper flakes (optional)

1. Prepare the casing (see page 28).

2. Cut the boar and fat into 1-inch cubes.

3. In a large bowl, combine the boar, fat, salt, fennel, black pepper, and the red pepper flakes (if using). Mix well, using your hands. Refrigerate the mixture for about 30 minutes to firm it up before grinding.

4. Grind the seasoned meat through the coarse disk of a meat grinder.

5. Stuff the mixture into the prepared casing, prick air pockets, and twist off into 3- to 4-inch lengths. Cut the links apart with a sharp knife.

6. Cook as directed for fresh pork sausages on page 36 to an internal temperature of 160°F (71°C) on an instant-read thermometer.

NOTE: If you don't have boar, use 5 pounds fresh pork ham, marinated according to the instructions in the box on page 146, then cubed.

Makes 5 pounds

Bison Bologna

This isn't a true bologna like the one you are accustomed to seeing in the deli case. It has a richer flavor and a fine texture.

5 feet medium hog casing

4 pounds bison (buffalo) meat, with fat

1 pound beef fat

2 tablespoons kosher or coarse salt

2 teaspoons sweet paprika

½ teaspoon cayenne pepper

2 cloves garlic, finely minced

2 teaspoons finely chopped shallots

1. Prepare the casing (see page 28).

2. Cut the bison and the beef fat into 1-inch cubes. Freeze the cubes for about 30 minutes to firm them up before grinding.

3. Grind the meat and fat together through the coarse disk of a meat grinder.

4. In a large bowl, combine the meat mixture, salt, paprika, cayenne, garlic, and shallots. Mix well, using your hands. Freeze the mixture for about 30 minutes.

5. Grind the seasoned mixture through the fine disk twice, freezing between grindings.

6. Stuff the mixture into the prepared casing, prick air pockets, and twist off into 3- to 4-inch links. Cut the links apart with a sharp knife. The links may be refrigerated, covered, for 2 to 3 days or frozen for up to 3 months.

7. Cook as directed for fresh sausage on page 36 to an internal temperature of 160°F (71°C).

Makes 5 pounds

BISON COMEBACK

Native to North America, bison (or buffalo), once numbered about 60 million but were hunted almost to extinction by the 1890s. USDA reports that about 150,000 of the animals are being raised across North America today, so farm-raised bison is available.

Dove Links

Since the usable meat on a single dove is just a couple of ounces, this sausage is more of a novelty item, something to serve as an hors d'oeuvre, perhaps, rather than a meal.

1 pound fresh dove meat (scraped from 8 to 10 doves)

¼ pound chicken fat

1 teaspoon kosher or coarse salt

½ teaspoon ground ginger

¼ teaspoon freshly ground black pepper (medium grind)

¼ teaspoon dried sage

¼ teaspoon dried thyme

1. Freeze the dove meat and chicken fat for 15 minutes.

2. Grind the meat and fat through the fine disk of a meat grinder.

3. In a medium-sized bowl, combine the meat, salt, ginger, pepper, sage, and thyme. Mix well, using your hands.

4. Grind the seasoned mixture through the fine disk of the grinder.

5. Wet your hands with cold water. Taking about 1 tablespoon of meat at a time, form little rolls of sausage.

6. Refrigerate the links until firm, about 30 minutes.

7. Cook as directed on page 36 for fresh sausages to an internal temperature of 160°F (71°C); panfrying is recommended.

Makes 1 pound

QUAIL INSTEAD

As quail farmers raise about 37 million quail on farms in the United States these days, it might be easier to come upon quail meat for this recipe instead of dove meat. A ready-to-cook quail weighs 3 to 7 ounces (including the giblets), so you'd need 3 to 5 birds to get the pound of meat needed.

Elk Sausage with Capers and Wine

Elk is an assertive meat, so we've added seasonings that will stand up to it.

5 feet medium hog casing

4 pounds elk meat, trimmed and cubed

1 pound beef fat

2 tablespoons kosher or coarse salt

2 teaspoons cayenne pepper

2 teaspoons freshly ground black pepper (coarse grind)

1 teaspoon crushed anise seed

2 tablespoons small capers, drained if in a vinegar brine and rinsed

2 cloves garlic, finely chopped

¼ to ⅓ cup dry red wine

1. Prepare the casing (see page 28).

2. Cut the meat and fat into 1-inch cubes. Refrigerate the cubes for about 30 minutes to firm them up before grinding.

3. Grind the meat and fat together through the coarse disk of a meat grinder.

4. In a large bowl, combine the ground meat, salt, cayenne, black pepper, anise seed, capers, and garlic. Mix in ¼ cup of the wine, then add a bit more if needed to achieve a stuffing consistency.

5. Stuff the mixture into the prepared casing, prick air pockets, and twist off into 4-inch links. Cut the links apart with a sharp knife. Use within 2 to 3 days, wrapped in plastic and refrigerated, or freeze for up to 3 months.

6. Cook as directed on page 36 for fresh sausages to an internal temperature of 160°F (71°C); roasting or grilling is recommended.

Makes 5 pounds

PUNGENT CAPERS

Capers stand up to the assertiveness of elk meat because of their pungent flavor. Capers are the flower bud of a bush native to the Mediterranean and some parts of Asia. They are sun-dried, then generally packed in salt or a vinegar brine. Rinse capers before using.

Goose-Neck Sausages

In this novel recipe, goose-meat sausage is stuffed into chicken-neck skins instead of hog casings. You can get at least 3 pounds of usable meat from a large wild goose.

2 pounds chicken necks (about 10)

2½ pounds fresh goose meat

½ pound chicken fat

1 tablespoon kosher or coarse salt

½ teaspoon dried marjoram

½ teaspoon freshly ground white pepper (medium grind)

½ teaspoon dried sage

½ teaspoon dried thyme

¼ teaspoon ground allspice

1 tablespoon vegetable oil

1. Carefully, so as not to tear them, remove the skins from the chicken necks so you have 10 tubes of skin. (Use the neck bones and meat to make stock.)

2. Cut the goose meat and chicken fat into 1-inch cubes. Freeze the cubes for about 30 minutes to firm them up before grinding.

3. In a large bowl, combine the goose meat, fat, salt, marjoram, pepper, sage, thyme, allspice, and oil. Freeze for 30 minutes.

4. Grind the mixture through the fine disk of a meat grinder.

5. Sauté the mixture in a large skillet until the meat is no longer pink, about 10 minutes. Let cool.

6. Preheat the oven to 375°F (190°C).

7. Tie one end of each of the neck skins shut with butcher's twine. Stuff the skins with the goose mixture and tie off the open ends.

8. Bake the sausages in a single layer in a baking dish for 45 minutes, until the skins are crisp and the meat reaches 165°F (74°C) on an instant-read thermometer. Serve warm.

Makes 3 pounds

Moose Sausage

If you like venison, you'll probably like moose. The meat has a distinctive, rich flavor and dark color. Here's another sausage in which the seasonings need to be assertive enough to balance the richness of the meat. Use the fat attached to the meat, or trim it away and substitute beef fat.

5 feet medium hog casing

5 pounds moose with fat or 4 pounds trimmed moose plus
    1 pound beef fat

2 teaspoons freshly ground black pepper (medium grind)

2 tablespoons kosher or coarse salt

1 teaspoon crushed red pepper

½ cup finely chopped red bell pepper

¼ cup finely chopped onion

4 cloves garlic, minced

¼ cup brandy

1. Prepare the casing (see page 28).

2. Cut the meat and fat into 1-inch cubes. Freeze the cubes for about 30 minutes to firm the meat up before grinding.

3. In a large bowl, combine the meat, fat, black pepper, salt, crushed red pepper, red bell pepper, onion, garlic, and brandy. Mix well, using your hands. Freeze for 30 minutes.

4. Grind the mixture through the coarse disk of a meat grinder.

5. Stuff the mixture into the prepared casing and prick air pockets. Twist off into 4-inch links. Cut the links apart with a sharp knife.

6. Arrange the links on a platter, cover, and refrigerate for 2 days to cure.

7. Cook as directed for fresh sausages on page 36, to an internal temperature of 160°F (71°C).

Makes 5 pounds

Partridge and Wild Rice Sausage

The boiled-down cider in the sausage mixture lends sweetness and helps bind and meld the ingredients. These sausages make a delicious luncheon or supper offering.

3 feet small hog or sheep casing

1½ pounds partridge meat

½ pound chicken fat

1 cup apple cider

1 cup cooked wild rice

½ cup golden raisins

2 teaspoons kosher or coarse salt

½ teaspoon freshly ground black pepper (medium grind)

¼ teaspoon ground allspice

¼ teaspoon ground cinnamon

1 tablespoon fresh lemon juice

1. Prepare the casing (see page 28).

2. Cut the partridge meat and the fat into 1-inch cubes. Freeze the cubes for about 30 minutes to firm them up before grinding.

3. Meanwhile, in a small saucepan, simmer the cider until it is reduced to about 3 tablespoons of syrupy liquid, 15 to 20 minutes. Remove from the heat and set aside.

4. Grind the meat and fat through the fine disk of a meat grinder.

5. In a large bowl, combine the ground meat and fat, reduced cider, rice, raisins, salt, pepper, allspice, cinnamon, and lemon juice. Mix well, using your hands.

6. Stuff the mixture into the prepared casing, prick air pockets, and twist off into 3-inch links. Cut the links apart with a sharp kinfe.

7. Arrange the links on a platter, cover, and refrigerate for several hours to meld the flavors. Use within 2 to 3 days or freeze for up to 3 months.

8. Cook to an internal temperature of 165°F (74°C) as directed for fresh sausages on page 36; panfrying is recommended.

Makes 2 pounds

MATT JOLIE
GAME SAUSAGE WITH A CHEF'S TOUCH

Matt is the chef at the well-regarded Hofbrauhaus in West Springfield, Massachusetts. The restaurant is noted for its monthly game dinners and its lavish Oktoberfest celebration every fall. Regulars at the restaurant love Matt's creativity with the menu, and especially with the sausage. Hot-smoked alligator andouille? Kangaroo? Matt has made them. Bratwurst, knockwurst, bauerwurst, venison in several guises, chicken and apple, all have appeared on the menu, which changes every two months.

Matt grew up in Boston and has fond memories of the tomato sausage his family always bought at a Syrian grocery. He is a self-taught sausage maker who still loves to experiment at home with his trusty KitchenAid mixer with meat-grinder attachment. At the restaurant, Matt usually makes 30-pound batches of sausage at a time, knowing that his customers will trust his judgment about a new sausage and happily order it.

Matt has also experimented with vegetarian sausage, using tofu as a carrier and adding carrots, celery, herbs, whole eggs, and bread-crumbs. He forms the mixture into sausage shapes and freezes them, then cooks them while still frozen to retain the shape. He says he appreciates that vegetarians usually are not looking for a meatlike taste, so he presents the vegetarian sausages as entrées in themselves, not as meat substitutes.

Matt encourages new sausage makers with this advice: "Don't be apprehensive about trying new things. I used a recipe the first time and haven't used one since. Just use flavors you enjoy."

So far, he has not been able to duplicate that Syrian tomato sausage from his youth. Perhaps, as with other childhood memories, it is meant to be elusive. Just don't be too surprised to find it, someday, on the menu at the Hofbrauhaus.

Rabbit Sausage

Although this recipe is specifically tailored to wild cottontail rabbits, you can substitute domestic rabbit, found in your grocer's meat case. The domestic meat will be milder, so you may wish to reduce the amounts of the seasonings.

3 feet small hog or sheep casing

2½ pounds rabbit meat

½ pound chicken or pork fat

1 tablespoon kosher or coarse salt

½ teaspoon freshly ground black pepper (medium grind)

½ teaspoon freshly ground white pepper (medium grind)

½ teaspoon dried thyme

2 tablespoons chopped fresh chives

2 tablespoons finely minced celery or lovage

2 tablespoons chopped fresh parsley

1 teaspoon freshly grated gingerroot

2 tablespoons dry white wine

1. Prepare the casing (see page 28).

2. Cut the meat and fat into 1-inch cubes. Freeze the cubes for about 30 minutes to firm them up before grinding.

3. In a large bowl, combine the meat, fat, salt, black and white peppers, thyme, chives, celery, parsley, gingerroot, and wine. Mix well, using your hands.

4. Grind the mixture through the fine disk of a meat grinder.

5. Stuff into the prepared casing, prick air pockets, and twist off into 3-inch links. Cut the links apart with a sharp knife. Use within 2 to 3 days or freeze for up to 3 months.

6. Cook as directed for fresh sausages on page 36; panfrying is recommended.

Makes 3 pounds

COTTONTAIL HANDLING

A wild cottontail usually weighs in at 2 to 4 pounds. Because wild rabbits are subject to tularemia, wear rubber gloves when skinning or handling the animal. Wash your hands before and after handling the raw meat, and be sure to wash in hot, soapy water all utensils and surfaces that came into contact with the meat.

Squirrel Sausage

Because of the paltry amount of meat found on a single squirrel, sweet and tasty though it may be, this sausage is another novelty item that is rarely made in large quantity. It's good served with honey-mustard sauce (see Note).

2 feet small sheep casing

1½ pounds squirrel meat (2 to 3 squirrels, dressed)

½ pound chicken or pork fat

2 tablespoons toasted pine nuts

2 teaspoons kosher or coarse salt

½ teaspoon freshly ground white pepper (medium grind)

¼ teaspoon ground allspice

¼ teaspoon ground cardamom

¼ teaspoon ground mace

1. Prepare the casing (see page 28).

2. Cut the meat and fat into 1-inch cubes. Freeze for 30 minutes. Grind the meat and fat through the fine disk of a meat grinder.

3. In a large bowl, combine the meat and fat, pine nuts, salt, pepper, allspice, cardamom, and mace. Mix well, using your hands. Freeze for 30 minutes.

4. Grind the seasoned mixture through the fine disk of the grinder.

5. Twist off into 2-inch links, about the size of cocktail franks. Cut the links apart with a sharp knife. Use within 2 to 3 days (store, wrapped in plastic, in the refrigerator) or freeze for up to 2 months.

6. Cook as directed for fresh sausages on page 36; steaming or poaching is recommended.

NOTE: To make honey-mustard sauce, combine 4 parts of mustard with 1 part each of honey and white wine vinegar. Season with Worcestershire sauce, pepper, and salt.

Makes 2 pounds

CHOICE QUARRY

Tree squirrels (the quarry of choice, as opposed to ground squirrels) can weigh anywhere from 1 to 2½ pounds "on the hoof." Be sure to wear gloves and remove intact the small glands in the small of the back and under each foreleg when skinning the animal. The glands will impart a bad flavor to the meat.

Wild Turkey Sausage

This recipe is geared to the use of wild turkey, not the domestic bird. The difference in the flavor of the two meats is as great as the difference in the birds' native intelligence.

> 5 feet small hog or sheep casing
> 3½ pounds wild turkey meat
> ½ pound turkey or chicken fat
> 1 tablespoon plus 2 teaspoons kosher or coarse salt
> 1 teaspoon celery seed
> 1 teaspoon freshly ground white pepper (medium grind)
> ½ teaspoon powdered bay leaf
> ¼ teaspoon ground cloves
> 2 tablespoons chopped fresh parsley
> 2 teaspoons grated lemon zest
> ¼ cup Wild Turkey bourbon

1. Prepare the casings (see page 28).

2. Cut the turkey and fat into 1-inch cubes. Freeze the cubes for about 30 minutes to firm up the meat before grinding.

3. In a large bowl, combine the turkey, fat, salt, celery seed, pepper, bay leaf, cloves, parsley, lemon zest, and bourbon. Mix well, using your hands.

4. Grind the mixture through the fine disk of a meat grinder.

5. Stuff the mixture into the prepared casing and prick air pockets. Twist off into 3-inch links. Cut the links apart with a sharp knife. Use within 2 to 3 days (wrapped in plastic and refrigerated) or freeze for up to 3 months.

6. Cook as directed for fresh sausages on page 36 to an internal temperature of 160°F (71°C); panfrying is recommended.

Makes 4 pounds

Herbed Game Sausage

Fresh herbs are the ticket to success in this recipe. Fortunately, even modest-size supermarkets carry packets of fresh herbs in the produce department these days. You can make up your own combination.

5 feet medium hog casing

1½ pounds venison, moose, bison, or elk meat

1 pound pork shoulder

½ pound pork fat

1 tablespoon kosher or coarse salt

1 teaspoon freshly ground black pepper (medium grind)

¼ cup chopped fresh parsley

3 tablespoons chopped fresh herbs (basil, chives, cilantro, marjoram, sage, savory, tarragon, thyme, in a combination you like)

5 cloves garlic, minced

½ cup dry red wine

1. Prepare the casing (see page 28).

2. Cut the game meat, pork, and fat into 1-inch cubes. Freeze the cubes for about 30 minutes to firm them up before grinding.

3. Grind the game meat and pork through the coarse disk of a meat grinder. Grind the fat through the coarse disk separately.

4. In a large bowl, combine the ground meats, fat, salt, pepper, parsley, herb combination, garlic, and wine. Freeze the mixture for 30 minutes.

5. Grind the seasoned mixture through the fine disk.

6. Stuff the mixture into the prepared casing, prick air pockets, and twist off into 5-inch links. Cut the links apart with a sharp knife.

7. Arrange the links on a platter, cover, and refrigerate for a couple of hours or overnight to meld the flavors. Use within 2 to 3 days or freeze for up to 3 months.

8. Cook as directed for fresh sausages on page 36 to an internal temperature of 160°F (71°C).

Makes 3 pounds

Venison Sausage

The recipe for this country-style sausage is versatile. You can substitute beef or pork for part of the venison, if needed. You can also shape the meat mixture into patties or meatballs instead of stuffing it into a casing.

4 feet medium hog casing

2½ pounds venison (from deer, elk, or caribou)

½ pound pork fat

1 cup fresh breadcrumbs

1 tablespoon kosher or coarse salt

1 teaspoon freshly ground black pepper (medium grind)

1 teaspoon dried sage

1 teaspoon dried thyme

2 teaspoons grated lemon zest

¼ cup dry white wine

1. Prepare the casing (see page 28).

2. Cut the meat and fat into 1-inch cubes. Freeze the cubes for about 30 minutes to firm them up before grinding.

3. Grind the venison and fat separately through the coarse disk of a meat grinder.

4. In a large bowl, combine the meat, fat, breadcrumbs, salt, pepper, sage, thyme, lemon zest, and wine. Mix well, using your hands. Freeze the mixture for 30 minutes.

5. Grind the seasoned mixture through the fine disk.

6. Stuff the mixture into the prepared casing, prick air pockets, and twist off into 4-inch lengths. Cut the links apart with a sharp knife. Or, shape the meat mixture into patties or meatballs.

7. Arrange the links, patties, or meatballs on a platter, cover, and refrigerate for several hours or overnight to meld the flavors. Use the sausage within 2 to 3 days or freeze for up to 3 months.

8. Cook as directed for fresh sausages on page 36 to an internal temperature of 160°F (71°C); grilling or panfrying is recommended.

Makes 3 pounds

Woodchuck Sausage

Some folks are just wild about woodchuck; some aren't. If you find a big ol' woodchuck ravaging your sweet corn, however, you might be tempted to try this recipe.

5 feet medium hog casing

4 pounds woodchuck meat

1 pound beef fat

2 teaspoons freshly ground black pepper (medium grind)

2 teaspoons kosher or coarse salt

1 teaspoon dried rosemary, crushed

½ teaspoon dried sage

½ teaspoon dried thyme

½ cup finely chopped onion

2 tablespoons chopped fresh parsley

2 cloves garlic, minced

1. Prepare the casing (see page 28).

2. Cut the meat and fat into 1-inch cubes. Freeze for about 30 minutes to firm up the cubes.

3. In a large bowl, combine the cubed meat and fat with the pepper, salt, rosemary, sage, thyme, onion, parsley, and garlic; mix well. Freeze the mixture for 30 minutes.

4. Grind the meat mixture through the coarse disk of a meat grinder. Freeze for 30 minutes. Then grind again through the fine disk.

5. Stuff the mixture into the prepared casing, prick air pockets, and twist off into 3-inch links. Cut the links apart with a sharp knife. Use within 2 to 3 days, stored in plastic wrap in the refrigerator, or freeze for up to 3 months.

6. Cook as directed for fresh sausages on page 36 to an internal temperature of 160°F (71°C); panfrying is recommended.

Makes 5 pounds

Duck Dogs

The wild duck meat in this recipe can stand up to the seasonings used here. The larger species of wild ducks will yield about 12 ounces of meat apiece, so you will need 3 ducks to make this recipe.

2 to 3 feet small hog or sheep casing

2 pounds fresh wild duck meat

2 teaspoons kosher or coarse salt

1 teaspoon ground coriander

1 teaspoon sweet paprika

½ teaspoon freshly ground white pepper (medium grind)

¼ teaspoon ground mace

2 tablespoons finely chopped fresh chives

2 cloves garlic, minced

1 egg white

1. Prepare the casing (see page 28).

2. Cut the meat into 1-inch cubes.

3. In a large bowl, combine the duck, salt, coriander, paprika, pepper, mace, chives, garlic, and egg white. Mix well, using your hands. Freeze for 30 minutes.

4. Grind the mixture through the fine disk of a meat grinder. Freeze the mixture to firm, about 30 minutes.

5. Stuff the mixture into the prepared casing, prick air pockets, and twist off into 4-inch links. Tie off each link with butcher's twine. Do not separate the links.

6. Bring a large pot of water to a boil, add the links, and reduce the heat to maintain a water temperature of 180 to 190°F (83 to 88°C). Simmer the sausages for 30 minutes.

7. Drain the sausages and let cool. Dry them thoroughly and wrap in plastic. Refrigerate for up to 1 week or freeze for up to 2 months.

8. The links may be served cold, or browned in a little oil and served warm.

Makes 2 pounds

Smoked Game Sausage

You can choose venison, elk, moose, or buffalo, alone or in combination, to make this hot-smoked sausage. It's delicious grilled or cut into chunks and added to a stew or hearty soup.

4 feet medium hog casing

2 pounds lean game meat of your choice

1 pound pork fat

1 tablespoon freshly ground black pepper (medium grind)

1 tablespoon kosher or coarse salt

2 teaspoons ground coriander

1 teaspoon whole mustard seed

1 small onion, finely chopped

⅓ cup finely chopped walnuts

3 cloves garlic, minced

½ cup dry red wine

1 tablespoon Worcestershire sauce

1. Prepare the casing (see page 28).

2. Cut the meat and fat into 1-inch cubes. Freeze the cubes for about 30 minutes to firm them up before grinding.

3. Grind the meat through the coarse disk of a meat grinder. Grind the pork fat through the fine disk.

4. In a large bowl, combine the meat, fat, pepper, salt, coriander, mustard seed, onion, walnuts, garlic, wine, and Worcestershire. Mix well, using your hands.

5. Stuff the mixture into the prepared casing, prick air pockets, and twist off into 6-inch links. Do not separate the links.

6. Arrange the sausages on a platter and mature, uncovered, in the refrigerator overnight.

7. In the morning, hot-smoke the sausages at 170 to 180°F (77 to 82.2°C) for about 4 hours, or until sausage reaches an internal temperature of 160°F (71°C).

8. Refrigerate the sausages, covered, for up to 3 days, or freeze for up to 2 months.

Makes 3 pounds

MAKING JERKY

To begin, what does *jerky* mean? Our English word *jerky* comes from the Spanish *charqui*, which means "dried meat." Basically, it's the oldest meat preservation technique known to mankind — sun-drying strips of meat. Evaporating the water from the meat stops enzyme reactions that lead to spoilage. Ancient Egyptians and others used the technique for any animal too big to eat all at once (elephant, crocodile, water buffalo, and so on).

Meat dries most quickly when it's cut into thin strips; salt and seasonings add flavor and help with preservation. In our more safety-conscious age, people who decide to make their own jerky (or even pemmican, a favorite of modern survivalists) first should abide by the recent advice from the USDA recommending that meat be precooked to 160°F (71°C) before drying.

The following recipe for beef jerky is a good starter effort. You can easily substitute venison, elk, bison, emu, or another meat for the beef.

> 1 pound round steak
> 1 teaspoon ground ginger
> ½ teaspoon onion powder, or 2 teaspoons onion juice
> ½ teaspoon freshly ground black pepper
> 2 garlic cloves, crushed
> ¼ cup soy sauce
> 2 tablespoons Worcestershire sauce
> 1 teaspoon hot sauce

1. Partially freeze the steak, then slice it into strips about 4 inches long and ⅛-inch thick. Combine the meat with the ginger, onion powder, pepper, garlic, soy sauce, Worcestershire sauce, and hot sauce. Marinate in a resealable plastic bag in the refrigerator at least 8 hours, turning frequently.

2. Run bamboo skewers through the ends of the strips and hang them from the oven rack with a pan underneath to catch the drips. Be sure to allow air space between the strips.

3. Start the oven at about 175°F (80°C) and turn it to its lowest setting (about 130 to 140°F, or 55 to 60°C) after an hour. Prop open the oven door with a wooden spoon and let the jerky bake until it is dry, 8 to 10 hours.

4. Cool completely. Jerky may be stored in an airtight container for 1 to 2 months.

Makes about 5 ounces

CHAPTER 8

Poultry Sausages

A highbrow is the kind of person who looks at

a sausage and thinks of Picasso.

— Sir Alan Patrick Herbert

D R. ROBERT C. BAKER OF CORNELL UNIVERSITY has the distinction of being known as the inventor of the so-called chicken dog. In the 1970s, he and his colleagues in Cornell's College of Agriculture and Life Sciences realized that poultry could be used for virtually any sausage that is traditionally made with beef or pork, and with the extra advantages of being cheaper and lower in fat. Since then, commercial sausage makers and consumers have adopted poultry sausages with enthusiasm.

Sausage is one application in which the inherent mild taste of chicken and turkey is a real advantage, for it encourages all kinds of creativity on the part of the home sausage maker. Fruit, herbs, zesty spices, sharp cheeses, wine, liqueurs, seeds, and grains can be added to poultry sausage with distinctive results. A larger proportion of dark meat to light meat seems to produce a more pleasing sausage, and the judicious addition of some skin and fat will enhance the flavors without creating a greasy product. Enjoy your experiments with poultry sausage, and say a word of thanks to the Father of the Chicken Dog, Dr. Baker.

Country Chicken Sausage

This sausage relies on the traditional "country sausage" combination of herbs and spices — sage, thyme, ginger, and savory.

2 feet small hog or sheep casing

2 pounds chicken meat (mixture of dark and light with skin)

2 teaspoons kosher or coarse salt

1 teaspoon freshly ground black pepper (medium grind)

½ teaspoon cayenne pepper (optional)

½ teaspoon ground ginger

½ teaspoon dried sage

½ teaspoon dried summer savory

½ teaspoon dried thyme

1. Prepare the casing (see page 28).

2. Grind the chicken through the fine disk of a meat grinder.

3. In a large bowl, combine the chicken, salt, pepper, cayenne (if using), ginger, sage, summer savory, and thyme. Mix well, using your hands.

4. Grind the mixture through the fine disk of a meat grinder.

5. Stuff the mixture into the prepared casing. Prick air pockets. Twist off into 2- to 3-inch links. Cut the links apart with a sharp knife. Use within 2 to 3 days, kept covered in the refrigerator, or freeze for up to 2 months.

6. Cook as directed for fresh poultry sausage on page 36 to an internal temperature of 165°F (74°C). Panfrying is recommended.

Makes 2 pounds

Roman-Style Chicken Sausage

This sausage gets it name from that classic trio of Roman flavorings: onions, sweet peppers, and freshly grated Romano cheese.

    4 feet small hog or sheep casing

    4 pounds chicken meat (mixture of dark
      and light with skin)

    2 teaspoons freshly ground black pepper
      (coarse grind)

    2 teaspoons kosher or coarse salt

    1 cup finely chopped onion, sautéed and
      cooled to room temperature

    ½ cup finely chopped green bell pepper

    ½ cup freshly grated Romano cheese

1. Prepare the casing (see page 28).

2. Grind the chicken through the coarse disk of a meat grinder.

3. In a large bowl, combine the chicken, pepper, salt, onion, green pepper, and cheese. Mix well, using your hands.

4. Grind the seasoned mixture through the coarse disk.

5. Stuff the mixture into the prepared casing. Prick air pockets. Twist off into 4-inch links. Cut the links apart with a sharp knife. Use within 2 to 3 days, kept covered in the refrigerator, or freeze for up to 2 months.

6. Cook as directed for fresh poultry sausage on page 36 to an internal temperature of 165°F (74°C). Panfrying is recommended.

Makes 4 pounds

Chicken Bratwurst

This mild-mannered sausage may not be the stuff that has inspired the bratwurst mania of Wisconsin sausage lovers, but it is a darn good low-fat sausage. Enjoy it grilled, panfried, or poached. And don't forget the mustard.

3 feet small hog or sheep casing

3 pounds chicken meat (mixture of dark and light with skin)

2 teaspoons kosher or coarse salt

1 teaspoon freshly ground white pepper (fine grind)

¾ teaspoon caraway seeds, crushed

¾ teaspoon dried marjoram

½ teaspoon ground allspice

1. Prepare the casing (see page 28).

2. Grind the meat through the fine disk of a meat grinder.

3. In a large bowl, combine the chicken, salt, pepper, caraway seeds, marjoram, and allspice. Mix well, using your hands. Refrigerate the mixture for 30 minutes.

4. Grind the seasoned mixture through the fine disk.

5. Stuff the mixture into the prepared casing. Prick air pockets. Twist off into 3-inch links. Cut the links apart with a sharp knife.

6. Arrange the links on a platter, cover, and refrigerate for at least 2 hours to meld the flavors. Use within 2 to 3 days or freeze for up to 2 months.

7. Cook as directed for fresh poultry sausage on page 36 to an internal temperature of 165°F (74°C).

Makes 3 pounds

WHAT'S IN A NAME?

bratwurst

Bratwurst is only one of many sausages brought to America by German immigrants. It's a mild yet distinctive-tasting sausage whose name can be translated simply as "roast sausage." The verb *braten* in German can mean to roast, broil, bake, fry, or grill, and bratwurst is good all of those ways. Today, the center of bratwurst culture in the United States is in Sheboygan, Wisconsin, where "brats" are made and consumed with gusto. (See page 114.) Pork is the dominant meat in bratwurst, but veal is a common addition.

Chicken Sausage with Chardonnay and Apples

The apples and wine add moisture, and the ginger sparks up the taste of this fine-textured sausage. It is delicious as an entrée or sliced and served warm with cheese and crackers.

2 feet small hog or sheep casing

2 pounds boneless chicken thighs with skin

2 teaspoons kosher or coarse salt

1 teaspoon ground ginger

½ teaspoon freshly ground black pepper (medium grind)

1 Granny Smith or other firm, tart apple, peeled and chopped

2 tablespoons minced onion

¼ cup Chardonnay

1. Prepare the casing (see page 28).

2. Grind the chicken and skin through the fine disk of a meat grinder.

3. In a large bowl, combine the chicken, salt, ginger, pepper, apple, onion, and Chardonnay. Mix well, using your hands.

4. Grind the seasoned mixture through the fine disk of the meat grinder.

5. Stuff the mixture into the prepared casing. Prick air pockets. Twist off into 3-inch links. Cut the links apart with a sharp knife. Arrange the links on a platter, cover, and refrigerate for at least 2 hours to meld the flavors. Use within 2 to 3 days or freeze for up to 2 months.

6. Cook as directed for fresh poultry sausage on page 36 to an internal temperature of 165°F (74°C). Panfrying is recommended

Makes 2 pounds

Curried Chicken Sausage

Those who love a fiery curry can double or triple the amount of cayenne. And those who can't take the heat will enjoy a mouth-cooling raita sauce served alongside; see box. (Those who like it really mild can cut the amount of cayenne in half.)

2 feet small hog or sheep casing

2 pounds chicken meat (mixture of dark and light, with skin)

2 teaspoons kosher or coarse salt

1 teaspoon cayenne pepper

1 teaspoon ground coriander

1 teaspoon ground ginger

1 teaspoon ground turmeric

½ teaspoon ground cardamom

½ teaspoon dry mustard

½ teaspoon freshly ground black pepper (medium grind)

2 tablespoons plain yogurt or sour cream

1. Prepare the casing (see page 28).

2. Grind the chicken and skin through the fine disk of a meat grinder.

3. In a large bowl, combine the chicken, salt, cayenne, coriander, ginger, turmeric, cardamom, mustard, pepper, and yogurt. Mix well, using your hands.

4. Grind the seasoned mixture through the fine disk of the meat grinder.

5. Stuff the mixture into the prepared casing. Prick air pockets. Twist off into into 3-inch links. Cut the links apart with a sharp knife.

6. Arrange the links on a platter, cover, and refrigerate for at least 2 hours to meld the flavors. Use within 2 to 3 days or freeze for up to 2 months.

7. Cook as directed for fresh poultry sausage on page 36 to an internal temperature of 165°F (74°C). Panfrying is recommended.

Makes 2 pounds

RAITA

Serve Curried Chicken Sausage with steamed basmati rice and a cool raita sauce made by combining 2 cups fresh yogurt with 1 large peeled and chopped cucumber, 1 tablespoon chopped fresh mint leaves, ½ teaspoon ground cumin, and ½ teaspoon kosher or coarse salt.

Herbes de Provence Chicken Sausage

The mixture of herbs in this classic blend — usually basil, fennel, lavender, marjoram, rosemary, sage, summer savory, and thyme — are said to reflect the Romans' influence on the south of France. Whatever the origin, herbes de Provence go beautifully with chicken in this chunky little sausage.

2 feet medium hog casing

2 pounds chicken meat (mixture of dark and light, with skin)

2 teaspoons herbes de Provence blend

1 teaspoon kosher or coarse salt

½ teaspoon freshly ground black pepper (medium grind)

1 tablespoon small capers, drained if in a vinegar brine and rinsed

1 tablespoon olive oil

2 teaspoons fresh lemon juice

1. Prepare the casing (see page 28).

2. Grind the chicken and skin through the fine disk of a meat grinder.

3. In a large bowl, combine the chicken, herbes de Provence, salt, pepper, capers, olive oil, and lemon juice. Mix well, using your hands.

4. Grind the seasoned mixture through the fine disk of the meat grinder.

5. Stuff the mixture into the prepared casing. Prick air pockets. Twist off into 3-inch links. Cut the links apart with a sharp knife.

6. Arrange the links on a platter, cover, and refrigerate for at least 2 hours to meld the flavors.

7. Cook as directed for fresh poultry sausage on page 36 to an internal temperature of 165°F (74°C). Panfrying is recommended.

Makes 2 pounds

Duck Sausage with Basil and Sun-Dried Tomatoes

The rich flavor of duck gets extra depth from the fresh basil and sun-dried tomatoes. The sausages are pretty to cut into, with their flecks of green and red.

2 feet small hog or sheep casing

2 pounds duck (mixture of leg and breast, with skin)

2 slices smoked bacon, chopped

1 teaspoon kosher or coarse salt

½ teaspoon freshly ground black pepper (medium grind)

¼ cup chopped fresh basil

3 tablespoons chopped sun-dried tomatoes packed in oil

2 tablespoons dry red wine

1 tablespoon tomato paste

1. Prepare the casing (see page 28).

2. Grind the duck through the fine disk of a meat grinder.

3. In a large bowl, combine the duck, bacon, salt, pepper, basil, tomatoes, wine, and tomato paste. Mix well, using your hands.

4. Grind the seasoned mixture through the fine disk of the meat grinder.

5. Stuff the mixture into the prepared casing. Prick air pockets. Twist off into 3-inch links. Cut the links apart with a sharp knife.

6. Arrange the links on a platter, cover, and refrigerate for at least 2 hours to meld the flavors. Use within 2 to 3 days or freeze for up to 2 months.

7. Cook as directed for fresh poultry sausage on page 36 to an internal temperature of 165°F (74°C).

Makes 2 pounds

Duck Kielbasa

Ducks and geese differ from chickens and turkeys in that their fat is incorporated in their skin (good insulation for waterfowl) rather than being deposited between the skin and the meat. In making sausage from ducks and geese, we can control the amount of fat in the final product to a great extent by controlling how much of the skin and its attendant fat finds its way into the sausage. Remember, some fat is necessary for taste and texture.

4 feet small hog casing

4 pounds domestic duck meat with skin, cubed

1 tablespoon plus 2 teaspoons kosher or coarse salt

1 tablespoon sweet paprika

2 teaspoons freshly ground black pepper (medium grind)

1 teaspoon dried marjoram

1 teaspoon dried summer savory

½ teaspoon ground allspice

4 cloves garlic, minced

1. Prepare the casing (see page 28).

2. Grind the duck meat through the fine disk of a meat grinder.

3. In a large bowl, combine the duck, salt, paprika, pepper, marjoram, summer savory, allspice, and garlic. Mix well, using your hands.

4. Grind the seasoned mixture through the fine disk of the meat grinder.

5. Stuff the mixture into the prepared casing. Prick air pockets. Twist off into 3- to 4-inch links. Cut the links apart with a sharp knife.

6. Wrap the links in plastic wrap. Use within 2 to 3 days or freeze for up to 2 months.

7. Cook as directed for fresh poultry sausage on page 36 to an internal temperature of 165°F (74°C).

Makes 4 pounds

Bohemian Duck Sausage

The relatively mild flavor of domestic duck meat is highlighted by the combination of herbs in this recipe.

4 feet small hog or sheep casing

4 pounds domestic duck meat with skin, cubed

1 tablespoon plus 2 teaspoons kosher or coarse salt

2 teaspoons freshly ground white pepper (medium grind)

1 teaspoon celery seed

1 teaspoon mustard seed

1 tablespoon chopped fresh chervil

1 tablespoon chopped fresh tarragon

1. Prepare the casing (see page 28).

2. Grind the duck meat through the coarse disk of a meat grinder.

3. In a large bowl, combine the duck, salt, pepper, chervil, celery seed, mustard seed, and tarragon. Mix well, using your hands.

4. Grind the seasoned mixture through the fine disk of the meat grinder.

5. Stuff the mixture into the prepared casing. Prick air pockets. Twist off into 3-inch or 4-inch links.

6. Wrap the links in plastic. Use within 2 to 3 days or freeze for up to 2 months.

7. Cook as directed for fresh poultry sausage on page 36 to an internal temperature of 165°F (74°C).

Makes 4 pounds

Goosewurst

Whether you use fresh or frozen goose meat, this may be one of the best wursts you've ever tasted.

    5 feet medium hog casing

    5 pounds goose meat with skin, cubed

    ½ cup Drambuie (Scotch-based liqueur)

    2 tablespoons kosher or coarse salt

    1 tablespoon sweet paprika

    2 teaspoons freshly ground white pepper (medium grind)

    1 teaspoon ground coriander

    1 teaspoon ground mace

    ½ teaspoon cayenne pepper

    ½ cup minced onion

    ¼ cup chopped fresh chives

1. Prepare the casing (see page 28).

2. Grind the goose through the coarse disk of a meat grinder.

3. In a large bowl, pour the Drambuie over the goose and mix well. Cover and refrigerate for at least 3 hours or overnight.

4. Add the salt, paprika, pepper, coriander, mace, cayenne, onion, and chives to the goose mixture. Mix well, using your hands.

5. Grind the seasoned mixture through the fine disk of the meat grinder.

6. Stuff the mixture into the prepared casing. Prick air pockets. Twist off into 3- to 4-inch links. Cut the links apart with a sharp knife.

7. Cook as directed for fresh poultry sausage on page 36 to an internal temperature of 165°F (74°C). Panfrying is recommended.

Makes 5 pounds

Turkey Sausage

The tried-and-true sausage seasonings of sage, thyme, marjoram, and black pepper combined with turkey make this sausage taste like Thanksgiving stuffing in a casing. For variety, you can substitute equal amounts of ground coriander, cumin, and cayenne for the sage, thyme, and marjoram.

2 feet small hog or sheep casing

2 pounds turkey meat (mixture of dark and light with skin)

2 teaspoons kosher or coarse salt

1 teaspoon freshly ground black pepper (medium grind)

½ teaspoon dried marjoram

½ teaspoon dried sage

½ teaspoon dried thyme

2 tablespoons white wine

1. Prepare the casing (see page 28).

2. Grind the turkey through the fine disk of a meat grinder.

3. In a large bowl, combine the turkey, salt, pepper, marjoram, sage, thyme, and wine. Mix well, using your hands.

4. Grind the seasoned mixture through the fine disk of the meat grinder.

5. Stuff the mixture into the prepared casing. Prick air pockets. Twist off into 2- to 3-inch links. Cut the links apart with a sharp knife. Cook and serve, or wrap and refrigerate for up to 3 days or freeze for up to 2 months.

6. Cook as directed for fresh poultry sausage on page 36 to an internal temperature of 165°F (74°C).

Makes 2 pounds

Turkey and Cranberry Sausage

This sausage smells like Thanksgiving when you cook it, so bring on the mashed potatoes!

2 feet medium hog casing

2 pounds turkey (mixture of dark and light, with skin)

2 teaspoons kosher or coarse salt

1 teaspoon dried marjoram

1 teaspoon dried sage

½ teaspoon freshly ground black pepper (medium grind)

2 tablespoons Grand Marnier or other orange-flavored liqueur

½ cup dried cranberries

¼ cup chopped chestnuts, roasted if fresh (see Note)

1. Prepare the casing (see page 28).

2. Grind the turkey through the fine disk of a meat grinder.

3. In a large bowl, combine the turkey, salt, marjoram, sage, pepper, and Grand Marnier. Mix well, using your hands.

4. Grind the seasoned mixture through the fine disk. Mix in the cranberries and chestnuts.

5. Stuff the mixture into the prepared casing. Prick air pockets. Twist off into 3-inch links.

6. Arrange the links on a platter, cover, and refrigerate for at least 2 hours to meld the flavors. Use within 2 to 3 days or freeze for up to 2 months.

7. Cook as directed on page 36 to an internal temperature of 165°F (74°C).

NOTE: Fresh chestnuts are generally available from Thanksgiving to New Year's. They can be purchased canned year-round.

Makes 2 pounds

QUICK "ROASTED" CHESTNUTS

To quickly prepare fresh chestnuts, slash the flat side of each nut with a knife and place them in a single layer in a glass pie plate. Microwave on high for about 6 minutes, until shell starts to peel back. Peel and rub the skins off while the nuts are still warm, then sauté in butter until nuts are golden and softened, about 10 minutes.

Southwestern Turkey Sausage

Perfect in a fajita, terrific in a black bean stew, and absolutely decadent with huevos rancheros, these sausages can add new life to your familiar Tex-Mex favorites. Roasting the chiles (under the broiler or over an open flame) is an extra step that intensifies the flavors of these spicy sausages.

3 feet medium hog casing

3 pounds turkey meat with skin, cubed

2 tablespoons chili powder

1 tablespoon kosher or coarse salt

2 teaspoons ground cumin

1 teaspoon freshly ground black pepper (medium grind)

1 Anaheim chile, roasted, seeded, and chopped

1 jalapeño chile, roasted, seeded, and chopped

¼ cup chopped fresh cilantro

2 teaspoons minced garlic

2 tablespoons red wine vinegar

1 tablespoon lime juice

1. Prepare the casing (see page 28).

2. Grind the turkey through the coarse disk of a meat grinder.

3. In a large bowl, combine the ground turkey, chili powder, salt, cumin, pepper, Anaheim chile, jalapeño, cilantro, garlic, vinegar, and lime juice. Refrigerate for 1 hour.

4. Grind the seasoned mixture through the coarse disk.

5. Stuff the mixture into the prepared casings. Prick air pockets. Twist off into 4- to 5-inch links. Cut the links apart with a sharp knife.

6. Chill sausages for at least 2 hours, or overnight, to meld the flavors. Use within 2 to 3 days or freeze for up to 2 months.

7. Cook as directed for fresh poultry sausage on page 36.

Makes 3 pounds

HANDLING CHILES

The seeds and membranes of chiles of all kinds contain oils that can severely irritate skin and eyes. The best bet to avoid irritation is to wear gloves while working with chiles. If you don't, be sure not to touch your mouth, nose, or eyes once you've cut a chile, then thoroughly wash your hands with soap and water after you've finished handling the chiles.

Thai-Flavored Turkey Sausage

All of the wonderfully exotic flavors of Thai cuisine — garlic, ginger, chiles, cilantro, lime juice, and fish sauce — are blended in these low-fat sausages. They can add incredible zest to your next stir-fry.

3 feet medium hog casing

3 pounds turkey meat (mixture of dark and light, with skin), cubed

1 tablespoon kosher or coarse salt

1 teaspoon freshly ground black pepper (medium grind)

½ teaspoon crushed red pepper

2 tablespoons chopped fresh basil

2 tablespoons chopped fresh cilantro

1 tablespoon chopped fresh mint

2 teaspoons minced garlic

2 teaspoons grated fresh ginger-root

1 tablespoon Asian fish sauce

1 teaspoon Thai green curry paste

1 teaspoon grated lime zest

1 tablespoon fresh lime juice

1. Prepare the casing (see page 28).

2. Put the turkey and skin through the coarse disk of a meat grinder.

3. In a large bowl, combine the turkey, salt, black pepper, crushed red pepper, basil, cilantro, mint, garlic, gingerroot, fish sauce, curry paste, lemon zest, and lime juice. Freeze for 30 minutes.

4. Grind the seasoned mixture through the fine disk of the meat grinder.

5. Stuff the mixture into the prepared casing. Prick air pockets. Twist off into 4- to 5-inch links. Cut the links apart with a sharp knife. Refrigerate, covered, for up to 2 to 3 days or freeze for up to 2 months.

6. Cook as directed for fresh poultry sausage on page 36 to an internal temperature of 165°F (74°C).

Makes about 3 pounds

Turkey Chorizo

As in all chorizo-style sausages, hot red pepper carries the day here. The curing process intensifies the flavors of the spices and wine.

5 feet small hog or sheep casings

5 pounds turkey meat with skin

2 tablespoons sweet paprika

1 tablespoon plus 2 teaspoons kosher or coarse salt

2 teaspoons cayenne pepper

2 teaspoons ground cumin

2 teaspoons oregano

2 teaspoons freshly ground black pepper (medium grind)

1 teaspoon ground coriander

1 teaspoon ground ginger

½ teaspoon celery seed

½ teaspoon ground cinnamon

Curing salt (use supplier's recommended quantity for 5 pounds of meat; see Note)

½ cup dry red wine

1. Prepare the casing (see page 28).

2. Grind the turkey through the fine disk of a meat grinder.

3. In a large bowl, combine the turkey, paprika, salt, cayenne, cumin, oregano, black pepper, coriander, ginger, celery seed, cinnamon, curing salt, and wine. Mix well, using your hands.

4. Cure the sausage, loosely covered, in the refrigerator for 24 hours.

5. Grind the seasoned mixture through the fine disk of the meat grinder.

6. Stuff the mixture into the prepared casing. Prick air pockets. Twist off into 3-inch links. Do not separate the links.

7. Hang the sausage to dry in a cold place for about 8 weeks. Refrigerate the cured sausage. To serve, cook as directed on page 36 to an internal temperature of 165°F (74°C).

NOTE: We recommend that you use a commercial premixed cure in any recipe for cured sausage. Premixed cures replace the saltpeter in older recipes.

Makes 5 pounds

Sicilian-Style
Turkey Sausage

*Sicilian sausages rely principally upon fennel seed for their distinctive taste.
The hot-smoking cooks the sausage and adds its own inimitable flavor.*

    5 feet small hog or sheep casing

    5 pounds turkey meat (mixture of dark and light,
        with skin), cubed

    2 tablespoons kosher or coarse salt

    2 teaspoons crushed fennel seed

    2 teaspoons whole fennel seed

    2 teaspoons freshly ground black pepper (medium grind)

    2 teaspoons crushed red pepper (optional)

    2 cloves garlic, minced

1. Prepare the casing (see page 28).

2. Grind the turkey through the fine disk of a meat grinder.

3. In a large bowl, combine the turkey, salt, crushed and whole fennel seed,
   black pepper, crushed red pepper (if using), and garlic.

4. Grind the mixture through the fine disk of the meat grinder.

5. Stuff the mixture into the prepared casing. Twist off into 3-inch links.

6. Hot-smoke at 180 to 190°F (83 to 88°C) for 2 to 4 hours, until internal
   temperature of the sausage is 165°F (74°C).

7. Refrigerate the sausage, covered, for up to 1 week, or freeze for up to
   2 months.

Makes 5 pounds

Chicken Dogs

Because the meat mixture is ground three times, the texture of this sausage is fine, almost like a commercial hot dog.

5 feet small hog or sheep casing

5 pounds chicken meat (mixture of dark and light), cubed

1 cup nonfat dry milk

1 tablespoon plus 2 teaspoons kosher or coarse salt

1 tablespoon onion powder

1 tablespoon paprika

1 tablespoon sugar

2 teaspoons finely ground coriander

1 teaspoon garlic powder

1 teaspoon ground mace

1 teaspoon dried marjoram

1 teaspoon finely ground mustard seed

¼ teaspoon ascorbic acid

Curing salt (use supplier's recommended quantity for 5 pounds of meat; see Note)

1. Prepare the casing (see page 28).

2. In a large bowl, combine the chicken, milk, salt, onion powder, paprika, sugar, coriander, garlic powder, mace, marjoram, mustard seed, ascorbic acid, and curing salt. Mix well, using your hands.

3. Grind the mixture through the coarse disk of a meat grinder. Freeze for 30 minutes.

4. Grind the mixture through the fine disk. Freeze for 30 minutes.

5. Grind the mixture through the fine disk a second time.

6. Stuff the mixture into the prepared casing. Prick air pockets. Twist off into 5-inch links. Do not separate the links.

7. Cold-smoke at about 110 to 120°F (44 to 49°C) for 2 hours.

8. Bring a large pot of water to a boil. Add the links and reduce the heat to maintain a water temperature of 180 to 190°F (83° to 88°C). Simmer the links for 30 minutes to an internal temperature of 165°F (74°C).

9. Drain the links and let them cool. Pat the links dry, cover, and refrigerate for 3 days to cure before heating and eating. Use within 1 week or freeze for up to 2 months.

NOTE: We recommend that you use a commercial premixed cure in any recipe for cured sausage. Premixed cures replace the saltpeter in older recipes.

Makes 5 pounds

THE TOP 10 HOT DOG-CONSUMING AMERICAN CITIES

Who eats the most hot dogs? The following U.S. cities, ranked by pounds of hot dogs sold in supermarkets, are the biggest consumers, according to a recent report from the National Hot Dog and Sausage Council:

1. Los Angeles, California
2. New York, New York
3. Chicago, Illinois
4. Philadelphia, Pennsylvania
5. San Antonio/Corpus Christi, Texas
6. Baltimore, Maryland/Washington, DC
7. Dallas/Fort Worth, Texas
8. Birmingham/Montgomery, Alabama
9. Houston, Texas
10. Miami/Fort Lauderdale, Florida

CHAPTER 9

Seafood Sausages

But there is something about meat or fowl or fish

that has been ground . . . then properly seasoned and

correctly cooked, that appeals to me immediately . . .

— Colman Andrews

FISH AND SEAFOOD MAY NOT BE the first ingredients that come to mind when you hear the word *sausage*, but the recipes in this chapter demonstrate that fish has several advantages over meat as the main component of sausage.

For one thing, there's ease of preparation. Most of the recipes in this chapter can quickly be made using a food processor to mince the ingredients. In fact, you don't even have to stuff the seasoned mixtures into casings: A simple wrap of buttered parchment paper or even plastic film will suffice for most, or the mixture can be shaped into patties.

There's the health angle: Seafood is low in saturated fat and high in the omega-3 oils that have been shown to be beneficial to coronary health and to brain development.

Finally, fish is an economical ingredient. There's practically no waste, and a low-priced species such as pollock can be used as an underpinning for the small amounts of lobster or shrimp that dress up a sausage. If you use frozen fillets, be sure to thaw and drain them first.

Seafood Herb Sausage

The fresh chives and parsley give this sausage a refreshing flavor.

4 feet small hog casings

2 pounds whitefish fillets, cubed and well chilled

1½ teaspoons kosher or coarse salt

½ teaspoon celery salt

½ teaspoon freshly ground black pepper (medium grind)

2 tablespoons chopped fresh chives

1 tablespoon chopped fresh parsley

1 teaspoon lemon juice

1 large egg or 2 large egg whites, lightly beaten

1. Prepare the casing (see page 28).

2. In a food processor, process the fish just until it is broken up, about 3 pulses.

3. Add the salt, celery salt, pepper, chives, parsley, lemon juice, and egg and process just until everything is well blended.

4. Stuff the mixture into the prepared casing, prick air pockets, and twist off into 3- to 4-inch links. Cut the links apart with a sharp knife.

5. Cook (see below) or refrigerate immediately, wrapped in plastic. Do not store the sausages for longer than 1 day.

Makes 2 pounds

COOKING SEAFOOD SAUSAGES

Fish sausage is highly perishable and should be used within 24 hours. To cook the sausages in this chapter, first poach them in gently simmering water for about 7 minutes. To serve, grill or broil long enough to reheat them and crisp the skins, about 5 minutes or until an instant-read thermometer reaches 160°F (71°C).

The uncooked sausages may also be microwaved (cook on high, covered, for 4 to 5 minutes) or panfried in butter or oil for about 10 minutes, until golden brown and cooked through. Use a light hand in cooking and handling seafood sausages.

Old Bay Sausage

Old Bay Seasoning is the proprietary name of a seafood blend that contains celery seed, dry mustard, paprika, and other flavorings. This classic combo of seasonings transforms the mild whitefish that is the "meat" of the sausage so much that you should try this recipe if your family isn't fond of fish.

4 feet small hog casing

2 pounds whitefish fillets, cubed and well chilled

1½ teaspoons kosher or coarse salt

1 teaspoon sweet paprika

½ teaspoon celery salt

¼ teaspoon ground bay leaf

¼ teaspoon ground cardamom

¼ teaspoon ground cloves

¼ teaspoon ground ginger

¼ teaspoon ground mace

¼ teaspoon crushed mustard seed

¼ teaspoon freshly ground black pepper (medium grind)

1 large egg or 2 large egg whites, lightly beaten

1 teaspoon lemon juice

1. Prepare the casing (see page 28).

2. In a food processor, process the fish just until it is broken up, about three pulses.

3. Add the salt, paprika, celery salt, bay leaf, cardamom, cloves, ginger, mace, mustard seed, pepper, egg, and lemon juice. Process just until everything is well blended.

4. Stuff the mixture into the prepared casing, prick air pockets, and twist off into 3- to 4-inch links. Cut the links apart with a sharp knife.

5. Cook (see page 187) or refrigerate immediately, wrapped in plastic. Do not store the sausages for longer than 1 day.

Makes 2 pounds

OLD BAY STORY

You can replace the herbs and spices in the Old Bay Sausage recipe with 2 teaspoons of authentic Old Bay Seasoning, the seafood herb-and-spice blend that was created in 1939 in Baltimore by a German-Jewish refugee named Gustav Brunn.

Gustav arrived with a spice grinder and the dream of starting a business. With a shop near the city's fish market, he developed a new recipe especially for the famous Chesapeake Bay crabs. The secret blend of more than a dozen herbs and spices — including bay leaf, celery salt, cloves, ginger, mustard, and red pepper — is very popular in the Mid-Atlantic area and is used on everything from seafood to hamburgers and even french fries.

Gustav was a man after a sausage maker's heart, grinding his own fresh spices and creating a new and delicious combination. His creation is available in the spice or seafood section of most supermarkets.

Zesty Citrus and Seafood Sausage

Anyone who has ever squeezed a lemon wedge over a serving of fish knows how compatible citrus and seafood can be, as they are in this sausage.

4 feet small hog casing

2 pounds whitefish fillets, cubed and well chilled

2 teaspoons kosher or coarse salt

½ teaspoon freshly ground black pepper (medium grind)

1 tablespoon chopped fresh parsley

1 sprig fresh thyme, leaves only

1 teaspoon grated lemon zest

1 teaspoon grated orange zest

2 large egg whites

1 tablespoon lemon juice

1. Prepare the casing (see page 28).

2. In a food processor, process the fish just until it has broken up, about three pulses.

3. Add the salt, pepper, parsley, thyme, lemon zest, orange zest, egg whites, and lemon juice. Process just until everything is well blended.

4. Stuff the mixture into the prepared casing, prick air pockets, and twist off into 3- to 4-inch links. Cut the links apart with a sharp knife.

5. Cook (see page 187) or refrigerate immediately, wrapped in plastic. Do not store the sausages for longer than 1 day.

Makes 2 pounds

Dilly Fish Sausage

This makes beautiful pink and green sausages fragrant with dill. For an elegant garnish, top with chunks of preseasoned salmon.

       4 feet small hog casings
       1 pound fresh salmon, cubed and well chilled
       1 pound whitefish fillets, cubed and well chilled
    1½ teaspoons kosher or coarse salt
       ½ teaspoon freshly ground black pepper (medium grind)
       1 tablespoon chopped fresh dill
       2 teaspoons chopped fresh chives
       2 teaspoons chopped fresh parsley
       1 large egg or 2 large egg whites, lightly beaten
       2 tablespoons sour cream

1. Prepare the casing (see page 28).

2. In a food processor, process the salmon and whitefish just until it is broken up, about three pulses.

3. Add the salt, pepper, dill, chives, parsley, egg, and sour cream and process just until everything is well blended.

4. Stuff the mixture into the prepared casing, prick air pockets, and twist off into 3- to 4-inch links. Cut the links apart with a sharp knife.

5. Cook (see page 187) or refrigerate immediately, wrapped in plastic. Do not store the sausages for longer than 1 day.

Makes 2 pounds

Smoked Salmon Sausage

The smoky flavor and rosy color of smoked salmon predominates in this recipe, even though whitefish is the main ingredient and no smoking is involved.

4 feet small hog casing

1½ pounds whitefish fillets, cubed and well chilled

¼ pound smoked salmon, chopped and well chilled

1½ teaspoons kosher or coarse salt

Pinch of cayenne pepper

2 tablespoons chopped fresh parsley

1 tablespoon minced onion

1 teaspoon fresh lemon juice

2 egg whites, lightly beaten

1. Prepare the casing (see page 28).

2. In a food processor, process the whitefish and salmon just until it is broken up, about three pulses. Add the salt, cayenne, parsley, onion, lemon juice, and egg whites, and process until well blended.

3. Stuff the mixture into the prepared casing, prick air pockets, and twist off into 3-inch or 4-inch links. Cut the links apart with a sharp knife.

4. Cook (see page 187) or refrigerate immediately, wrapped in plastic. Do not store the sausages for longer than 1 day.

Makes 1¾ pounds

DIPPING SAUCE

Smoked Salmon Sausage is a hit when sliced and served warm with a savory dipping sauce. For the sauce, lightly beat together ¼ cup sour cream, ¼ cup plain yogurt, 1 tablespoon chopped fresh dill weed, and 1 teaspoon capers.

Squid Sausage

This "sausage" was inspired by the Mediterranean dish of stuffed squid. The sausage is unique in that it is stuffed into the body of the squid itself.

8 medium squid, 6 to 7 inches long

1 teaspoon freshly ground black pepper (medium grind)

1 teaspoon kosher or coarse salt

½ teaspoon dried oregano

1 cup chopped fresh parsley

1 clove garlic, minced

1 cup fresh breadcrumbs

¼ cup plus 1 tablespoon olive oil

½ cup dry vermouth

2 cups crushed tomatoes

1. Clean the squid. For each squid, cut off the tentacles and reserve. Cut off and discard the mouth, which is in the center of the tentacles. Under cold running water, peel off the outer skin and discard. Squeeze the body to push out the insides, pulling off the head when the insides are out. Pull out the center bone (it looks like a piece of clear plastic) and discard. Turn the body inside out and rinse well. Turn back and rinse again. Dry on paper towels.

2. Chop the tentacles coarsely in a food processor. Add the pepper, salt, oregano, parsley, and garlic. Process until blended.

3. Add the breadcrumbs and 1 tablespoon of the olive oil. Mix well.

4. Fill the bodies of the squid between half and three-quarters full. (Do not overfill, or they will burst during cooking.)

5. Skewer the openings shut with toothpicks.

6. Heat the remaining ¼ cup of olive oil in a large skillet over medium heat and add the squid. Panfry until lightly browned, turning often to prevent them from sticking, about 10 minutes.

7. Add the vermouth and cook until the wine has nearly evaporated, about 3 minutes. Add the crushed tomatoes and simmer the mixture for 20 minutes, uncovered. Serve warm, and remind diners to watch out for the toothpicks.

Makes 4 servings

Louisiana Crayfish Sausage

The succulent freshwater crustacean of the Louisiana bayou country is more tender than lobster, more delicate than shrimp. It finds its way into chili, mousse, the spicy stew called étouffée, and other dishes, so why not sausages? Enjoy them with a glass of cold Dixie beer.

4 feet small hog casing

1 pound picked-over crayfish tail meat

1 pound whitefish fillets, cubed and well chilled

2 teaspoons kosher or coarse salt

½ teaspoon cayenne pepper

½ teaspoon freshly ground black pepper (medium grind)

1 tablespoon minced celery

1 tablespoon minced green bell pepper

1 tablespoon minced shallot

2 tablespoons chili sauce

1 egg or 2 egg whites

1 tablespoon lemon juice

1. Prepare the casing (see page 28).

2. In a food processor, process the crayfish and whitefish just until broken up, about three pulses.

3. Add the salt, cayenne, black pepper, celery, green pepper, shallot, chili sauce, egg, and lemon juice. Process just until everything is well blended.

4. Stuff the mixture into the prepared casing, prick air pockets, and twist off into 3- to 4-inch links. Cut the links apart with a sharp knife.

5. Cook (see page 187) or refrigerate immediately, wrapped in plastic. Do not store the sausages for longer than 1 day.

Makes 2 pounds

THAT FISHY SMELL

If you rinse your hands under cold water before you handle fish, they won't smell as fishy. And rubbing your hands, knife, and cutting board with lemon wedges will help remove fish odor.

Lobster Sausage

You won't need to mortgage the farm for this recipe, since lobster accounts for only a small portion of the ingredients. Its distinctive flavor, however, permeates the entire sausage.

    4 feet small hog casing
 1½ pounds whitefish fillets, cubed and well chilled
    2 teaspoons kosher or coarse salt
    1 teaspoon paprika
  ½ teaspoon ground coriander
  ½ teaspoon ground mustard seed
  ½ teaspoon freshly ground white pepper (medium grind)
    1 teaspoon lemon juice
    1 large egg or 2 large egg whites, lightly beaten
  ½ pound lobster meat, coarsely chopped

1. Prepare the casing (see page 28).

2. In a food processor, process the fish just until it is broken up, about three pulses.

3. Add the salt, paprika, coriander, mustard seed, pepper, lemon juice, and egg. Process until blended.

4. In a large mixing bowl, mix together the fish mixture and the lobster.

5. Stuff the mixture into the prepared casing, prick air pockets, and twist off into 3- to 4-inch links. Cut the links apart with a sharp knife.

6. Cook (see page 187) or refrigerate immediately, wrapped in plastic. Do not store the sausages for longer than 1 day.

Makes 2 pounds

Shrimp Sausage

Fresh or frozen shrimp are preferred for this recipe. You can use canned shrimps as a last resort, but rinse them well under cold running water to get rid of the slight "tinny" taste.

4 feet small hog casing

1½ pounds whitefish fillets, cubed and well chilled

2 teaspoons kosher or coarse salt

1 teaspoon sweet paprika

2 tablespoons chopped fresh parsley

2 teaspoons minced onion

1 egg or 2 egg whites, lightly beaten

1 teaspoon lemon juice

½ pound small shrimp, peeled and chopped

1. Prepare the casing (see page 28).

2. In a food processor, process the fish just until it is broken up, about three pulses.

3. Add the salt, paprika, parsley, onion, egg, and lemon juice. Process until well blended.

4. In a large mixing bowl, mix together the fish mixture and the shrimp until well blended.

5. Stuff the mixture into the prepared casing, prick air pockets, and twist off into 3- to 4-inch links. Cut the links apart with a sharp knife.

6. Cook (see page 187) or refrigerate immediately. Do not store the sausages for longer than 1 day.

Makes 2 pounds

SEAFOOD STOCK

For the frugal among us, here's an idea that yields a delicious dividend: flavorful seafood stock. Freeze shrimp and lobster shells after you've removed their meat. When you've amassed a bunch, simmer them in a mixture of water, bottled clam juice, chopped celery leaves, onion skins, and peppercorns. Add other spices to suit your imagination. Let the liquid reduce to concentrate its flavor, then strain the stock and use for fish soup, paella, or a seafood casserole.

Scampi Sausage

Shrimp, in Italian, is translated as gamberetto, *but as all patrons of Italian-American restaurants know, shrimp shows up as scampi on the menus. And where there is scampi, there is also garlic. Technically, scampi are a type of crustacean related to the shrimp, found in the Adriatic. But who are we to argue? These sausages, a blend of delicious shellfish and garlic, bring to mind the popular Italian-American favorite shrimp scampi. Try them on top of pasta.*

4 feet small hog casing

1 pound whitefish fillets, cubed and well chilled

2 teaspoons kosher or coarse salt

½ teaspoon ground allspice

1 tablespoon minced garlic

2 teaspoons minced onion

2 large eggs or ½ cup egg whites, lightly beaten

1 teaspoon butter, melted

1 teaspoon lemon juice

1 teaspoon vegetable oil

½ pound small shrimp, peeled

¼ pound crabmeat, shredded

¼ pound bay scallops or quartered sea scallops

1. Prepare the casing (see page 28).

2. In a food processor, process the fish just until it is broken up, about three pulses.

3. Add the salt, allspice, garlic, onion, eggs, butter, lemon juice, and vegetable oil. Process until well blended.

4. Add the shrimp, crab, and scallops. Process just until blended. Do not overprocess.

5. Stuff the mixture into the prepared casing, prick air pockets, and twist off into 3- to 4-inch links. Cut the links apart with a sharp knife.

6. Cook (see page 187) or refrigerate immediately, wrapped in plastic. Do not store the sausages for longer than 1 day.

Makes 2 pounds

Clam Dogs

A "Down East" (that would be Maine) favorite is the clam roll — fried clams heaped into a toasted hog dog bun (New England–style, split at the top) and topped with tartar sauce. You might want to eat your clam dogs in the same manner.

    4 feet small hog casing

1½ pounds whitefish fillets, cubed

    2 teaspoons kosher or coarse salt

    ½ teaspoon dried basil

    ½ teaspoon freshly ground black pepper (medium grind)

    2 tablespoons chopped fresh parsley

    2 teaspoons minced onion

    2 cloves garlic, minced

    1 large egg or 2 large egg whites, lightly beaten

    2 cans (6 ounces each) chopped clams, drained

1. Prepare the casing (see page 28).

2. In a food processor, process the fish just until it is broken up, about three pulses.

3. Add the salt, basil, pepper, parsley, onion, garlic, and egg. Process until well blended.

4. In a mixing bowl, mix together the fish mixture and the clams until well blended.

5. Stuff the mixture into the prepared casing, prick air pockets, and twist off into 4- or 5-inch links. Cut the links apart with a sharp knife.

6. Cook (see page 187) or refrigerate immediately, wrapped in plastic. Do not store the sausages for longer than 1 day.

Makes 2 pounds

Conch Sausage

The conch is a marine mollusk probably best known for its attractive shell, which people put to their ear to "hear" the sound of crashing waves. Although you can use fresh conch in this recipe, the canned variety is more readily available and has been tenderized by the canning process.

4 feet small hog casing

1½ pounds whitefish fillets, cubed

2 teaspoons kosher or coarse salt

1 teaspoon crushed red pepper

½ teaspoon dried oregano

½ teaspoon dried rosemary

1 large egg or 2 egg whites, lightly beaten

1 teaspoon lemon juice

2 cans (6 ounces each) conch, drained

1. Prepare the casing (see page 28).

2. In a food processor, process the fish just until it is broken up, about three pulses.

3. Add the salt, red pepper, oregano, rosemary, egg, and lemon juice. Process until well blended. Transfer the mixture to a large bowl.

4. In the food processor, pulse the conch until it has the texture of minced clams. Stir the conch into the fish mixture; mix well.

5. Stuff the mixture into the prepared casing, prick air pockets, and twist off into 3- to 4-inch links. Cut the links apart with a sharp knife.

6. Cook (see page 187) or refrigerate immediately, wrapped in plastic. Do not store the sausages for longer than 1 day.

Makes 2 pounds

Oyster Sausage

Fresh oysters are preferred here, although canned may be substituted in a pinch.

> 4 feet small hog casing
>
> 2 pounds shucked oysters, drained, liquid reserved
>
> 2 cups fresh breadcrumbs
>
> 1½ teaspoons kosher or coarse salt
>
> 1 teaspoon freshly ground black pepper (medium grind)
>
> 1 egg or 2 egg whites, lightly beaten
>
> ¼ cup chopped fresh parsley
>
> 1 clove garlic, minced

1. Prepare the casing (see page 28).

2. In a food processor, process the oysters until they are coarsely chopped, about three pulses.

3. Add the breadcrumbs, salt, pepper, egg, parsley, and garlic; process until well blended. Add enough of the reserved oyster liquor to the mixture to make a stiff paste.

4. Stuff the mixture into the prepared casing, prick air pockets, and twist off into 3- to 4-inch links. Cut the links apart with a sharp knife.

5. Cook (see page 187) or refrigerate immediately, wrapped in plastic. Do not store the sausages for longer than 1 day.

Makes 2 pounds

CHAPTER 10

Vegetarian Sausages

*Sir Andrew Aguecheek: "I am a great eater of
beef, and I believe that does harm to my wit."
Sir Toby Belch's reply: "No question."*

— William Shakespeare, *Twelfth Night*

IF YOU, LIKE SIR ANDREW, THINK IT WORTHY to cut
back a bit on your consumption of beef, or other meats,
for that matter, this chapter is for you. The dedicated
carnivore may regard the term *vegetarian sausage* as an oxy-
moron. But those of us who love vegetarian cooking — and
perhaps Sir Toby — know that the same herbs and spices that
taste so great in pork sausage or chicken dogs go equally well
with the grains, legumes, and vegetables that are the mainstays
of vegetarian sausage. Perhaps you have a vegetarian member
of your family and want to share your love of sausage with
your loved one. Maybe you cook vegetarian occasionally in the
interest of more healthful eating. Either way, the recipes in
this chapter are sure to appeal.

VEGETARIAN INGREDIENTS

Each of the vegetarian sausages in this chapter includes the following components:

Foundation ingredients. Cooked beans or legumes; cooked barley, rice, or other grains; tempeh, tofu, TVP (texturized vegetable protein), or other soy products. These foundation ingredients are usually grated, mashed, or ground and replace ground meat in a meat sausage.

Vegetables and fruits. Fresh carrot, celery, garlic, onion, squash, apples, dried apricots, dates, and so on. They are usually minced or grated, and sometimes sautéed before they are added to the sausage mixture.

Moistening and binding ingredients. Usually eggs or egg whites act as a binder. Sometimes butter, oil, brandy, wine, or reduced cider are used to moisten the mixture.

Thickeners. Breadcrumbs, flour, rolled oats, wheat germ, or other ingredients thicken and "bulk up" the mixture so it can be shaped. Breadcrumbs are probably the most versatile.

Seasonings. Parsley, sage, rosemary, thyme, salt, pepper, and the whole cast of characters used in traditional meat sausages are used in vegetarian sausages. Please feel free to personalize our recipes to suit your own tastes. As with meat sausages, seasonings provide the greatest opportunity for experimentation.

Casings. Researchers at several universities are reportedly experimenting with vegetarian casings, but so far none has come onto the market. (Hog casings don't quite fit the definition of "vegetarian," although you could use them if you are not making vegetarian sausage for reasons of principle.)

Fortunately, Mother Nature has provided some excellent casings in the form of cabbage leaves, chard leaves, corn husks, the outer layer of leeks, and other leaves that can give your mixture a sausage shape and stand up during cooking. Get creative: Wrap your sausage mixtures in lavash bread, phyllo dough, or tortillas. Parchment paper, foil, and plastic wrap can be used as nonedible casings. When forming sausages, use about ½ cup of mixture and shape it into a sausage that's about ¾ inch thick and 3 to 4 inches long.

Most of the vegetarian mixtures can also be shaped into sausage rolls, patties, or balls and sautéed without any casing at all. Generally, you would form about ½ cup of the sausage mixture at a time and should shape the mixture into patties that are about ½-inch thick and 3 inches in diameter.

Cooking Vegetarian Sausages

Because they are made from precooked or quick-cooking ingredients, vegetarian sausages tend to cook quickly, usually about 10 minutes on the stovetop. Depending on the size, shape, and makeup of the vegetarian sausage, panfrying, grilling, or poaching may be used as the cooking method. Individual recipes provide specific cooking instructions. In general, vegetarian sausages are more delicate than meat sausages and should be handled gently.

Refrigerate any unused vegetarian sausages and use within 3 days. They may also be frozen, well wrapped, for up to 3 months.

AMIE AND JENNY NICHOLS
SAUSAGES THAT HARMONIZE

Amie and Jenny have an earlier edition of this book and were inspired enough to develop their own recipes for fresh sausage. They recited two of their tasty-sounding inventions:

"We do Simon and Garfunkel Lamb Sausage made from 5 pounds ground lamb; 2 teaspoons coarse black pepper; 1 tablespoon each parsley, sage, rosemary, and thyme; 1 tablespoon salt; and 1 tablespoon garlic.

"We also do Sweet Sicilian Lamb Sausage made from 5 pounds ground lamb; 1 tablespoon each of salt, garlic, fennel seed, and coarse black pepper; and 1 teaspoon each crushed red pepper, anise seed, and caraway seed.

"We love the book!"

Vegetarian Breakfast Sausage

There is any number of different "vegetarian breakfast links" sold in the freezer case of the supermarket, right next to the convenient pork sausage "brown 'n' serves." What makes them breakfast sausages? The same seasonings that go into breakfast sausages go into the vegetarian sausages in the freezer case — and into this recipe. If you find it more convenient, you can prepare and shape the sausages the night before, to save time on a busy morning.

1½ cups cooked white or navy beans, or 1 can (15 ounces) drained and rinsed

1 cup cooked brown lentils

¼ cup raw or toasted wheat germ

1 teaspoon kosher or coarse salt

½ teaspoon dried marjoram

½ teaspoon freshly ground black pepper (medium grind)

½ teaspoon dried sage

½ teaspoon dried thyme

½ cup minced celery

2 teaspoons chopped fresh parsley

2 tablespoons butter, melted, or 2 tablespoons vegetable oil

¼ cup fresh breadcrumbs, or more as needed

⅔ cup milk

1 large egg, lightly beaten

1 cup cornmeal

1. Mash the beans and lentils in a large bowl. Stir in the wheat germ, salt, marjoram, pepper, sage, thyme, celery, parsley, and butter and knead together until well blended. Add the breadcrumbs as needed to make a mixture that holds its shape.

2. With wet hands, roll small handfuls of mixture into sausage shapes about ¾ inches in diameter and 3 to 4 inches long and place on a platter; refrigerate for about 1 hour to firm up.

3. Preheat the oven to 450°F (230°C) and grease an oblong roasting pan.

4. In a shallow bowl, combine the milk and egg. Sprinkle the cornmeal in a pie plate. Dip each sausage into the egg mixture, then roll in the cornmeal. Arrange in the pan and roast for about 10 minutes, until golden brown, turning frequently. Serve hot.

Makes about 10 sausages

Black Bean and Smoked Corn Sausage Patties

Grilling the sweet corn over a charcoal fire gives the sausage patties a smoky edge. These sausages are terrific in a tortilla, dressed up with guacamole and salsa.

2 ears sweet corn, husked

¼ cup minced onion

2 cloves garlic, minced

1 teaspoon ground cumin

1 tablespoon olive oil

1½ cups cooked black beans, or 1 can (15 ounces), drained and rinsed

½ cup dry breadcrumbs

½ teaspoon freshly ground black pepper (medium grind)

½ teaspoon kosher or coarse salt

2 tablespoons chopped fresh cilantro

1 egg, lightly beaten

2 tablespoons salsa, plus additional for serving

Guacamole, to serve (optional)

1. Over a medium-hot charcoal fire, grill the corn, turning frequently, until the ears are lightly browned on all sides, about 5 minutes. Set aside.

2. In a frying pan on top of the grill, sauté the onion, garlic, and cumin in the olive oil until the onion is transparent, about 5 minutes. Remove the pan from the grill.

3. Using a sharp knife, slice the kernels from the grilled corn.

4. In a food processor, combine the corn, onion mixture, beans, breadcrumbs, pepper, salt, cilantro, egg, and 2 tablespoons of the salsa. Pulse until the ingredients are blended and the mixture holds together.

5. With wet hands, shape the mixture into patties about ½-inch thick and 3 inches in diameter. Refrigerate for about 1 hour to firm up.

6. To cook, panfry over medium heat or grill, and serve with salsa and guacamole (if using).

Makes 5 to 6 sausage patties

> ### HOMEMADE BREADCRUMBS
>
> Make your own dry breadcrumbs from good-quality whole-grain bread. Four slices of toasted bread whirled in a food processor will make about 1½ cups breadcrumbs.

Italian Bulgur and Bean Sausage Rolls

These sausages are rolled up in chard leaves and poached. Serve with pasta and a hearty marinara sauce.

1⅓ cups boiling water

⅔ cup uncooked bulgur

1½ cups cooked red kidney beans, or 1 can (15 ounces), drained and rinsed

¼ cup chopped fresh parsley

2 tablespoons chopped fresh basil

1 teaspoon chopped fresh oregano

1 teaspoon small capers, drained and rinsed

1 teaspoon minced garlic

½ cup dry breadcrumbs

½ teaspoon freshly ground black pepper (medium grind)

½ teaspoon kosher or coarse salt

1 egg, lightly beaten

1 tablespoon olive oil

1 tablespoon tomato paste

6 to 8 fresh chard leaves

Vegetable broth or water

1. In a medium-sized bowl, pour the boiling water over the bulgur. Cover and let steam for about 10 minutes.

2. In a food processor, combine the beans, parsley, basil, oregano, capers, and garlic. Process until fairly smooth.

3. Drain any unabsorbed water from the bulgur. Add the bulgur, bread-crumbs, pepper, salt, egg, oil, and tomato paste to the bean mixture and pulse just until combined. Refrigerate for about 30 minutes.

4. Steam the chard leaves until pliable, 30 to 60 seconds.

5. Form about ½ cup of the sausage mixture at a time into a sausage shape and roll it up in a chard leaf, as if making an egg roll, tucking in the sides of the leaf. Fasten each roll with a toothpick. Repeat until all the filling and leaves are used.

6. To cook, bring a saucepan of broth to cover the sausage rolls to a simmer. Add the rolls and simmer for about 10 minutes, until heated through. Lift out the rolls with a slotted spoon and serve on a bed of pasta.

Makes 6 to 8 sausage rolls

Portobello Sausage

Portobello mushrooms are everyone's favorite meat substitute. These easy-to-make sausages demonstrate why.

12 ounces portobello mushrooms, cut into chunks

½ cup chopped onion

2 cloves garlic, chopped

1 tablespoon olive oil

1½ cup cooked black beans, or 1 can (15 ounces), drained and rinsed

¼ cup chopped fresh parsley

1 teaspoon kosher or coarse salt

½ teaspoon freshly ground black pepper (medium grind)

1 tablespoon lemon juice

½ cup fresh breadcrumbs

2 tablespoons grated Parmesan cheese

Salsa and sour cream, to serve (optional)

1. Preheat the oven to 450°F (230°C).

2. In a medium-sized baking dish, toss the mushrooms, onion, and garlic with the oil until well coated. Roast for 8 to 10 minutes, until the mushrooms release their juices and brown.

3. Spoon the mixture, including juices, into a food processor and add the beans, parsley, salt, pepper, and lemon juice. Process briefly, until the ingredients are combined but the mixture is still chunky.

4. Transfer the mixture into a bowl, add the breadcrumbs and Parmesan, and mix well.

5. With wet hands, shape ½ cup of the mixture into patties about ½-inch thick or sausage shapes about 3 inches long.

6. Panfry over medium heat or grill the sausages until crisp and heated through, about 5 minutes per side. Serve hot with salsa and sour cream (if using).

Makes 6 to 8 sausages or patties

Wild Mushroom Sausage with Walnuts

If you are lucky enough to find a source of morels, puffballs, oyster, or other wild mushrooms, treat the delicate beauties kindly and incorporate them into a vegetarian sausage. You can substitute domestic mushrooms, but they won't have that same earthy flavor.

1 tablespoon butter

8 ounces wild mushrooms

2 tablespoons chopped shallots

1 cup cooked white beans

½ cup cooked white or brown rice

1 teaspoon kosher or coarse salt

½ teaspoon freshly ground black pepper (medium grind)

¼ cup chopped toasted walnuts

2 tablespoons chopped scallions

½ cup fresh breadcrumbs

1 egg, lightly beaten

¼ cup milk

1. Melt the butter in a large skillet over medium heat. Add the mushrooms and shallots; sauté until the mushrooms release juices, about 5 minutes.

2. In a food processor, combine the mushroom mixture, beans, rice, salt, pepper, walnuts, and scallions. Process until combined but still a bit chunky.

3. Transfer the mixture to a large bowl and stir in the breadcrumbs, egg, and milk until combined.

4. Form ½ cup of the mixture into ½-inch-thick patties or 3-inch-long sausage shapes. Arrange on a plate, cover, and refrigerate for about 1 hour to firm up the sausages.

5. To cook, panfry over medium heat in a small amount of oil until hot and crisp, about 5 minutes per side.

Makes 6 to 8 patties or sausages

GATHERING MUSHROOMS

When collecting wild mushrooms, gather only young specimens for eating. Gather whole mushrooms, including the base of the stems, to be sure of proper identification. Many wild mushrooms are poisonous, so it's important to know which species are edible. If you have any doubt at all about a mushroom, don't eat it.

Store in paper bags in the refrigerator, and simply wipe clean before eating.

Spicy Tempeh Sausage

Tempeh is made from fermented cooked soybeans and sometimes grains, pressed into a firm cake. It can be crumbled or grated to use as a meat substitute, and it's famous for absorbing the flavors of whatever it is combined with. Find tempeh in the refrigerated section of most natural food stores. Serve this sausage with salsa and corn tortilla chips.

8 ounces tempeh

½ cup cooked brown rice

1 teaspoon chili powder

½ teaspoon kosher or coarse salt

1 Anaheim or poblano chile, seeded and minced

2 tablespoons chili sauce

2 tablespoons tomato or V-8 juice

2 tablespoons vegetable oil

1 large egg white

Dash of Tabasco sauce

1. Steam the tempeh over boiling water for about 10 minutes. Cool, then grate with the coarse side of a box grater.

2. In large bowl, combine the tempeh, rice, chili powder, salt, chile, chili sauce, tomato juice, oil, egg white, and Tabasco. Mix well, using your hands.

3. With wet hands, form ½ cup of the mixture at a time into ½-inch-thick patties or 3-inch-long sausage shapes and refrigerate for about 1 hour, until firm.

4. To cook, panfry over medium heat in a small amount of oil until browned on all sides, about 10 minutes. Serve hot.

Makes 10 to 12 sausages or small patties

STEAMER BASKETS

Steamer baskets, found at kitchen-supply stores and many department stores, adjust to fit most 2-quart and larger saucepans and are a handy gadget in the kitchen. Food cooked in a steamer over simmering water retains more nutrients and does not get waterlogged.

Be sure to cover the pan tightly when steaming, and use no more than 1 inch of water.

Steamer baskets are available in stainless steel or bamboo, the type used in Chinese and Japanese cooking.

Apple Tofu Sausage

*This savory low-fat mixture makes a delicious breakfast or lunch offering.
Serve for breakfast with cornbread or grits; for lunch with a crusty baguette.*

2 teaspoons vegetable oil

½ cup chopped onion

2 tart apples, peeled, grated,
and tossed with 1 teaspoon
lemon juice

1 pound extra-firm tofu, drained
(see box below)

1 cup fresh breadcrumbs

1½ teaspoons dried sage

1 teaspoon kosher or coarse salt

½ teaspoon ground allspice

½ teaspoon freshly grated
nutmeg

½ teaspoon freshly ground black
pepper (medium grind)

¼ teaspoon ground ginger

2 large egg whites

1. Heat the oil in a medium-sized skillet over medium-high heat. Add the
   onion and sauté until softened, about 3 minutes. Add the grated apples
   and sauté for 3 minutes longer. Transfer the mixture to a large bowl to
   cool.

2. Crumble or grate the tofu into the bowl; toss to combine with the onion
   mixture. Add the breadcrumbs, sage, salt, allspice, nutmeg, pepper, ginger, and egg whites. Mix together well.

3. With wet hands, form ½ cup of the mixture into ½-inch-thick patties or
   3-inch-long sausage shapes and arrange on a large plate. Refrigerate for
   about 1 hour, or until firm.

4. To cook, preheat the oven to 450°F (230°C). Grease a baking sheet.

5. Bake the sausages for 10 to 15 minutes, until the outsides are golden
   brown and the insides are
   cooked through and firm.

**Makes 10 to 12 patties
or sausages**

HOW TO DRAIN TOFU

To remove most of the excess moisture
from tofu, cut it into three horizontal
slabs. Put folded paper towels between
the layers and put a heavy plate on top
of the tofu for about 15 minutes.

Vegetarian Kishke in Leek Casings

Kishke is a Jewish-American sausage made from flour, matzo meal, fat, onions, and ground beef. This tasty version replaces the meat with a flavorful mix of carrots, celery, and leeks. And instead of the pedestrian beef casing, the outer leaves of the leeks form an elegant wrapper for these sausages. Serve with a mix of roasted vegetables for an outstanding vegetarian dinner.

6 leeks, 1 to 1½ inches in diameter

2 celery stalks, chopped

1 large carrot, grated

3 tablespoons vegetable or olive oil

1 cup matzo meal or fresh breadcrumbs

¼ cup raw wheat germ

1 teaspoon kosher kosher or coarse salt

½ teaspoon freshly ground pepper

1 large egg

12 long chive stems with blossoms (optional)

1. Trim off the root end of the leeks, leaving about 6 inches of the green part intact. Blanch the leeks in simmering water for 2 minutes, then plunge them into cold water. Carefully push out the centers of the leeks, leaving the outer skins whole. Roughly chop the white portions of the centers.

2. Combine the leek centers, celery, and carrot in a food processor and pulse until finely chopped. Add the oil, matzo meal, wheat germ, salt, pepper, and egg and pulse until the mixture holds together.

3. Preheat the oven to 350°F (175°C). Grease a baking sheet.

4. Carefully fill the leek skins with the filling mixture. (If any of the mixture is left over, you can roll it in blanched cabbage leaves or squares of aluminum foil.)

5. Arrange the leek sausages on the baking sheet, cover with foil, and bake for 25 minutes.

6. If desired, tie each of the baked sausages with two chive stems and decorate with chive blossoms.

Makes 6 sausages

Polish-Flavored Tempeh Sausage

Why not use the classic kielbasa seasonings in a vegetarian sausage? These might not fool your Polish grandmother, but they're good on their own. Tempeh is found in the refrigerated section of most natural food stores.

8 ounces tempeh

1½ cups red kidney beans, or
   1 can (15 ounces), drained
   and rinsed

½ cup chopped onion

2 cloves garlic, minced

½ cup fresh breadcrumbs

1 teaspoon sweet paprika

1 teaspoon freshly ground black
   pepper (medium grind)

1 teaspoon kosher or coarse salt

½ teaspoon dried marjoram

½ teaspoon dried summer savory

¼ teaspoon ground allspice

2 large egg whites

2 tablespoons canola oil

1. Steam the tempeh over boiling water for about 10 minutes. Cool, then grate with the coarse side of a box grater.

2. Combine the tempeh, beans, onion, and garlic in a food processor and pulse until well mixed. Add the breadcrumbs, paprika, pepper, salt, marjoram, savory, allspice, egg whites, and oil. Pulse until thoroughly blended.

3. With wet hands, form mixture into ½-inch-thick patties or 3-inch-long sausage shapes. Refrigerate for about 1 hour, until firm.

4. Preheat the oven to 400°F (200°C). Grease a baking sheet.

5. Arrange the sausages on the baking sheet, cover with foil, and bake for 20 to 25 minutes, until browned. Serve hot.

Makes about 12 patties or sausages

EASIER LINKS

You can shape vegetarian sausage mixtures into sausage-size links and freeze them so they hold that shape. Panfry in a small amount of butter or oil without defrosting.

Part Three

Cooking with Sausage

CHAPTER 11

Sausage for Breakfast or Brunch

What? Sunday morning in an English family

and no sausages? God bless my soul,

what's the world coming to, eh?

— Dorothy L. Sayers

IT'S NOT JUST THE ENGLISH who enjoy a breakfast featuring sausage. And there's no reason to limit yourself to perfectly browned sausage links alongside two over easy. (Although there's nothing wrong with that.) After all, if there is anything more versatile than sausage, it would have to be the traditional breakfast egg. Here, we share recipes for sausages paired with eggs in omelettes, starring in quiches, studding pancakes, and more.

If these recipes are too athletic for busy weekday mornings at your house, certainly they deserve star billing at a weekend brunch, an occasion to show off your sausage-making skills to all your friends. They'll be duly impressed.

Country-Style Eggs with Sausage

Here is a simple recipe for one serving that pairs the versatile egg with sausage; it can be multiplied for as many people as you have to serve.

1 teaspoon olive or vegetable oil
¼ pound country-style breakfast sausage, removed from casings
2 large eggs, well beaten
1 tablespoon grated Parmesan cheese
1 tablespoon milk
1 teaspoon fresh snipped chives
Freshly ground black pepper
Kosher or coarse salt

1. Heat the oil in a medium-sized skillet over medium-high heat. Add the sausage and sauté, crumbling it with the back of a spoon, until it is browned/cooked through, about 10 minutes. Drain off almost all the grease; set aside the skillet.

2. In a mixing bowl, combine the eggs, Parmesan, milk, chives, pepper, and salt to taste. Mix well.

3. Return the skillet with the sausage to the burner over medium heat. Pour in the egg mixture and cook, stirring constantly until the eggs are set, about 2 minutes. Serve immediately.

Serves 1

FAVORITE OMELETTE COMBINATIONS

For creative adaptions of the Sausage Omelette recipe on the next page, add the following additional ingredients with the ½ cup of cooked sausage.

Swiss Miss. Use ¼ cup grated Swiss cheese and 1 tablespoon *each* of chopped fresh parsley and chives. Especially good with cooked bratwurst.

Tex-Mex. Use ¼ cup grated Monterey Jack cheese, 2 tablespoons salsa, 2 tablespoons cooked pinto or black beans, and 1 tablespoon finely chopped green bell pepper. Especially good with chorizo or other spicy sausage.

California Dreamin'. Use 2 tablespoons crumbled fresh goat cheese; half of a peeled ripe avocado, diced; ¼ cup chopped ripe tomatoes; and 1 tablespoon chopped ripe olives. Try it with chicken sausage or lobster sausage.

Chinese, Please. Use 2 scallions, chopped; ½ cup fresh bean sprouts; 1 clove garlic, minced; 1 tablespoon soy sauce; and ½ teaspoon five-spice powder. Use Chinese sausage or a spicy pork sausage.

Maple Apple. Peel and chop 1 large apple and sauté in 1 tablespoon butter until softened; remove from heat and stir in 1 tablespoon real maple syrup. Pair with spicy breakfast sausage or smoked ham.

Sausage Omelette

The basic omelette is the perfect show-case for any fresh homemade sausage.

    1 teaspoon olive or vegetable oil
4 to 5 ounces fresh sausage meat,
        removed from casings
    2 teaspoons butter
    3 large eggs, beaten until light
    Freshly ground black pepper
    Salt

1. Heat the oil in a medium-sized skillet over medium-high heat. Add the sausage and sauté, crumbling it with the back of a spoon as it cooks, until it is browned and cooked through, about 10 minutes. Drain off almost all the grease; set aside the skillet.

2. Heat a medium omelette pan or nonstick skillet over medium-high heat. Add the butter, swirling to coat the pan. Add the eggs to the pan. With one hand, shake the pan back and forth while stirring the eggs with your other hand. Stir, using a fork held flat so as not to break through the bottom of the omelette. When the eggs begin to form curds and set along the bottom, stop stirring. With the back of the fork, spread the eggs evenly around the pan.

3. Spoon the sausage across the middle of the omelette. Sprinkle with pepper and salt. Cook for another minute.

4. Tilt up the pan and use the fork to roll the top third of the omelette onto the sausage filling. If you want the omelette lightly browned, let it sit for a few seconds.

5. Tilt the pan over a serving platter and make a second fold by sliding the omelette out of the pan, seam-side down, onto a platter. Serve immediately.

Serves 1 to 2

Norwegian Omelette

This recipe is adapted from the Lefse Omelette on the menu at the Norske Nook, a restaurant in Osseo, Wisconsin. The town was settled by Norwegian dairy farmers, who still fill the tables every morning at breakfast time and inspire the specialties of the house. For the uninitiated, lefse is like a Norwegian tortilla, only softer and thinner. It makes a wonderful envelope for an omelette.

    4 large russet or Idaho potatoes,
        peeled and cut into 1-inch
        pieces
    1 teaspoon kosher or coarse salt
    2 tablespoons butter, melted
    2 tablespoons half-and-half
½ to ¾ cup all-purpose flour
    1 tablespoon plus 1 teaspoon olive
        or vegetable oil
    1 pound spicy sausage, removed
        from its casings
    2 cups frozen hash brown potatoes,
        thawed and patted dry
6 to 8 large eggs
    1 tablespoon milk
    1 teaspoon butter
    1 cup hollandaise sauce, warmed
        (optional; recipe follows)

1. In a saucepan cover potatoes with water by 1 inch, add the salt, and simmer until very tender, 10 to 15 minutes. Drain, then return the potatoes to the pan. Shake the pan over medium heat to dry the potatoes thoroughly.

2. Mash the potatoes with the butter and half-and-half. Stir in the flour, a little at a time, to make a dough that is soft but not sticky. Cover the dough and refrigerate for a couple of hours or overnight.

3. Preheat oven to 200°F (93°C).

4. In a large ovenproof skillet, heat 1 teaspoon of the oil over medium-high heat. Add the sausage and sauté, crumbling it with the back of a spoon as it cooks, until it is cooked through and browned, about 10 minutes. Drain off almost all the grease, then put the skillet in the oven to keep the sausage warm.

5. In another large ovenproof skillet, heat the remaining 1 tablespoon oil over medium-high heat. Add the hash browns in a single layer and cook until crispy, turning occasionally so the potatoes brown evenly, about 10 minutes. Put the pan in the oven to keep the potatoes warm.

6. Form about ¼ cup of the lefse dough into small balls. Roll out each ball on a floured surface into a thin circle 8 to 10 inches in diameter.

7. Heat a dry griddle or cast-iron frying pan over medium-high heat. Cook each dough circle for about a minute on each side, until brown and bubbled. As they are removed from the griddle, stack the lefse with squares of parchment paper between the layers and put in the oven to keep warm.

8. Whisk the eggs and milk together in a medium-sized bowl. Melt the 1 teaspoon of butter in a medium-sized nonstick skillet, add the egg mixture, and cook over low heat, stirring constantly, until the eggs are softly scrambled.

9. To assemble the omelette, fill each lefse with some of the scrambled eggs, sausage, and hash brown potatoes. Roll or fold to cover the filling. Serve topped with a dollop of hollandaise sauce (if using).

NOTE: If you don't have ovenproof skillets, transfer the sausage and potatoes after they are cooked to a large shallow baking pan to keep them warm in the oven.

Serves 6 to 8

HOLLANDAISE SAUCE

Hollandaise sauce has a tendency to curdle, but that can be avoided by using a blender to make it.

Combine 3 egg yolks, 2 tablespoons lemon juice, ¼ teaspoon kosher or coarse salt, and a pinch of freshly ground white pepper in a blender and blend until smooth. With the blender running, pour in ½ cup (1 stick) melted butter in a thin, steady stream. To reheat hollandaise, warm it in the top of a double boiler over gently simmering water.

Sausage Quiche

The best excuse I can think of for using up a few eggs is to make a quiche. No doubt, you have enjoyed a quiche Lorraine, the rich concoction of custard, cheese, and bacon. This dish is a variation on that theme.

PASTRY

1 cup sifted all-purpose flour
¼ teaspoon kosher or coarse salt
⅓ cup chilled vegetable shortening, cut into marble-sized pieces
About ¼ cup cold water

FILLING

1 teaspoon vegetable oil
½ pound Italian-style sweet sausage, removed from its casings
½ pound fresh mushrooms, sliced
1 small onion, chopped
½ small green bell pepper, cored, seeded, and chopped
3 large eggs, well beaten
Pinch of cayenne pepper
Kosher or coarse salt
Freshly ground black pepper
2 cups half-and-half
¼ cup grated Romano cheese
4 ounces mozzarella or Gruyère cheese, shredded

1. To make the pastry, sift the flour together with the salt into a medium-sized bowl. Using a pastry blender, mix the shortening into the flour mixture.

2. Sprinkle the water on, a little at a time, while mixing continuously with the pastry blender. Form the dough into a ball.

3. On a lightly floured surface, roll out the pastry into a 10-inch-diameter circle. Fold the pastry onto itself, then gently drape the dough over a 9-inch pie plate. Unfold the dough, fit the pastry into the plate, then crimp the edges with your finger or a fork.

4. Preheat oven to 400°F (200°C).

5. To make the filling, heat the oil in a large skillet over medium-high heat. Crumble the sausage into the skillet and cook, crumbling it with the back of a spoon, until the sausage is browned, about 10 minutes. Remove the sausage with a slotted spoon and set it aside.

6. To the sausage drippings remaining in the skillet add the mushrooms, onions, and pepper, and sauté over medium heat until they are crisp-tender, about 5 minutes. Remove them with a slotted spoon and set them aside. Discard the drippings.

7. In a medium-sized bowl, beat the eggs. Continuing to beat, add the cayenne, salt and black pepper to taste, and half-and-half.

8. Sprinkle the sausage in the pastry shell. Layer the mushroom mixture evenly over the sausage. Spread the grated and shedded cheeses over all. Finally, pour the egg mixture over everything.

9. Bake for 30 minutes, or until firm and lightly browned. Let the quiche cool for about 10 minutes before slicing.

Serves 4 as an entrée

Sausage and Apple Pancake Roll-ups

Sausages and pancakes go together like bread and butter. Pancake roll-ups, stuffed with sausage and apples, with some real down-home maple syrup dribbled on top, make for a super breakfast dish or a quick supper. Make your own pancakes from scratch, using the recipe here or your own favorite mix.

FILLING

1 teaspoon olive or vegetable oil
1 pound country-style pork breakfast sausage, removed from its casings
2 large apples, peeled, cored, and chopped coarsely
½ cup apple jelly

PANCAKES

2 cups buttermilk
3 large eggs, well beaten
4 tablespoons butter, melted
2 cups sifted all-purpose flour
1½ teaspoons baking powder
1 teaspoon baking soda
Kosher or coarse salt (optional)
Pure maple syrup, to serve

1. Heat the oil in a large skillet over medium-high heat. Add the sausage and sauté, crumbling it with the back of a spoon as it cooks, until it is cooked through and browned, about 10 minutes. Drain off the fat.

2. Add the apples to the skillet and sauté until tender, about 5 minutes longer.

3. Stir in the apple jelly; cook just until it is melted. Remove the pan from the heat and keep warm.

4. To make the pancakes, whisk together the buttermilk, eggs, and butter. In a separate bowl, whisk together the flour, baking powder, baking soda, and salt (if using). Stir the flour mixture into the egg mixture with a wooden spoon until blended, but do not overbeat. A few lumps are okay.

5. Lightly coat a griddle with oil and heat over medium-high heat until a drop of water sizzles into steam when you flick it on. Ladle the pancake batter onto the griddle. Turn each pancake when the bottom is golden brown and the sides begin to look dry.

6. As each pancake is done, spoon some of the sausage mixture on it, roll it up, dribble on some maple syrup, and serve immediately.

Serves 4

SAUSAGE AND APPLES

Pork and apples are natural companions. The tartness of the apples contrasts with the mildness of the meat, bringing out the best in both. Any fresh pork sausages in this book can be used to advantage with apples to create a hearty and satisfying meal.

Sausage Pipérade

A pipérade is a Basque dish of tomatoes and peppers. Eggs can be added to make an open-faced omelette. This recipe is a variation on that theme.

- 2 tablespoons plus 1 teaspoon olive or vegetable oil
- 1 pound Italian-style sweet sausage, removed from its casing
- 1 small onion, finely chopped
- 4 cloves garlic, finely chopped
- ½ cup chopped green bell pepper
- ½ cup chopped red bell pepper
- ½ cup chopped yellow bell pepper
- 2 to 3 ripe tomatoes, peeled, seeded, and sliced
- ½ teaspoon dried basil
- ½ teaspoon dried marjoram
- ½ teaspoon dried oregano
- ½ teaspoon dried rosemary, crumbled
- ½ teaspoon dried sage
- ½ teaspoon dried summer savory
- ½ teaspoon dried thyme
- Freshly ground black pepper (medium grind)
- Kosher or coarse salt (optional)
- 8 large eggs
- 1½ tablespoons butter

1. Heat 1 teaspoon of the oil in a medium-sized skillet over medium-high heat. Add the sausage and sauté, crumbling it with the back of a spoon as it cooks, until it is cooked through and browned, about 10 minutes. Remove the sausage with a slotted spoon. Discard the drippings.

2. In the same skillet, heat the remaining 2 tablespoons of oil over medium-high heat. Add the onion and garlic and sauté until the onions are translucent, about 5 minutes.

Add the peppers and sauté for 5 minutes. Add the tomato slices and sauté, shaking the pan, until the tomato juices have mostly evaporated.

3. Add the sausage, basil, marjoram, oregano, rosemary, sage, savory, thyme, pepper, and salt to taste (if using). Cook, stirring, until the vegetables are soft, about 5 minutes longer. Set aside in the skillet.

4. Beat the eggs lightly. Melt the butter in a second skillet, add the eggs, and quickly scramble the eggs until they are creamy and moist, about 4 minutes.

5. Spread the eggs over the vegetables in the first skillet and serve immediately.

Serves 4

Breakfast Sausage Crêpes

This is a unique way to have your pancakes and sausage for breakfast.

- 12 crêpes (recipe follows)
- 1 teaspoon olive or vegetable oil
- 1 pound country-style breakfast sausage, removed from its casings
- Maple syrup

1. Prepare the crêpes and keep them warm.

2. Heat the oil in a large skillet over medium-high heat. Add the sausage and sauté, crumbling it with the back of a spoon as it cooks, until it is cooked through and browned, about 10 minutes. Remove the sausage with a slotted spoon and keep warm.

3. Roll the sausage inside the crêpes on individual plates and serve immediately. Pass the syrup at the table.

Serves 4

CRÊPES

These very thin pancakes can be used in a variety of ways to enfold food from strawberries and whipped cream to savory sausage and vegetable fillings. You will need a small nonstick skillet or a seasoned crêpe pan.

> ½ cup all-purpose flour
> Pinch of kosher or coarse salt
> ½ cup milk
> ¼ cup lukewarm water
> 2 large eggs
> 2 tablespoons butter, melted
> Butter, for frying

1. In a bowl or blender, combine the flour, salt, milk, water, eggs, and melted butter. Beat or blend until the batter is smooth. Let the batter stand for 30 minutes, or refrigerate for up to 2 days.

2. Lightly butter a skillet and preheat it over medium-high heat.

3. Add about 2 tablespoons of batter to the pan and spread it to the edges. Brown on the bottom. Gently turn the crêpe, being careful not to tear it, and cook the other side. The top side will be firm (not wet) to the touch when the crêpe is done. Repeat until all the batter is used. Stack the cooked crêpes between sheets of wax paper.

Makes about 12 crêpes

Salami Crêpes

We enjoy serving these for brunch — a refreshing change from the ham and cheese or bacon so often served at brunch gatherings.

> 1 dozen Crêpes (see recipe this page)
> Dijon mustard
> ¼ pound thinly sliced homemade hard salami, such as Genoa Salami or Italian-Style Dry Sausage
> ¼ pound Swiss cheese, shredded

1. Prepare the crêpes.

2. Preheat oven to 425°F (220°C).

3. Spread a thin layer of mustard on each crêpe. Layer equal amounts of salami and cheese on each crêpe. Roll up the crêpes jelly-roll fashion.

4. Arrange the crêpes on a baking sheet and bake for 10 minutes, or until the cheese is melted. Serve hot.

Serves 4

Sausage, Onion, and Pepper Crêpes

Stuffing the classic combination of sausage, onions, and peppers in a crêpe rather than a grinder roll makes a hearty dish for breakfast or brunch.

    1   dozen Crêpes (page 221)
    1   teaspoon olive or vegetable oil
    ¾   pound sweet Italian-style sausage,
        removed from the casing
    1   small onion, chopped
    1   small green bell pepper, cored,
        seeded, and chopped

1. Prepare the crêpes.

2. Preheat oven to 425°F (220°C).

3. Heat the oil in a large skillet over medium-high heat. Add the sausage and sauté, crumbling it with the back of a spoon as it cooks, until it is cooked through and browned, about 10 minutes. Remove the sausage with a slotted spoon and divide it equally among the crêpes.

4. In the sausage drippings over medium-high heat, sauté the onion and pepper until they are crisp-tender, about 5 minutes. Remove the vegetables with a slotted spoon and divide among the crêpes.

5. Roll up the crêpes jelly-roll fashion and arrange on a baking sheet. Bake for about 10 minutes, or until warmed through. Serve hot.

Serves 4

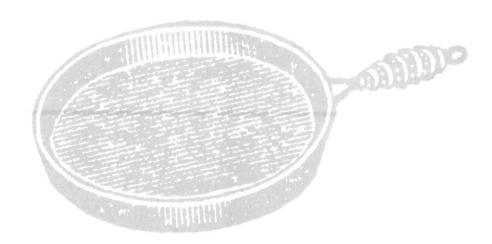

CHAPTER 12

Sausage Starters

A document from the Spanish Vice-regent

in Palermo on January 30, 1415,

shows that lamb, pork, or sausages were bought

thirteen days out of the month and

macaroni only once a month.

— Clifford A. Wright

SAUSAGE AND GOOD TIMES GO TOGETHER like wine and cheese, like the Fourth of July and fireworks. Sausage is a fun food, and as popular today as in Palermo in 1415. We told you in the beginning of this book that sausage is fun to make and, we trust, we've convinced you of that. We make sausage part of our good times by including sausage in our hors d'oeuvres when we entertain.

After all, next to the cracker, one of the most frequently used ingredients in many before-meal treats is some kind of sausage. This attests to sausage's versatility and indicates that it can be prepared alone or in conjunction with other ingredients that tempt the palate. May your guests' palates be pleased!

Composed Antipasto Platter

In Italy, nearly all antipasto dishes are prepared ahead and served slightly warm or at room temperature. Here is a suggestion for an eye-catching and appetizing arrangement. The quantities of each ingredient are up to you — it depends on how many people you are serving. Allow 2 to 4 ounces of meat, cheese, and eggs per person and 2 to 4 ounces of each vegetable.

> Sliced hard-cooked eggs
> Anchovy fillets or capers
> Strips of red and green bell peppers
> Olive oil
> Lemon juice
> Genoa salami, prosciutto, bologna, and other cured meats
> Provolone cheese, sliced
> Marinated artichoke hearts
> Marinated mushrooms
> Cured black olives, pitted
> Pimiento-stuffed green olives
> Crusty bread, sliced about ½-inch thick
> 1 clove garlic, cut in half

1. On a platter or beautiful plate (the biggest you have for a large crowd), arrange the ingredients according to the shape of the platter. That is, arrange in circles for a round dish or racetrack shape for an oval platter. In the center of the plate, arrange the egg slices, then top them with the anchovies. Circle the eggs with the pepper strips, then sprinkle olive oil and few drops of lemon juice on them. Around the peppers, arrange overlapping slices of salami, prosciutto, bologna, and Provolone, interleaving the meats with the cheese. Spoon a row of artichokes around the meat and cheese. Circle the artichokes with the mushrooms. Arrange the olives around the mushrooms, alternating trios of black and green.

2. Rub both sides of each slice of bread with the garlic and arrange the bread in a basket.

3. Serve the basket alongside the antipasto platter.

Marinated Antipasto Platter

There are as many different combinations possible for this dish as there are recipes for spaghetti sauce. Here, the components of the platter are marinated before serving.

What is really nice about this recipe is that you can vary it every time you make it, depending upon what you have on hand.

This dish shows off your homemade salamis. The more variety, the better. The exact quantities are up to you. Allow 2 to 4 ounces of meat and cheese per person and 2 to 4 ounces of each vegetable. The only rule to follow is to be creative!

> Salami (at least two different varieties), cut into ½-inch cubes
> Cheese — Asiago, mozzarella, provolone, Scamorze, Swiss — any combination, cut into ½-inch cubes
> Sliced celery (optional)
> Sliced carrots (optional)

Bell peppers (red, green, yellow, and purple), cut into strips (optional)

Mushrooms, fresh buttons or slices (optional)

Cauliflower, broken into florets (optional)

Tomatoes, medium-sized ones, quartered, or cherry (optional)

Scallions, trimmed (optional)

Olive oil

Lemon juice

Red wine vinegar

Basil leaves, fresh, shredded

Oregano, one or two fresh sprigs, chopped

Freshly ground black pepper and kosher or coarse salt

Crusty French or Italian bread

1. In a mixing bowl large enough to hold all the ingredients, mix together the salamis, cheeses, and whatever vegetables you choose to use.

2. Pour in just enough olive oil to coat the mixture lightly. Dribble in a small amount of lemon juice and red wine vinegar and mix well. Add the basil, oregano, salt, and pepper.

3. Refrigerate the mixture for at least 2 hours before serving to allow the flavors to blend. Taste and adjust the seasoning, adding more herbs, pepper, and salt as needed.

4. Serve with the bread.

WHAT'S IN A NAME?

antipasto

Antipasto literally means "before the meal" in Italian, and refers to a whole range of dishes that are served to stimulate the appetite and please the eye. The three basic types of antipasto are *anitpasto misto*, which includes mixed raw vegetables, cold meats, fish, and cheese; *di pesce*, featuring fish; and *affettato*, which highlights sliced pork products such as prosciutto and salami sliced thin and often accompanied by breadsticks or crusty bread.

Focaccia Stuffed with Sausage

This double-layer focaccia is baked at a slightly lower temperature than its close relative, pizza, so that the interior ingredients cook evenly and thoroughly. The filling features your own homemade sausage — either salami or classic Italian sausage. If you want to prepare a traditional focaccia, freeze half the dough and use the filling as a topping.

DOUGH

2 packages (¼ ounce each) active dry yeast
1½ cups warm (105 to 115°F; 41 to 46°C) water
3¾ to 4 cups all-purpose flour
1 tablespoon olive oil
1 teaspoon kosher or coarse salt
1 teaspoon sugar

FILLING

1 large egg, beaten lightly
½ pound mozzarella cheese, shredded
1 cup grated Parmesan or Asiago cheese
½ pound fresh mushrooms, thinly sliced
1 red onion, thinly sliced
6 cloves garlic, chopped
¼ cup chopped fresh basil
½ pound salami, thinly sliced, or hot Italian sausage, crumbled and sautéed until brown
2 tablespoons olive oil

TOPPING

1 tablespoon olive oil
Kosher or coarse salt
1 tablespoon chopped fresh rosemary leaves

1. To make the dough, dissolve the yeast in the warm water in a large bowl. Stir in 2 cups of the flour and the oil, salt, and sugar. Stir 50 times in one direction.

2. Put a plate on top of the bowl and let the dough rest for 30 to 60 minutes. (If you are in a hurry, you can skip this step, but it helps to develop the flavor and texture of the bread.)

3. Stir in the remaining 1¾ to 2 cups of the flour, ½ cup at a time, to make a soft dough.

4. Knead the dough on a lightly floured surface for about 5 minutes, until smooth and elastic. Transfer the dough to a greased bowl, turn greased-side up, cover, and let rise in a warm spot for 1 hour.

5. Gently deflate the dough. If you are ready to make the focaccia, turn it out onto a floured surface. If you are not ready, refrigerate the dough, covered, for up to 24 hours, punching down as needed.

6. Preheat the oven to 375°F (170°C). Grease two baking sheets.

7. On a floured surface, divide the dough into four equal portions. Press or roll two of the portions into 12-inch circles and transfer to the baking sheets.

8. For the filling, brush the egg around the edge of each circle. Arrange half of the cheeses, mushrooms, onion, garlic, basil, and salami on each circle. Drizzle each half with 1 tablespoon of the olive oil.

9. Press or roll the remaining portions of dough into 12-inch circles. Place over the fillings. Press the edges together with a fork or your fingers to seal.

10. To top the focaccia, brush the tops of each with half of the remaining 1 tablespoon of olive oil and sprinkle each one with salt and chopped rosemary.

11. Bake for about 30 minutes, until golden brown. Serve hot.

Serves 6 to 8

Guacamole Dip with Chorizos

A ripe avocado is creamy and rich, making an excellent addition to grilled sandwiches and salads. (In salads, sprinkle the cut pieces with fresh lemon juice so the fruit doesn't turn brown.)

But given a ripe avocado or two, most of us think about making guacamole. This classic Mexican dip doesn't usually have meat in it, but our version is an excellent vehicle for showing off your homemade chorizos. You can tailor the recipe to either fresh or dried chorizos.

 1 teaspoon olive or vegetable oil (optional)
 ½ pound fresh or dried chorizos
 1 ripe avocado
 1 medium-sized tomato, cored, peeled, seeded, and finely diced
 2 cloves garlic, finely minced
 ¼ cup mayonnaise
 ¼ cup sour cream
 Dash of hot pepper sauce
 Kosher or coarse salt and freshly ground black pepper
 Tortilla chips, for serving

1. If you are using fresh chorizos, heat the oil in a medium-sized skillet over medium-high heat. Remove the sausage from its casing, then add the sausage and sauté, crumbling it with the back of a spoon as it cooks, until it is cooked through and browned, about 10 minutes. If you are using dry chorizos, cut them into ½-inch cubes and process them in a food processor until they are finely crumbled.

2. Cut the avocado in half lengthwise, cutting all the way around the pit. Twist the halves in opposite directions until they separate. Pull the pit out with your finger; if it does not budge, carefully strike it with edge of a sharp, heavy knife, then turn the knife to dislodge the pit. Scoop out the flesh with a spoon. Mash the avocado in a bowl, using the back of a fork, or process in a food processor. Mash or process until you get a smooth purée.

3. Stir the tomato into the avocado until combined. Mix in the chorizo, garlic, mayonnaise, sour cream, hot pepper sauce, salt, and pepper.

4. Serve with tortilla chips.

NOTE: Cover the freshly made guacamole with plastic wrap so that air doesn't get to the surface. This will keep the mixture from oxidizing and turning brown.

Serves 8 to 10

Double-Sausage Calzones

Calzones are an Italian invention that can be a main dish, a hearty snack, or a delicious appetizer. As appetizers, they can be quite filling, so they are best served when a relatively light meal is to follow. Serve them piping hot, but warn your guests to be careful not to burn their mouths on the bubbling cheese inside.

The dough for calzones is a standard Neopolitan pizza dough. (You can also substitute a frozen bread or pizza dough — just thaw according to package directions.)

DOUGH

1 package (¼ ounce) active dry yeast
¾ cup plus ½ cup warm (105° to 115°F; 41 to 46°C) water
1 teaspoon kosher or coarse salt
3 cups all-purpose flour
1 tablespoon olive oil

FILLING

2 tablespoons plus 1 teaspoon olive oil
1 pound Italian-style sweet sausage, removed from its casings
1 small onion, diced
½ pound pepperoni, salami, or dry sausage, or a combination of these, cut into ¼-inch cubes
1 tablespoon chopped fresh Italian parsley
Chopped pitted black olives (optional)
Mashed anchovies (optional)
Capers (optional)
Chopped red, green, or yellow bell peppers (optional)
Crushed red pepper (optional)
Freshly ground black pepper and kosher or coarse salt

2 cups shredded mozzarella cheese (may be part skim)

1. To make the dough, mix the packet of yeast into the ¾ cup warm water. Let stand for 15 minutes, until bubbles form.

2. In a large bowl, stir the salt into the flour. Gradually add the yeast mixture and the oil. Turn the dough onto a floured surface. Gradually add the remaining ½ cup of water, while kneading the dough for about 10 minutes. The dough should be smooth and elastic.

3. Transfer the dough to a lightly greased bowl, turning to coat. Cover the bowl and set aside in a warm place until the dough doubles in size, about 1 hour.

4. To make the filling, heat 1 teaspoon of the oil in a large skillet over medium-high heat. Add the sausage and sauté, crumbling it with the back of a spoon as it cooks, until it is cooked through and browned, about 10 minutes. Remove the sausage with a slotted spoon to a large mixing bowl.

5. Add the onion to the pan with the sausage drippings and sauté until it is translucent, about 5 minutes. Drain the onion and add it to the sausage. Stir in the pepperoni, parsley, any optional filling ingredients you are using, and pepper and salt to taste.

6. Preheat the oven to 450°F (230°C). Lightly oil a baking sheet.

7. To assemble the calzones, on a floured work surface divide the dough into eight equal portions. Roll out each portion to form a circle about ⅛-inch thick. Brush the middle of each circle with some of the remaining olive oil, leaving a 1-inch border bare. Divide the sausage mixture equally among the circles of dough, placing it to one side of center. Sprinkle an equal amount of mozzarella on each. Carefully fold over each piece of dough to form a semicircle and press to seal the edges.

8. Brush the tops of the calzones with olive oil and arrange them, 1 inch apart, on the baking sheet.

9. Bake the calzones for 25 minutes, or until they are golden brown. Serve piping hot.

NOTE: To make calzones for a main course, make four calzones instead of eight.

Serves 8

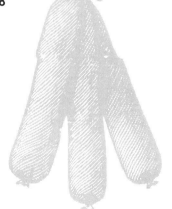

Chorizo Tostadas

This recipe is a three-alarmer — or four — depending on how hot you make your chorizos. A tostada is a tortilla that is crisp-fried and covered with all sorts of yummy toppings. To give these a four-alarm flavor, use more jalapeño.

> 2 teaspoons olive or vegetable oil
> 15 to 20 six-inch corn or flour tortillas
> 1 pound fresh chorizo, removed from its casing
> ½ pound Monterey Jack or Cheddar cheese, shredded
> ½ cup chopped black olives
> ¼ cup seeded and chopped jalapeño chiles

1. Coat a large skillet with 1 teaspoon of the oil and heat over medium heat. Add the tortillas and fry, one at a time, until they are crisp and golden, turning once, about 1 minute per side. Drain on paper towels, then transfer to baking sheets.

2. In the same skillet over medium-high heat, heat the remaining 1 teaspoon of oil. Add the sausage and sauté, crumbling it with the back of a spoon as it cooks, until it is cooked through and lightly browned, about 10 minutes. Drain well on paper towels.

3. Preheat the broiler.

4. Sprinkle an equal amount of sausage, cheese, olives, and jalapeños, onto each tortilla. Broil the tostadas for 1 to 2 minutes, or just until the cheese melts.

5. To serve, cut the tostadas into wedges. Serve warm.

Serves 10

DAVID GINGRASS
A LOVE FOR CHARCUTERIE

Go through the heavy iron gates on Hawthorne Lane in San Francisco, next door to the Museum of Modern Art, and enter a brick courtyard with flowers spilling out of planters and pots. You have arrived at Hawthorne Lane, one of the city's finest restaurants, and perhaps an unlikely place to find the humble sausage.

David Gingrass, cofounder and general manager of the posh restaurant, grew up in Milwaukee, so he got a good start in life, sausagely speaking. He studied charcuterie at the Culinary Institute of America in Hyde Park, New York, and learned more about it at top restaurants on both the East and West Coasts before starting Hawthorne Lane in the 1990s.

Although the restaurant is known mostly for its Asian-influenced California cuisine, David likes to serve his own dry-cured salami as an appetizer at the restaurant's fancy oval cherrywood bar. He often offers a fresh sausage on the lunch menu, and makes pancetta for his pizza.

"In a different menu, I'd do a lot more with sausage," he says. "Sausages are so good, but they're not quite what people have in mind when they come here. Too earthy, perhaps. We've done a lot with fresh sausage on the lunch menu — duck with dried fruit, a smoked lamb sausage with lots of garlic, a curried pork, and chicken and pork in an 80:20 mixture with sun-dried tomatoes, Parmesan, and basil. We also like to offer terrines, which are basically uncased sausage."

Not everyone can afford dinner at Hawthorne Lane, but sausage lovers in the Bay area know they can sit at the bar and eat David's home-cured salami or come for lunch and find their favorite food on the menu.

Potato Sausage Balls

In this dish, the sausage is on the inside.

1 pound country-style breakfast
    sausage, removed from its casing
2 to 3 cups slightly stiff mashed potatoes
2 eggs, beaten
2 tablespoons water
1 cup dried breadcrumbs
1 teaspoon freshly ground white
    pepper (fine grind)
½ teaspoon dried basil
½ teaspoon dried oregano
Pinch of cayenne pepper
2 tablespoons grated Parmesan
    cheese
1 tablespoon chopped fresh parsley
Oil, for frying

1. Shape the sausage meat into 1-inch balls. Enclose each ball in mashed potatoes to make a ball about 2 inches in diameter.

2. Whisk together the eggs and water in a small shallow bowl.

3. In a second shallow bowl, combine the breadcrumbs, white pepper, basil, oregano, cayenne, Parmesan, and parsley.

4. Dip each sausage ball into the egg mixture, then gently roll it in the seasoned breadcrumbs. Arrange the balls on a baking sheet. Refrigerate for 1 hour to allow the crumb coating to set.

5. Heat several inches of oil in a deep saucepan to 375°F (190°C). Fry the sausage balls, a few at a time and turning occasionally, until they are golden, about 3 minutes. Drain on paper towels. Serve hot.

Serves 8 to 10

Salami Log

This appetizer is just the thing to impress guests both with your sausage-making skills and with your flair for the creative.

1 package (3 ounces) cream
    cheese, at room temperature
½ pound hard salami, such as
    Genoa Salami or Italian-Style
    Dry Sausage, thinly sliced
1 teaspoon drained and chopped
    capers in vinegar brine
1 teaspoon chopped fresh chives
1 teaspoon chopped sweet gherkin
1 teaspoon chopped fresh parsley

1. Spread the cream cheese on the slices of salami.

2. Sprinkle the capers, chives, gherkin, and parsley evenly over all the slices.

3. Roll up the first slice of salami, but before it is completely rolled, overlap the end by about 1 inch on the next slice of salami and continue to roll. Repeat until you have rolled up all the slices.

4. Refrigerate for several hours, then cut into ¼-inch slices with a very sharp knife.

5. Arrange the slices on a platter and serve cold.

Serves 6 to 8

Sausage-Stuffed Mushrooms

This hors d'oeuvre is convenient. It looks as if it took a long time to prepare, but anyone who knows his or her way around a kitchen can fix this dish in half an hour. It can be refrigerated, then reheated just before guests arrive. The recipe works best with mushrooms at least 1½ inches in diameter.

18 large mushroom caps
2 tablespoons butter
¼ pound sweet Italian or country-style sausage, removed from its casing
2 tablespoons finely minced onions
2 tablespoons olive oil
¼ cup dried breadcrumbs
½ teaspoon dried oregano
Freshly ground black pepper (medium grind) and kosher or coarse salt
2 tablespoons dry sherry
1 tablespoon chopped fresh parsley
1 clove garlic, very finely minced
¼ pound mozzarella, grated

1. Clean the mushrooms and remove the stems. Chop the stems finely and set aside.

2. Melt the butter in a large skillet over medium heat, add the mushroom caps, and gently sauté them for 2 to 3 minutes, just until they are slightly golden but not noticeably shrunken. Remove them with a slotted spoon and drain on a paper towel.

3. Add the sausage and onions to the skillet and sauté, crumbling the sausage with the back of a spoon as it cooks, until it is cooked through and lightly browned, and the onions are crisp-tender, about 10 minutes. Stir the oil and chopped mushroom stems into the mixture in the skillet; sauté 2 minutes longer.

4. Remove the skillet from the heat. Add the breadcrumbs, oregano, pepper and salt to taste, and sherry; mix well.

5. Preheat the broiler. Grease a baking sheet.

6. Stir the cheese into the sausage mixture.

7. Divide the mixture evenly among the mushroom caps and arrange the caps on the baking sheet, filling-side up.

8. Broil for 1 to 2 minutes, until the cheese bubbles. Serve hot or refrigerate for up to 1 day. Reheat when needed.

Serves 6 to 8

Snowball Liverwurst Pâté

Pâté de foie gras is a famous (or infamous, if you look at it from the goose's point of view) French delicacy. In order to produce it, geese are put through the rather indelicate procedure of being force-fed until their livers become enlarged. Whether you are squeamish about what they do to geese to produce the pâté or simply don't want to spend what's necessary for the pricey product, you can still eat your pâté: Chicken livers and homemade liverwurst fill the bill nicely.

3 tablespoons butter
¼ pound chicken livers
2 cloves garlic, minced
2 scallions with tops, minced
1 tablespoon fresh chopped basil, or 1 teaspoon dried
¼ pound liverwurst, diced
Freshly ground black pepper
Kosher or coarse salt
1 tablespoon Drambuie or brandy
1 package (3 ounces) cream cheese
¼ cup chopped fresh parsley
Bread or crackers, to serve

1. Heat the butter in a large skillet over medium heat. Add the chicken livers and sauté for about 15 minutes, until they are uniformly colored. Add the garlic, scallions, and basil and sauté until the garlic and scallions are softened but not browned, 1 to 2 minutes longer. Stir the liverwurst into the liver mixture. Remove the skillet from the heat.

2. Process the mixture in a food processor until it is puréed, then add pepper and salt to taste and the Drambuie; pulse until blended.

3. Lightly oil a small gelatin mold. Pack the mixture into it firmly. Cover and refrigerate the mold for at least 4 hours.

4. Whip or beat the cream cheese until it is smooth.

5. Unmold the pâté onto a serving dish and frost it with the cream cheese.

6. Gently press the chopped parsley into the cheese frosting. Refrigerate for about 1 hour to set the frosting.

7. Serve chilled, with the bread or crackers.

NOTE: If you like, add an extra teaspoon of liqueur and a little finely minced garlic to the cream cheese frosting for extra flavor.

Serves 8 to 10

Braunschweiger Meatballs

This is an easy, quick-to-prepare party dish that can be prepared a day or two ahead and refrigerated until needed.

½ pound Braunschweiger (page 80)
2 teaspoons freshly grated onion
½ teaspoon finely minced garlic
Dash of hot pepper sauce
Freshly ground black pepper (medium grind)
Kosher or coarse salt
2 tablespoons chopped fresh parsley

1. Mash the braunschweiger with a fork and add the onion, garlic, hot pepper sauce, pepper, and salt to taste. Mix well.

2. Form the mixture into 20 or 25 little meatballs and roll each one in the parsley to coat.

3. Insert a toothpick into each ball and refrigerate for at least 2 hours before serving.

Serves 4 to 6

Thuringer Spears

You can use any hard or semi-hard sausage for this recipe; the Thuringer stands up well to the pickled onion and olive flavors.

> ½ pound Thuringer or other hard or semi-hard sausage, cubed
> Pickled cocktail onions, plus 1 teaspoon liquid from the pickled onions
> Pitted black olives
> 1 tablespoon olive oil
> ½ teaspoon sugar

1. Alternate chunks of sausage with onions and olives on toothpicks.

2. Combine the oil, pickling liquid, and sugar, and mix well. Pour over the spears and serve.

Serves 6 to 8

Toasted Salami Skewers

Assemble these hors d'oeuvres ahead of time and store them in the refrigerator. To serve, allow them to come to room temperature and pop them under the broiler or into the toaster oven just before company comes.

> 4 slices thinly sliced hard salami
> 20 green stuffed olives
> 20 cocktail onions
> 1 cup pineapple juice
> 1 tablespoon olive oil

1. Cut the salami into strips. You should get about five strips from each slice.

2. Push a toothpick through one end of a strip of salami. Skewer an olive and bring the salami over the skewer to cover one side of the olive. Skewer an onion and repeat the process with the salami so that the salami forms an S shape around the olives and onions. Arrange the spears on the broiler pan.

3. Combine the pineapple juice and oil; brush some of the mixture onto each skewer.

4. Just before serving, preheat the broiler. Broil the spears for about 2 minutes, or until warmed through. Serve hot.

Serves 6 to 8

Sausage and Cheese Pumpernickel Canapés

Use any cured or dried sausage you have on hand, such as kielbasa or bologna, for this recipe.

> ½ pound sliced cured or dried sausage
> ½ pound sliced Swiss, provolone, Muenster, or mozzarella cheese, cut into 1-inch squares
> 5 slices pumpernickel bread
> 7 large pitted black or green stuffed olives, sliced

1. Cut the sausage and cheese slices into 1-inch squares. Cut each slice of bread into quarters.

2. Arrange one slice of sausage, one slice of cheese, and one slice of olive on each bread square.

Serves 8 to 10

CHAPTER 13

Sausage for Lunch or Dinner

There is no love sincerer

than the love of food.

— George Bernard Shaw

ONE OF THE MARVELOUS THINGS ABOUT SAUSAGE is that it is so eminently adaptable. There is hardly a vegetable or fruit that doesn't go well with some kind of sausage. Part of sausage's versatility stems from the fact that it can be prepared in so many different ways. There isn't a single cuisine in the civilized world that doesn't include as part of its repertoire at least some kind of sausage.

There can be no such thing as the definitive sausage recipe book. For every idea about how to use sausage, there is an infinite number of variations around that theme. One needn't be a culinary genius to come up with one's own variations.

In this section, we are going to treat sausage as the main ingredient in a meal. The recipes in this chapter are family favorites. They range from the most simple to quite elaborate. They all have two things in common: They all rely on some kind of sausage as an integral ingredient and they are all delicious. As we said earlier about making sausage — make these recipes your own. Try them our way first, and then experiment to suit your taste, as well as your family's taste. Consider them our gift to you: your reward for being a *wurstmacher!*

Pepperoni, Salami, and Sausage Pizza

A pizza for sausage lovers! Three different types of sausage top this tasty pie.

    1 tablespoon plus 1 teaspoon
      olive oil
    ¼ pound sweet Italian-style sausage,
      removed from its casing
    1 small onion, chopped
    2 cloves garlic, minced
    ¼ cup chopped red and green sweet
      peppers
    ¼ cup pepperoni, diced
    ¼ cup hard salami, diced
    Basic Pizza Dough (see next page)
    ½ pound mozzarella, shredded
    ¼ cup Italian Tomato Sauce (page
      247)
    ¼ cup grated Parmesan cheese
    Freshly ground black pepper
      (medium grind)
    Kosher or coarse salt

1. Heat the oil in a large skillet over medium-high heat. Add the sausage and sauté, crumbling it with the back of a spoon as it cooks, until it is cooked through and browned, about 10 minutes. Remove it with a slotted spoon and set it aside in a large bowl.

2. Drain off all but 1 tablespoon of the drippings, add the onion, garlic, and bell peppers, and sauté until tender-crisp, about 5 minutes. Remove the vegetables with a slotted spoon and combine with the sausage. Discard the drippings.

3. Preheat oven to 425°F (220°C).

4. Add the pepperoni and salami to the sausage mixture. Mix well.

5. On a floured surface, roll out the dough to form a 12-inch circle. Transfer the circle to a baking sheet or perforated pizza pan. Sprinkle a thin layer of mozzarella on the dough. Distribute the sausage mixture evenly over the cheese. Dot with the tomato sauce and then sprinkle with the Parmesan cheese. Sprinkle with pepper and salt to taste. End with a layer of mozzarella.

6. Bake for about 25 minutes, until the top is golden and bubbling.

Serves 6 to 8

Greek Pizza

Lamb, olives, and feta cheese give a decidedly Greek accent to this pizza. The Lamb, Rosemary, and Pine Nut Sausage (page 95) is a good choice here.

    2 tablespoons olive oil
    ½ pound fresh lamb sausage,
      removed from its casing
    1 small onion, chopped
    2 cloves garlic, minced
    ½ cup chopped ripe olives (prefer-
      ably brine-cured)
    Basic Pizza Dough (see next page)
    ½ pound mozzarella, shredded
    1 cup crumbled feta cheese
    1 tablespoon chopped fresh basil
    1 tablespoon chopped fresh
      oregano
    Freshly ground black pepper
      (medium grind)
    Kosher or coarse salt

1. Heat the oil in a large skillet over medium-high heat. Add the sausage and sauté, crumbling it with the back of a spoon as it cooks, until it is cooked through and browned, about 10 minutes. Remove it with a slotted spoon and set it aside in a large bowl.

2. Drain off all but 1 tablespoon of the drippings, add the onion and garlic, and sauté 2 to 3 minutes, until they are tender-crisp. Remove the vegetables with a slotted spoon and add to the sausage. Discard the drippings.

3. Preheat oven to 425°F (220°C).

4. Add the olives to the sausage mixture. Mix well.

5. On a floured surface, roll out the dough to form a 12-inch circle. Transfer the circle to a baking sheet or perforated pizza pan. Sprinkle a thin layer of mozzarella on the dough. Distribute the sausage mix-ture evenly over the cheese. Dot with the crumbled feta cheese. Sprinkle with the basil, oregano, and pepper and salt to taste. End with a layer of mozzarella.

6. Bake for about 25 minutes, until the top is golden and bubbling.

Serves 6 to 8

BASIC PIZZA DOUGH

To save time, why not double this recipe each time you prepare it, then freeze half of the dough for another night?

- 1 package (¼ ounce) active dry yeast
- ¾ cup plus ½ cup warm (105°F to 115°F; 41° to 46°C) water
- 1 teaspoon kosher or coarse salt
- 3 cups all-purpose flour
- 1 tablespoon olive oil

1. Mix the packet of yeast into the ¾ cup of warm water. Let stand for 15 minutes, until bubbles form.

2. In a large bowl, stir the salt into the flour. Gradually add the yeast mixture and the oil. Turn the dough onto a floured surface. Gradually add the remaining ½ cup of water while kneading the dough, for about 10 minutes. The dough should be smooth and elastic.

3. Transfer the dough to a lightly greased bowl, turning to coat. Cover the bowl and set aside in a warm place until the dough doubles in size, about 1 hour.

1 pizza shell

WHAT'S IN A NAME?

pizza

Literally translated, *pizza* means "pie." The popular round savory tart made with crisp yeast dough and topped with tomato sauce, mozzarella cheese, and any number of vegetables or meats became popular in the United States after World War II. Soldiers who served in Italy brought their passion for pizza home with them, and a new American favorite was born.

ASHLEY GORMAN
"OUR SAUSAGE SINGS WITH FLAVOR"

Ashley Gorman isn't bragging when he says that the sausage he makes at Gorman's Meat Market in Mesquite, Texas, "sings with flavor." He's simply stating a fact and quoting a happy customer.

Ashley, a third-generation sausage maker, has a passion for sausage making. "I don't want to sell something I wouldn't take home and put on my plate and be proud of," he says. He makes as much as 30,000 pounds of sausage a year by hand, much of it venison brought in by hunters and all of it made with the best and freshest ingredients.

Ashley's grandfather started making sausage at the market in 1958, drawing on his German and French heritage and turning out hot links and smoked sausages for the citizens of Mesquite. Ashley's uncle Scott took Ashley into the business when he was only 9 years old (Ashley went to full time after he graduated from high school in 1986) and together they started improving on the recipes.

"My uncle Scott was most interested in the final product, but I always liked the actual 'dirty work' of grinding and mixing and refining the recipe," Ashley says. When people from Louisiana started moving into Mesquite in the 1980s, they brought their love for boudin, and Ashley added that to the market's repertoire. "We took the idea of boudin and, instead of making it so greasy, we used 72 percent lean pork butts; no junk meat; and added red, yellow, and green peppers, onions, and other ingredients. Now the Louisiana people love ours better than their sausage at home!"

Ashley is justly proud of his jalapeño and cheese hot links, his Mettwurst, and the Cajun and teriyaki jerky that he smokes over genuine mesquite, keeping a constant eye on the fire so it doesn't get too hot and burn the edges of the jerky. He's fussy; he won't put anything in the meat case that he's not completely happy with.

During hunting season in the fall, Gorman's Meat Market becomes "Processing Central" for those lucky enough to bag a deer. It's not hard for Ashley to convince most of them to devote a goodly part of the carcass to his spicy venison-pork breakfast sausage.

Hot Italian Sausage and Ricotta Pizza

The ricotta cheese adds creaminess and richness to this pizza.

- 3 tablespoons olive oil
- ½ pound hot Italian sausage, removed from the casing
- 1 small onion, chopped
- 2 cloves garlic, minced
- 8 ounces white mushrooms, sliced
- Basic Pizza Dough (page 237)
- 1 cup Italian Tomato Sauce (page 247)
- 2 cups fresh ricotta cheese
- 1 tablespoon chopped fresh basil
- Freshly ground black pepper (medium grind)
- Kosher or coarse salt

1. Heat 1 tablespoon of the oil in a large skillet over medium-high heat. Add the sausage and sauté, crumbling it with the back of a spoon, until it is cooked through and browned, about 10 minutes. Remove the sausage with a slotted spoon into a large bowl.

2. Add the remaining 2 tablespoons of oil to the skillet. Add the onion, garlic, and sliced mushrooms and sauté until the mushrooms and onions are softened, about 5 minutes. Remove the vegetables with a slotted spoon and add to the sausage. Discard the oil. Mix the sausage and vegetables.

3. Preheat oven to 425°F (220°C).

4. On a floured surface, roll out the dough to form a 12-inch circle. Transfer the circle to a baking sheet or perforated pizza pan. Spread a layer of tomato sauce on the dough. Distribute the sausage mixture evenly over the sauce. Spoon dollops of ricotta over the sausage mixture. Sprinkle with the basil and pepper and salt to taste.

5. Bake for about 25 minutes, until the top is golden and bubbling.

Serves 6 to 8

TOP FIVE SAUSAGE-EATING PLACES

According to the National Hot Dog and Sausage Council, fanciers of boudin and other sausages made in the New Orleans area top the list for sausage consumption in the United States. The statistics are based on one year's worth of supermarket purchases; imagine how many more pounds would have been consumed had they counted all the sausage made by home *wurstmachers!*

1. New Orleans, Louisiana/Mobile, Alabama	20.8 million pounds
2. Los Angeles, California	19.6 million pounds
3. San Antonio/Corpus Christie, Texas	19.1 million pounds
4. Dallas/Fort Worth, Texas	16.7 million pounds
5. Houston, Texas	15.0 million pounds

Sausage-Stuffed Artichokes

An artichoke is eminently stuffable, especially with the product of the wurst maker's effort.

4 large artichokes
1 lemon, quartered
6 cloves garlic; 4 crushed and 2 finely minced
4 bay leaves
¼ cup plus 1 teaspoon olive oil
1 pound country-style breakfast sausage or sweet Italian-style sausage, removed from its casing
½ cup dried breadcrumbs
¼ cup grated Parmesan cheese
1 teaspoon dried thyme
Pinch of cayenne pepper
Freshly ground black pepper (medium grind)
Kosher or coarse salt
¼ cup minced onion
1 tablespoon chopped capers
1 large egg, well beaten
½ cup dry white wine
½ cup lemon juice

1. Bring a medium-sized pot of water to a boil for the artichokes.

2. To prepare the artichokes, cut off the stems, leaving a flat base on each. Reserve the stems. Remove any bruised outer leaves. Cut about 1 inch off the top of each artichoke with a sharp knife. With a pair of kitchen scissors, snip off the tip of each outer leaf.

3. Add the artichokes, reserved artichoke stems, lemon, crushed garlic, and bay leaves and boil, covered, for about 30 minutes, until the leaves are

tender at their thickest part. Drain and let cool.

4. While the artichokes are cooking, heat 1 teaspoon of the oil in a large skillet over medium-high heat. Add the sausage and sauté, crumbling it with the back of a spoon as it cooks, until it is cooked through and browned, about 10 minutes. Remove with a slotted spoon and set aside.

5. In the sausage drippings, sauté the minced onion until it is translucent, about 5 minutes.

6. In a medium-sized bowl, combine the sausage, breadcrumbs, Parmesan, thyme, cayenne, black pepper and salt to taste, onion, capers, egg, and wine. Mix well.

7. Chop the cooked artichoke stems finely; stir them into the sausage mixture.

8. Preheat the oven to 350°F (175°C).

9. Pull back the leaves from the artichokes and remove the inner choke. Stuff the sausage mixture into the artichokes. If you have enough stuffing, place some between the large leaves at the base. Arrange the artichokes in a large baking pan.

10. Whisk together the lemon juice and remaining ¼ cup oil in a small bowl; stir in the minced garlic. Pour the lemon juice mixture over the artichokes.

11. Cover and bake for about 20 minutes, or until the base leaves are very tender. Serve hot with the pan juices for dipping.

Serves 4

Sausage-Stuffed Apples

Nothing chases away the chill of a cool, crisp autumn evening like big juicy apples begging to be stuffed and baked. The seasonings suggested are optional so that you can match the seasoning to the type of sausage you use.

  1 tablespoon oil
  1 pound fresh pork sausage, removed from its casing
  1 cup chopped celery
  1 small onion, finely chopped
3–5 cups fresh breadcrumbs (the amount depends on how big the apples are)
  ½ teaspoon ground cinnamon or ginger OR ½ teaspoon dried marjoram, ½ teaspoon dried sage, and ½ teaspoon dried thyme
  ¼ teaspoon ground allspice (optional)
  ½ cup hot water
  ½ cup dry white wine
  6 very large baking apples (Golden Delicious, Cortland, Northern Spy, Rome, Winesap, McIntosh)

1. Heat the oil in a large skillet over medium-high heat. Add the sausage and sauté, crumbling it with the back of a spoon as it cooks, until it is cooked through and browned, about 10 minutes. Remove the sausage with a slotted spoon and set it aside.

2. In the drippings remaining in the skillet, sauté the celery and onion until they are tender-crisp, about 5 minutes. Drain off the fat.

3. Return the sausage to the skillet and add the breadcrumbs, water, wine, and the desired seasonings. Mix well and remove from the heat.

4. Preheat the oven to 375°F (190°C). Grease a 13- by 9-inch baking pan.

5. Core the apples and peel each one about a third of the way down. Stuff the centers of the apples with equal amounts of sausage mixture.

6. Arrange the apples in the pan. Bake for about 45 minutes, until the apples are tender. Serve hot.

Serves 6

Sausage-Filled Piroshki

Piroshki is a Russian dish of filled dumplings made from a raised dough that is traditionally baked or fried. We prefer to boil ours, as we have done here, but you can do it your way.

DOUGH

- 1 package (¼ ounce) active dry yeast
- ½ cup warm (105 to 115°F; 41 to 46°C) water
- 2½ cups sifted all-purpose flour
- 1 large egg, well beaten
- 2 tablespoons vegetable oil

FILLING

- 1 tablespoon olive or vegetable oil
- 1 pound fresh sausage, any variety, removed from its casing
- 1 small onion, chopped
- 1 large egg, well beaten

TO SERVE

Melted butter
Chopped fresh parsley
Freshly ground black pepper (medium grind)
Kosher or coarse salt

1. To make the dough, mix the yeast with the warm water and let it rest for 15 minutes, or until it becomes frothy.

2. In a large bowl, mix together the flour, egg, and oil. Stir the yeast mixture into the flour mixture to make a soft dough.

3. Place the dough in a greased bowl, cover, and let the dough rise until double in size, about 1 hour.

4. While the dough is rising, make the filling. Heat the oil in a large

skillet over medium-high heat. Add the sausage and sauté, crumbling it with the back of a spoon as it cooks, until it is cooked through and browned, about 10 minutes. Remove the sausage with a slotted spoon and set it aside.

5. In the drippings remaining in the skillet, sauté the onion until it is tender, about 5 minutes. Remove with a slotted spoon and add to the sausage.

6. Add the egg to the sausage mixture; blend thoroughly.

7. Begin heating a large pot of salted water for the piroshki.

8. Punch down the dough and roll it out on a floured surface until it is about ⅛ inch thick. With a biscuit cutter or glass, cut the dough into circles about 3 inches in diameter.

9. Place about 1 tablespoon of the sausage mixture on each circle of dough; fold over to form half moons. Pinch the edges tightly to seal.

Dough prepared for folding.

Half-moon shape.

Pinched edges.

10. Slip the piroshki, a few at a time, into the boiling water and cook for 3 to 4 minutes, until the piroshki float. Remove with a slotted spoon to a large bowl and cover with foil to keep the piroshki warm. Continue cooking piroshki until all are cooked.

11. When all the piroshki are done, put them in a large bowl, toss them with butter, parsley, pepper, and salt and serve warm.

Serves 4 to 6

Sausage-Stuffed Egg Rolls

Commercially prepared egg roll skins will work very well in this recipe. Plan ahead to allow refrigeration time for the egg rolls to firm up before they are fried. Serve these with Chinese (hot) mustard or your favorite dipping sauce.

- 1 tablespoon olive or vegetable oil
- ½ pound fresh country-style breakfast sausage, removed from its casing
- 1 cup finely shredded cabbage
- 1 cup finely chopped celery
- 1 cup finely chopped scallions
- ½ cup finely shredded carrots
- ½ cup finely chopped mushrooms
- ¼ cup finely chopped green bell pepper
- 1 tablespoon grated fresh gingerroot
- ½ teaspoon freshly ground white pepper (medium grind)
- 2 teaspoons soy sauce
- 1 large egg
- 1 large egg white, lightly beaten
- 10 to 12 egg roll wrappers
  Oil for deep-frying

1. Heat the oil in a large skillet over medium-high heat. Add the sausage and sauté, crumbling it with the back of a spoon as it cooks, until it is lightly browned, about 10 minutes. Drain off most of the fat.

2. Add the cabbage, celery, scallions, carrots, mushrooms, green pepper, gingerroot, white pepper, soy sauce, and egg to the skillet and sauté for 2 minutes, stirring. Remove the mixture from the heat; let cool.

3. To assemble the egg rolls, spoon about ¼ cup of the filling onto the center of an egg roll skin and fold two sides over to meet in the center. Brush the two sides and the two open ends with the egg white, then roll up the skin, beginning at one end, to enclose the center. Carefully place the egg rolls on a baking sheet. Refrigerate for 2 hours.

4. Heat 3 inches of oil to 375°F (190°C). Deep-fry the egg rolls until they are crisp and golden, about 5 minutes. Drain on paper towels. Serve hot.

10 to 12 egg rolls

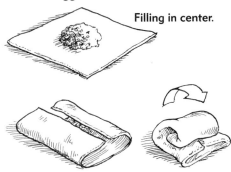

Filling in center.

Sides folded over.   Roll up the skin.

Turkey Sausage Strudel

Make strudel dough according to your favorite recipe, or use ready-made phyllo dough, available in your grocer's freezer section.

- 1 tablespoon vegetable oil
- ¾ pound fresh turkey sausage, removed from its casing
- ¼ pound fresh mushrooms, finely chopped
- ¼ cup finely minced onion
- 2 cloves garlic, finely minced
- ¼ cup finely minced fresh parsley
- 2 ounces cream cheese, softened
- 4 sheets (12 by 16 inches each) phyllo or strudel leaves
- 2 tablespoons butter, melted
- ¼ cup dried breadcrumbs

1. In a large skillet, heat the oil over medium-high heat. Add the sausage and sauté, crumbling it with the back of a spoon as it cooks, until it is cooked through and browned, about 10 minutes. Remove the sausage with a slotted spoon and set aside in a large bowl.

2. In the same skillet, sauté the mushrooms, onion, and garlic until soft, about 10 minutes. Transfer the mixture to the bowl with the sausage. Add the parsley and cream cheese and mix well.

3. Preheat oven to 400°F (200°C). Lightly grease a baking sheet.

4. Lay one sheet of phyllo on a work surface. Cover the remaining phyllo so it won't dry out. Brush the single sheet with some of the melted butter. Sprinkle some of the bread-crumbs evenly over the sheet of phyllo. Add another sheet on top of the first, brush with butter, and dust with crumbs. Continue in the same manner with the third and fourth sheets.

5. Spread the sausage mixture evenly over the top sheet of phyllo, leaving a 1½-inch border all around. Tuck in the sides. Carefully roll up the phyllo, jelly-roll fashion. Place the roll seam-side down on the prepared baking sheet.

6. Bake for about 15 minutes, until the strudel is evenly browned. Cool slightly before slicing.

Serves 4 to 6

DEBRA FRIEDMAN

TEACHING PEOPLE WHERE THEIR FOOD COMES FROM

A visit to Old Sturbridge Village (OSV) in central Massachusetts is like stepping back into a small New England village of the 1830s. Clapboard houses line the common, a blacksmith pumps bellows to make cast iron red hot and malleable, and sturdy horses pull wagons around a working farm. The village, created in the 1930s to depict preindustrial rural life, annually draws half a million visitors, who walk the herb gardens and absorb the rhythms of a simpler age.

As coordinator for the foodways program at OSV, Deb Friedman demonstrates cooking using the same tools, ingredients, and recipes that a New England farm wife of the 1830s would have used. She makes sausage in December, when the farm's pigs are slaughtered.

"The pigs were always slaughtered last," Deb says, "after the cows had dried off. Once there was no whey or skim milk left after cheese making and butter making, the pigs had nothing to eat, so they were butchered and made into sausage, ham, bacon, and salt pork." The pigs are killed humanely before OSV opens for the day, but visitors can watch Deb turn and clean the intestines to use for sausage casings.

"We make a simple pork sausage flavored with sage, about two-thirds meat and one-third fat," Deb says. "We chop the meat by hand in a bowl using a curved blade. Our stuffer is a tin tube with a wooden plunger that pushes the meat into the intestines."

Some of the sausage mixture is stuffed into muslin sleeves and hung in the attic, where it freezes and lasts until spring (or a January thaw). The rest is stuffed into casings, twisted off into links, packed into a crock, and covered with rendered lard, as would have been done in the 1830s. The crocks are stored in a cold pantry. (Since none of the houses at OSV has central heat, there is little danger of spoilage.)

Deb reports that visitors to OSV really love learning about their food heritage, especially sausage. "Earthy foods are chic," she says, "and sausage is an earthy food."

Meat-Filled Ravioli in Sausage Sauce

Ravioli is one of the easiest forms of pasta to make because you roll out the dough in large sheets rather than cutting or shaping it into trickier styles. If you have a rolling pin, you are in business. Be sure to use real semolina flour for the pasta.

DOUGH

2½ to 3 cups semolina flour
1 teaspoon kosher or coarse salt
2 large eggs, well beaten
About ¼ cup water

MEAT FILLING

½ pound finely ground beef
½ pound finely ground pork
½ pound finely ground veal
¼ cup grated Romano cheese
½ teaspoon dried basil
½ teaspoon freshly ground black pepper (medium grind)
½ teaspoon kosher or coarse salt
¼ teaspoon ground nutmeg
¼ cup finely chopped fresh parsley
2 tablespoons minced onion
1 clove garlic, minced
2 large eggs, well beaten

SAUSAGE SAUCE

1 tablespoon olive or vegetable oil
1 pound sweet Italian-style sausage, removed from its casing
4 cups Italian Tomato Sauce (recipe follows)

ASSEMBLY

½ cup grated Parmesan cheese
½ cup grated Romano cheese
2 tablespoons chopped fresh parsley

1. To make the dough, mix the semolina and salt. Mound 2½ cups of the semolina on a pastry board or work surface and make a well in the center. Pour the eggs into the well and mix them, using your fingers or a fork, into the flour a little at a time. Add the water, a few tablespoons at a time, until you have a dough that can be shaped into a ball. Knead it for 5 to 7 minutes, adding up to ½ cup flour a little at a time, if necessary, to prevent sticking. The dough should be stiff but pliable. Place the dough in a bowl and cover it with a cloth or plastic wrap until you are ready to roll it out.

2. To make the filling, in a large bowl combine the beef, pork, veal, parsley, onion, garlic, Romano, basil, pepper, salt, nutmeg, and eggs. Mix well, using your hands. Refrigerate until you are ready to make ravioli.

3. To make the sauce, heat the oil in a large skillet over medium-high heat. Add the sausage and sauté, crumbling it with the back of a spoon as it cooks, until it is cooked through and browned, about 10 minutes.

4. Add the tomato sauce; gently simmer until it is bubbly, about 10 minutes.

5. To make the ravioli, roll out a piece of dough about the size of a lemon on a floured board to a rectangle that is about the thickness of a knife blade (between ⅛ and ¹⁄₁₆ of an inch). Lay the dough across the serrated plate of a ravioli maker. (If you don't have a ravioli maker, mark a 1½-inch-square grid with the dull side of a chef's knife.) Spoon 1 teaspoon of meat filling on top of each square.

6. Roll out a second sheet of dough to the same shape and thickness and lay it over the filling. Press down around the sides of each mound of filling. With a serrated pastry cutter, cut the squares apart. Set them on a lightly floured surface.

7. Repeat with the remaining dough to make about 6 dozen ravioli.

8. Bring a large pot of salted water to a boil for the ravioli. Preheat the oven to 400°F (200°C).

9. Cook the ravioli in batches in the rapidly boiling water for 4 to 5 minutes, or until the pasta is opaque. Handle them gently. Drain.

10. In a large baking dish or individual ramekins, layer the sauce, ravioli, and Parmesan and Romano cheeses. Bake, uncovered, for about 15 minutes, until the sauce is bubbly.

11. Garnish with chopped parsley and serve.

Serves 8 to 10

ITALIAN TOMATO SAUCE

For this sauce, use either dead-ripe plum tomatoes from your garden, peeled and chopped, or best-quality canned crushed tomatoes packed in juice. This all-purpose sauce tastes wonderful over pasta, in lasagne, dolloped onto pizza, or anywhere you want a good tomato flavor.

- 1 tablespoon olive oil
- 3 cloves garlic, crushed
- 4 cups peeled and chopped ripe plum tomatoes or 1 can (28 ounces) crushed tomatoes in juice
- 1 teaspoon kosher or coarse salt
- ½ teaspoon sugar
- ¼ cup red wine
- 2 tablespoons chopped fresh basil

1. In a heavy 4-quart soup pot, heat the oil over low heat. Add the garlic and sauté just long enough to take the edge off the raw taste, about 1 minute.

2. Add the tomatoes, salt, sugar, and wine and simmer, uncovered, for about 30 minutes (20 minutes for canned tomatoes). Tomato sauce has a way of erupting and splashing the cook, so keep the heat low and stir frequently.

3. If you used fresh tomatoes, mash any chunks against the side of the pot with a wooden spoon.

4. Add the basil and cook for another minute or two. Remove from heat and use as needed. The sauce can be frozen for up to 6 months.

Makes 4 cups

Scampi Sausage with Fettuccine

Linguine or fettuccine is the traditional pasta accompaniments to an Italian fish sauce. Use either in this recipe, but the fettuccine, because it is slightly wider, provides a better foil to the sausage.

- 2 tablespoons olive oil
- 2 cloves garlic, crushed
- ¼ cup finely chopped shallots
- ¼ cup finely minced fresh parsley
- 2 pounds Scampi Sausage (page 197)
- 1 cup dry white wine
- 3 cups Italian Tomato Sauce (page 247)
- Freshly ground black pepper
- Kosher or coarse salt
- 1 pound fettuccine
- 2 tablespoons butter

1. Start heating a large pot of salted water for the pasta.

2. In a large skillet, heat the oil over medium-high heat. Add the garlic and sauté until it is lightly browned, about 2 minutes. Discard the garlic.

3. Sauté the shallots in the olive oil until they are softened, about 5 minutes. Add the parsley and stir.

4. Add the sausage and sauté, turning the sausages until they are lightly browned all over, about 10 minutes.

5. Stir in the tomato sauce, wine, and pepper and salt to taste. Simmer for 10 minutes.

6. Meanwhile, cook the fettuccine until al dente in the rapidly boiling water. Drain, toss with butter, and arrange on a platter.

7. Pour the sauce over the fettuccine and arrange the sausages on top. Serve immediately.

Serves 6 to 8

Sausage and Rigatoni

This is a classic combination.

- 1 tablespoon olive oil
- 1 pound sweet Italian-style sausage links
- 1 small green bell pepper, seeded, cored, and chopped
- 1 small onion, chopped
- 4 cups Italian Tomato Sauce (page 247)
- 1 tablespoon chopped fresh parsley
- 1 pound rigatoni
- ¾ pound mozzarella cheese, shredded
- ½ cup grated Romano cheese

1. Start heating a large pot of salted water for the pasta.

2. Heat the oil in a large skillet over medium heat. Add the sausages and panfry, turning the sausages until they are lightly browned, about 15 minutes. Set aside the sausages to cool slightly and drain off all but 2 tablespoons of the drippings.

3. Add the pepper and onion to the drippings remaining in the skillet and sauté until they are tender-crisp, about 5 minutes.

4. Add the tomato sauce and parsley and simmer over medium heat until heated through, about 10 minutes.

5. Slice the sausages into 1-inch pieces and add them to the sauce.

Simmer for 10 minutes.

6. Meanwhile, cook the rigatoni in the rapidly boiling water until al dente, then drain.

7. Preheat the oven to 425°F (220°C). Grease a large baking dish.

8. Layer the sauce, rigatoni, and mozzarella in the baking dish. Sprinkle the Romano cheese on top.

9. Bake, uncovered, until the sauce is bubbly and the top layer of cheese is browned, about 20 minutes.

Serves 4 to 6

Chicken and Sausage Cacciatore

Cacciatore *means something fixed "in the style of the hunter." And there are as many cacciatore recipes as there are hunters. This hearty dish is rich in flavor, easily assembled, and good for family meals and company dinners.*

    1 broiler-fryer chicken (3 pounds),
        cut into 6 to 8 serving pieces
    ¼ cup vegetable or olive oil
    1 pound Italian-style sausage
    1 medium-sized onion, sliced thin
    1 medium green, yellow, or red bell
        pepper, cut into ¼-inch strips
    2 cloves garlic, minced
    4 cups peeled, cored, seeded, and
        chopped Italian plum tomatoes
    2 teaspoons dried oregano
    1 teaspoon dried basil
    1 bay leaf
    1 whole dried hot red pepper or
        1 teaspoon crushed red pepper
    Freshly ground black pepper
        (medium grind)

    Kosher or coarse salt
    1 pound spaghetti or spaghettini
    1 tablespoon butter
    Freshly grated Parmesan cheese
    Chopped fresh parsley

1. In a large skillet over medium-high heat, brown the chicken on all sides in the oil, about 20 minutes. Remove the chicken to a platter; cover with foil to keep it warm.

2. Panfry the sausages in the same skillet, about 20 minutes. Remove and keep warm.

3. Discard all but 2 tablespoons of the drippings. Add the onion, bell pepper, and garlic; sauté until the onions and peppers are tender-crisp, about 5 minutes.

4. Add the tomatoes, oregano, basil, bay leaf, red pepper, and black pepper and salt to taste. Bring the sauce to a simmer and return the chicken and sausage to the sauce. Simmer while you cook the pasta.

5. Bring a large pot of salted water to a boil to cook the pasta.

6. Cook the pasta until al dente in the rapidly boiling water; drain, then toss with the butter.

7. Arrange the pasta on a large platter. Using tongs, take the chicken and sausage out of the sauce and arrange the meat on top of the pasta. Pour the sauce over all. Sprinkle the Parmesan cheese on top and garnish with the chopped parsley.

Serves 6 to 8

Sausage and Chicken Casserole

Here is another perfect culinary marriage of chicken and sausage. Choose any spicy sausage for this dish.

1½ pounds spicy sausage links
1 broiler-fryer chicken (3 pounds), cut into 6 to 8 serving pieces
1 cup all-purpose flour
Freshly ground black pepper (medium grind)
Kosher or coarse salt
Vegetable oil (optional)
12 small potatoes, peeled
5 carrots, cut into 1-inch pieces (about 2 cups)
2 cups pearl onions, peeled
2 whole tomatoes, peeled, cored, seeded, and chopped
1 red or green bell pepper, cut into strips
2 cloves garlic, minced
1 teaspoon dried oregano
½ cup dry white wine

1. In a large skillet with enough water in it just to cover the bottom, simmer the sausages over medium heat until the water evaporates, the sausage gives up some of its fat, and it begins to brown, about 15 minutes. Remove with a slotted spoon.

2. In a shallow bowl, season the flour with pepper and salt. Dip the chicken pieces in the seasoned flour, being sure to coat all sides. Brown the pieces on all sides in the sausage drippings over medium heat, about 20 minutes. (If the sausage was exceptionally lean, coat the bottom of the skillet with a little vegetable oil before adding the chicken.) Using tongs, remove the chicken and keep warm.

3. In the same skillet, sauté the potatoes over medium-high heat, turning frequently so they brown evenly, about 5 minutes.

4. Preheat oven to 375°F (190°C).

5. Transfer the sausage, chicken, and potatoes to a large casserole dish.

6. Sprinkle the carrots, onions, tomatoes, bell pepper, garlic, oregano, and wine over the chicken and potatoes.

7. Bake, covered, for about 1 hour, or until an instant-read thermometer inserted into the thickest part of a chicken thigh reaches 180°F (82°C).

Serves 6 to 8

Sausage and Chicken Sautéed in Red Wine Sauce

This dish is a variation on a venerable French dish: coq au vin. *Serve it with lots of crusty bread to sop up the juices.*

- ¼ cup olive oil
- 1 broiler-fryer chicken (about 3 pounds) cut into 6 to 8 serving pieces
- 1 pound fresh Garlic Sausage (page 55)
- 18 small new potatoes in their jackets
- 2 carrots, cut into 1-inch pieces
- 1 cup pearl onions
- ¼ cup minced celery
- 2 cloves garlic, crushed
- 2 cups dry red wine
- 1 cup chicken stock
- 1 bay leaf
- Bouquet garni (see box)
- Freshly ground black pepper (medium grind)
- Kosher or coarse salt

1. Heat the olive oil in a Dutch oven over medium-high heat and brown the chicken pieces on all sides, about 20 minutes. With a slotted spoon, transfer the chicken pieces to a large bowl; cover with aluminum foil to keep warm.

2. Add the sausage to the Dutch oven and brown, about 20 minutes. Add the sausage to the bowl with the chicken.

3. Sauté the potatoes, carrots, onions, celery, and garlic in the Dutch oven until the vegetables are browned, about 10 minutes.

4. Return the sausages and chicken to the pot. Stir in the wine, chicken stock, bay leaf, bouquet garni, and pepper and salt to taste.

5. Bring to a simmer and cook, covered, for about 1 hour, until the chicken is tender; an instant-read thermometer inserted into the thickest part of a chicken thigh should read 180°F (82°C). Before serving, remove the bay leaf and the bouquet garni.

Serves 6 to 8

BOUQUET GARNI

To make the bouquet garni for Sausage and Chicken Sautéed in Red Wine Sauce, put 2 sprigs fresh parsley, 1 teaspoon dried marjoram, 1 teaspoon dried thyme, and 6 peppercorns in a small square of cheesecloth or muslin. Tie the corners together with a string.

A more traditional method would be to tie together fresh herbs.

Alternatively, you can purchase bouquet garni mixtures in the spice section of most supermarkets. In that case, use 1 tablespoon of the mixture.

Stuffed Roast Chicken

There are few meals as eminently satis-fying as a well-roasted chicken served with stuffing, mashed potatoes, and gravy. It doesn't get much better. And your whole house smells like the Sunday dinner of your dreams. Here are three ideas for stuffings that star — what else? — sausage.

1 roasting hen or capon (4 to 5 pounds)
1 teaspoon kosher or coarse salt
1 recipe Herb and Sausage Stuffing; Sausage, Corn Bread, and Cranberry Stuffing; or Wild Rice Stuffing with Sausage and Chestnuts
2 tablespoons olive oil or butter, melted

1. Preheat oven to 450°F (230°C).

2. Wash the chicken in cold running water. Pat dry and sprinkle the salt in the cavity.

3. Stuff the bird with the stuffing recipe of your choice. Do not ram the stuffing in too tightly, for it will expand during cooking. Close up the cavity using poultry pins, or sew it with heavy cotton thread.

4. Set the stuffed bird on a rack in a roasting pan. If you roast it breast-side down, you will not run the risk of drying out the breast meat; how-ever, the presentation will not be quite as elegant.

5. Rub the top of the chicken with the oil.

6. Put the roasting pan in the oven, then immediately reduce the tem-perature to 350°F (175°C). Roast for about 20 minutes per pound, basting frequently with the juices after the first 30 minutes. The chicken is done when the skin is golden brown and juices run clear if the thigh is pricked with the tip of a knife. (The tempera-ture on an instant-read thermometer will be about 180°F (82°C).

7. Transfer the chicken to a platter to rest for 15 minutes before carving. Use the drippings to make gravy, if desired.

Serves 8 to 10

HERB AND SAUSAGE STUFFING

1 teaspoon olive or vegetable oil
½ pound fresh sausage, removed from its casing
2 cups fresh breadcrumbs or stale bread cubes
¼ cup finely chopped celery, includ-ing leaves
2 teaspoons chopped fresh basil (or 1 teaspoon dried)
2 teaspoons chopped fresh oregano (or 1 teaspoon dried)
2 teaspoons chopped fresh parsley
1 tablespoon Parmesan cheese
½ teaspoon freshly ground black pepper (medium grind)
½ cup white wine or chicken stock, or more as needed

1. Heat the oil in a medium-sized skillet over medium-high heat. Add the sausage and sauté, crumbling it with the back of a spoon as it cooks, until it is cooked through and browned, about 10 minutes. Drain on paper towels, if necessary.

2. In a large bowl, toss together the sausage, breadcrumbs, celery, basil, oregano, parsley, Parmesan, pepper, and wine. Add more wine, if needed, to make the mixture moist.

2 to 3 cups

SAUSAGE, CORN BREAD, AND CRANBERRY STUFFING

- 1 teaspoon olive or vegetable oil
- ½ pound fresh sausage, removed from its casing
- 1 apple, peeled and chopped
- 1 small onion, chopped
- 2 cups day-old corn bread, cut into cubes (or use prepared corn bread stuffing mix)
- ½ cup chopped fresh cranberries
- ½ cup white wine or chicken stock, or more as needed

1. Heat the oil in a medium-sized skillet over medium-high heat. Add the sausage and sauté, crumbling it with the back of a spoon as it cooks, until it is cooked through and browned, about 10 minutes. Add the apple and onion and cook for about 5 minutes, until they are softened. Drain on paper towels, if necessary.

2. In a large bowl, toss together the sausage mixture, corn bread, cranberries, and wine. Add more wine, if needed, to make the mixture moist.

2 to 3 cups

WILD RICE STUFFING WITH SAUSAGE AND CHESTNUTS

- 1 teaspoon olive or vegetable oil
- ½ pound fresh sausage, removed from its casing
- 1 tablespoon butter
- 1 cup boiled chestnuts
- ¼ cup chopped celery
- 1 tablespoon chopped shallots
- 2 cups cooked wild rice
- ½ cup chicken stock, if needed

1. Heat the oil in a medium-sized skillet over medium-high heat. Add the sausage and sauté, crumbling it with the back of a spoon as it cooks, until it is cooked through and browned, about 10 minutes. Drain the sausage on paper towels and wipe out the skillet.

2. Melt the butter in the skillet. Add the chestnuts, celery, and shallots and sauté for about 5 minutes to soften them.

3. In a large bowl, combine the sausage, chestnut mixture, and wild rice. Add the chicken stock, a little at a time, if needed, to moisten the stuffing.

2 to 3 cups

Chicken Sausage Tandoori

To be truly authentic, this dish would have to be cooked in a tandoor oven, a rounded-top oven made of brick and clay that's used throughout India and has such high heat that meat cooks very quickly. But this recipe is delicious, regardless of where it is baked.

1 tablespoon plus 1 teaspoon ground cumin seed
2 teaspoons cayenne pepper
2 teaspoons ground coriander
2 teaspoons sweet paprika
Freshly ground black pepper (medium grind)
Kosher or coarse salt
1 tablespoon finely minced fresh gingerroot
3 cloves garlic, very finely minced
1 cup plain yogurt
2 pounds chicken sausage, such as Curried Chicken Sausage

1. In a medium-sized bowl, mix together the cumin seed, cayenne, coriander, paprika, pepper, and salt. Stir in the gingerroot, garlic, and yogurt.

2. Put the sausage in a casserole dish, then pour the yogurt mixture over the sausage, coating it well.

3. Marinate, covered and refrigerated, overnight.

4. Preheat the broiler or prepare the grill for high heat.

5. Lift the sausages out of the marinade. Discard the marinade. Broil or grill the sausage for about 20 minutes, turning frequently, until it is evenly browned and cooked through.

Serves 6

Roast Duckling with Sausage

Luganega sausage would be a good choice to use in this recipe because the lemon-orange flavor blends well with the duck.

1 duckling (4 to 5 pounds) with giblets
¾ cup water
¾ pound fresh mushrooms, chopped
1 small onion, chopped
2 cloves garlic, minced
Freshly ground black pepper (medium grind)
Kosher or coarse salt
2½ cups dry red wine
1 pound Luganega (page 57)

1. Preheat oven to 425°F (220°C).

2. Set aside the giblets. Wash and pat the duckling dry. Cut it into quarters. Cut off as much fat from the tail section as possible. Prick the skin in several places to allow fat to escape as the duck cooks.

3. Arrange the pieces of duckling on a rack in a shallow roasting pan and roast, uncovered, for 30 minutes.

4. In a small saucepan, bring the giblets and the water to a boil. Reduce the heat to maintain a low boil and cook until the liquid is reduced to ½ cup, about 30 minutes. Discard the giblets and reserve the liquid.

5. Remove the duckling from the oven. Using tongs, remove the pieces from the pan. Drain off the accumulated drippings and remove the rack from the pan. Return the duck to the roasting pan.

6. Combine the mushrooms, onion, garlic, pepper, salt, wine, and giblet liquid. Pour the mixture over the duck pieces. Add the sausages to the roasting pan.

7. Reduce the oven to 375°F (190°C) and roast, uncovered, for 45 minutes, until the sausages and duck pieces are well browned and the liquid is bubbling.

8. Serve the duck and sausage on a platter with the wine sauce poured over them.

Serves 4

Duck Sausage Bourguignonne

Classic boeuf bourguignonne *(meaning "beef as prepared in Burgundy") derives its delicious flavor from slow simmering and lots of red wine. Although this recipe needs less simmering because the meat doesn't need tenderizing, the flavor is just as distinctive.*

   2 pounds Bohemian Duck Sausage (page 176)
   3 tablespoons olive oil
   6 cups thinly sliced onions
   ¾ pound fresh mushrooms, sliced
   1 bay leaf
   1 teaspoon dried marjoram
   1 teaspoon dried thyme
   2 cloves garlic, finely minced
   2 cups dry red wine
   2 cups chicken stock
   1 tablespoon arrowroot or cornstarch
   ¼ cup brandy
   Freshly ground black pepper (medium grind)
   Kosher or coarse salt

1. Into a large skillet, pour enough water to just cover the bottom. Over medium-high heat, panfry the sausages until the water evaporates and the sausages are nicely browned, 15 to 20 minutes. Remove the sausages with a slotted spoon and drain on paper toweling.

2. Heat the olive oil in a Dutch oven over medium-high heat. Sauté the onions and mushrooms until they are slightly wilted, 3 to 5 minutes.

3. Add the bay leaf, marjoram, thyme, garlic, wine, and stock. Bring to a boil, reduce the heat, add the sausages, and simmer for 30 minutes. Season to taste with pepper and salt.

4. Mix the arrowroot with the brandy, bring the bourguignonne to a boil, and add the brandy mixture, stirring, until the mixture thickens. Serve hot.

Serves 6

Braciola

Braciola is an Italian dish traditionally made from flank steak, a versatile and flavorful cut that benefits from tenderizing and braising. This dish can be prepared with thinly sliced round steak but the flavor won't be quite the same. Lots of black pepper is one of the secrets of this dish.

- 1 flank or bottom round steak (about 1 pound)
- 1 teaspoon freshly ground black pepper (coarse grind)
- ½ teaspoon dried basil
- ½ teaspoon dried mint
- ½ teaspoon dried oregano
- ½ teaspoon crushed red pepper
- ¼ cup chopped flat-leaf parsley
- 2 tablespoons chopped onion
- 2 tablespoons grated Parmesan or Romano cheese
- 1 clove garlic, minced
- 2 links hot Italian-style sausage
- 2 tablespoons vegetable oil
- 2 to 3 cups Italian Tomato Sauce (page 247)

1. With the side of a meat cleaver or mallet, flatten the steak to ¼-inch thick. The meat should be rectangularly shaped.

2. In a small bowl, mix together the black pepper, basil, mint, oregano, crushed red pepper, parsley, onion, Parmesan, and garlic. Sprinkle the mixture evenly over the meat.

3. Lay the sausages end to end across the narrower end of the steak and roll it up jelly-roll fashion. As you get toward the end, tuck the sides in.

4. With butcher's twine, tie the roll tightly at 2-inch intervals.

5. Heat the oil in a large skillet over medium-high heat, then brown the roll on all sides, about 10 minutes.

6. Reduce the heat to medium-low. Pour the tomato sauce over the roll and simmer, partially covered, gently turning occasionally until tender, about 90 minutes.

7. To serve, cut into ½-inch slices. Spoon the sauce over the slices.

Serves 4 to 6

Double-Thick Stuffed Pork Chops

There is only one way to stuff a pork chop so that the stuffing stays put. With a very sharp pointed knife, pierce the chop in the center of the edge opposite the bone, then thrust the knife all the way to the bone. Without making that opening any larger, work a pocket into the chop by moving the knife first in one direction and then, turning it over, the other. Be careful not to poke a hole in the wall of the chop and to leave about a ¼-inch margin along the chop's outer edge. Fill the chop with stuffing by using a pastry tube or small funnel.

- 6 double-thick (1½-inch) center-cut loin pork chops
- ¼ pound fresh country-style breakfast sausage, removed from its casing
- ¼ cup diced bits of any cured sausage, such as pepperoni or salami
- ½ cup dried breadcrumbs

1 teaspoon ground ginger
1 tablespoon minced onion
1 teaspoon chopped fresh parsley
2 tablespoons dry white wine
2 tablespoons olive oil
Freshly ground black pepper
  (medium grind)
Kosher or coarse salt

1. Prepare the pockets in the chops, as described above.

2. Preheat the oven to 375°F (190°C).

3. In a medium-sized bowl, mix together the fresh sausage, cured sausage, breadcrumbs, onion, ginger, parsley, and wine.

4. Divide the mixture into six portions. With a pastry tube or small funnel, fill each chop with one portion of the stuffing.

5. Brush the chops with the oil, then dust with pepper and salt.

6. Arrange the chops on a rack in a roasting pan and roast, uncovered, for about 45 minutes, until browned and tender. Baste frequently with the pan juices to prevent the chops from drying out. Serve hot.

Serves 6

Bratwurst Cooked in Beer

Whether bratwurst cooked in beer is better than brats cooked any other way because the beer adds something intrinsic to the meat or simply because the vapors rising from the pot whet the appetite is a matter of conjecture. Suffice it to say that it is better.

1 bottle (12 ounces) beer or ale
1 cup water
1 pound Bratwurst (page 115)
2 cups sauerkraut, rinsed and
  drained
½ teaspoon caraway seed
4 hot dog rolls

1. In a large saucepan, pour the beer and water over the bratwurst. Bring to a boil, then reduce the heat so that the liquid barely simmers. Cook for 10 minutes.

2. Set a colander or vegetable steamer over the pan with the bratwurst, then spoon the sauerkraut into it. Sprinkle the caraway seed on the sauerkraut. Cover and allow the steam to heat the sauerkraut, about 10 minutes.

3. To serve, make a bed of sauerkraut in each roll and place a brat on top. Instant picnic!

Serves 4

Seafood Sausage with Orange Butter

Citrus flavors meld well with seafood and this recipe is no exception. Serve it with rice pilaf and green beans.

> 1 pound seafood sausage
> 4 tablespoons clarified butter (see box)
> 2 tablespoons finely chopped shallots
> ¼ cup orange juice
> ¼ cup orange liqueur
> ¼ cup heavy cream
> 1 tablespoon grated orange zest
> Freshly ground black pepper (medium grind)
> Kosher or coarse salt)

1. Sauté the sausage in the butter over medium heat until it is evenly browned and cooked through, about 10 minutes. Remove with tongs and drain on paper towels.

2. Sauté the shallots in the butter until soft, about 5 minutes.

3. Add the orange juice and orange liqueur. Cook over medium-high heat until the mixture is reduced by half, about 15 minutes. Add the cream and continue to cook, stirring, until the mixture is slightly thickened, about 3 minutes.

4. Stir in the orange zest, pepper, and salt.

5. Return the sausages to the pan to reheat briefly. With tongs, remove the sausages from the pan and arrange them on a platter. Pour the sauce over all.

Serves 4

CLARIFYING BUTTER

To make 4 tablespoons clarified butter, melt 6 tablespoons butter in a 2-cup microwave-safe container on low power (30%) for 2 to 3 minutes, or until completely melted. Let the butter stand for 3 to 4 minutes, then skim the foam from the top. Slowly pour off the yellow oil or clarified butter and discard the milky solids at the bottom.

Eggplant Parmesan with Vegetarian Sausage

Can eggplant Parmesan be improved upon? This is a favorite main dish for vegetarians. But meat-eaters may wish for a heartier main course. In that case, add vegetarian sausage to the casserole and make everyone happy.

> 1 medium-sized eggplant
> 1 cup flour
> Freshly ground black pepper (medium grind)
> Kosher or coarse salt
> ¼ cup plus 1 tablespoon olive oil
> 6 to 8 links vegetarian sausage
> 4 cups Italian Tomato Sauce (page 247)
> ¾ pound mozzarella cheese, grated
> ¼ cup grated Parmesan cheese

1. Wash, dry, and cut the eggplant into ¼-inch-thick slices.

2. In a small bowl, season the flour with pepper and salt. Dust the eggplant with the seasoned flour.

3. Heat ¼ cup of the oil in a large skillet over medium-high heat and sauté the eggplant, a few slices at a time, until they are golden, 5 to 7 minutes. Drain on paper towels and set aside.

4. Add the sausage to the skillet and sauté, turning often, until it is lightly browned, about 10 minutes. Remove with tongs and set aside.

5. Preheat oven to 375°F (190°C).

6. Cut the cooked sausages into 1-inch chunks.

7. Spread a thin layer of tomato sauce over the bottom of a 13- by 9-inch baking pan. Arrange about half the eggplant slices over the sauce. Layer half the sausage chunks over the eggplant, followed by half the mozzarella and Parmesan cheeses. Add another layer of sauce and repeat the layering process. End with a layer of sauce. Drizzle the remaining 1 tablespoon olive oil over the top.

8. Bake, covered, for 30 minutes. Remove the cover and bake an additional 30 minutes, or until browned and bubbling.

Serves 4 to 6

Seafood Sausage Chili

You can increase the "bite" of this dish by increasing the amount of cayenne pepper or adding some chopped fresh jalapeño peppers.

- ¼ cup olive oil
- 2 large onions, coarsely chopped
- 1 cup chopped celery
- ¼ cup grated carrot
- 2 tablespoons minced garlic
- 1 tablespoon cumin seed
- 1 tablespoon dried oregano
- 2 teaspoons cayenne pepper
- Kosher or coarse salt
- 1 can (28 ounces) crushed Italian-style tomatoes in purée
- 2 cups dry red wine
- 1 cup bottled clam juice
- 2 green bell peppers, cored, seeded, and diced
- 2 pounds seafood sausage

1. Heat the olive oil in a Dutch oven over medium-high heat. Add the onion, celery, carrot, and garlic and sauté until slightly softened, about 10 minutes.

2. Add the cumin, oregano, cayenne, salt to taste, tomatoes, wine, and clam juice. Bring the mixture to a boil, reduce the heat, and simmer for 30 minutes.

3. Stir in the green peppers and simmer for 20 minutes longer.

4. Add the sausage; simmer for 30 minutes longer, or until the sausage is cooked through. Serve hot.

Serves 6 to 8

Sausage Tortellini Soup

Chunks of sausage and cheesy tortellini simmer in a hearty broth. This soup is virtually a meal in itself; serve with a crusty bread and big glass of wine on a cold winter night.

- 1 tablespoon olive oil
- 1 pound fresh Italian sausage, sweet or hot, cut into ½-inch slices
- 2 small zucchini, chopped
- 2 carrots, chopped
- 1 onion, chopped
- 3 cloves garlic, minced
- 1 can (28 ounces) peeled whole tomatoes in juice
- 4 cups chicken broth
- 2 cups water
- 1 pound fresh cheese tortellini
- 1 package (10 ounces) frozen chopped spinach, thawed and squeezed dry
- 2 teaspoons dried basil, or 1 table-spoon chopped fresh basil
- 1 teaspoon dried oregano
- ½ teaspoon cayenne pepper
- Freshly ground black pepper (medium grind)
- Kosher or coarse salt
- Grated Parmesan or Asiago cheese, to serve

1. In a large soup pot over medium-high heat, heat the oil. Sauté the sausage chunks until browned and cooked through, about 10 minutes. Add the zucchini, carrots, onion, and garlic; sauté until the vegetables start to soften, about 10 minutes longer, stirring and turning the vegetables.

2. Add the tomatoes, chicken broth, and water and bring the mixture to a simmer. Cook for about 30 minutes, until the vegetables are tender.

3. Add the tortellini and simmer for about 10 minutes, until al dente.

4. Stir in the spinach, basil, oregano, and cayenne and simmer for 5 minutes longer. Sample a spoonful and add pepper and salt to taste.

5. To serve, ladle into bowls and top with the grated cheese.

Serves 6 to 8

Split Pea Soup with Kielbasa

A smoky, flavorful sausage like kielbasa seems to bring out extra "meatiness" in the green split peas. This is delicious with rye bread and butter.

- 1 pound dried green split peas
- 8 cups cold water
- 3 medium-sized onions, chopped
- 2 carrots, chopped
- 2 potatoes, peeled and cubed
- 1 teaspoon dried thyme
- 1 pound kielbasa
- 1 teaspoon freshly ground black pepper (medium grind)
- ½ teaspoon Kosher or coarse salt

REMOVING FAT

If fat floats on the top of a soup or other dish that contains sausage, you can gently dab with paper towels to absorb the fat, repeating until the dish no longer looks greasy.

1. Rinse the peas and remove any discolored ones.

2. In a large soup pot, cover the peas with the water. Bring to a boil, reduce the heat, and simmer for 20 minutes.

3. Stir the onions, carrots, potatoes, and thyme into the soup pot, lower the heat to a gentle simmer, and cover. Cook for about 45 minutes, stirring frequently so the peas don't stick on the bottom.

4. Cut the kielbasa into ½-inch slices and add to the soup, along with the pepper and salt. Simmer for about 30 minutes longer.

5. Taste the soup and add salt and pepper as needed. Serve hot.

Serves 8

Southwestern Stew with Meat or Vegetarian Sausage

This stew is made from garlic, chickpeas, and lots of south-of-the-border heat. It can be made with chicken broth and a spicy meat sausage, or vegetable broth and our Black Bean and Corn vegetarian sausage patties. Serve with corn bread.

- 1 pound Southwestern Pork Sausage (page 66) or Chorizo (page 63) or Black Bean and Corn Sausage (page 205)
- 10 cloves garlic, chopped
- 2 onions, chopped
- 2 tablespoons corn oil

- 1 can (2 ounces) chopped green chiles
- 1 fresh jalapeño chile, seeded and chopped
- 2 cups chicken or vegetable broth, or more as needed
- 1½ cups cooked chickpeas, or 1 can (15 ounces), rinsed and drained
- 1 teaspoon ground coriander
- 1 teaspoon ground cumin
- 1 teaspoon freshly ground black pepper (medium grind)
- 1 teaspoon Kosher or coarse salt
- 4 radishes, trimmed and sliced thin, to serve
- 2 scallions, sliced thin, to serve
- ¼ pound Monterey Jack cheese, grated, to serve
- 1 lime, cut into wedges, to serve

1. Cut the meat sausage into ½-inch slices. If you are using vegetarian sausage patties, cut into eight pieces per patty.

2. In a heavy soup pot over medium-high heat, sauté the sausage, garlic, and onions in the oil until the onions are softened, about 5 minutes. Stir in the green chiles, jalapeño, and broth and simmer for 10 minutes.

3. Sir in the chickpeas, coriander, cumin, pepper, and salt. Simmer for about 20 minutes longer, stirring frequently so the mixture doesn't stick. Add a small amount more of broth or water if it is too thick.

4. Ladle the hot stew into bowls. Garnish with radish slices, scallions, and cheese. Serve with lime wedges on the side.

Serves 4

Beef and Sausage Stew

Stew is always a heart-warmer on a cold blustery day and the addition of sausage in this recipe makes it even more so.

> 2 tablespoons vegetable oil
> 1 pound beef stew meat, cut into 1-inch cubes
> 1 pound pork sausage, in links
> 2 cups beef broth
> 2 cups canned tomato sauce
> ½ cup dry red wine
> 2 large potatoes, peeled and cubed
> 2 carrots, sliced
> 1 cup small white onions, peeled
> 1 cup green peas (fresh or frozen)
> 1 tablespoon chopped fresh parsley
> Freshly ground black pepper (medium grind)
> Kosher or coarse salt

1. Heat the oil in a Dutch oven over medium-high heat. Add the beef cubes and sausage and sauté until they are browned, about 20 minutes.

2. Stir in the beef broth, tomato sauce, and wine. Reduce the heat and simmer gently, covered, for 1 hour.

3. Add the potatoes, carrots, onions, peas, and parsley. Simmer until the vegetables are tender, about 30 minutes.

4. Taste the stew and add pepper and salt to taste. Serve hot.

Serves 4 to 6

Minestrone

The sausage adds flavor and richness to this classic Italian soup.

> 4 tablespoons extra-virgin olive oil
> 1 pound sweet Italian-style sausage links, cut into 1-inch pieces
> 4 very ripe tomatoes, peeled, cored, seeded, and chopped (retain the juices), or 1 can (28 ounces) diced tomatoes with their liquid
> 2 carrots, cut into ¼-inch slices
> 2 celery stalks, cut into ¼-inch slices
> 2 medium onions, chopped
> 1 small zucchini, sliced
> 6 cloves garlic, minced
> 6 to 8 cups water
> 2 cups chopped fresh green cabbage
> 2 tablespoons chopped fresh basil
> 2 tablespoons chopped fresh parsley
> 1 sprig (4 inches) fresh rosemary
> 1 can (15 ounces) chickpeas or pinto beans, rinsed and drained
> 1 cup orzo or small pasta shells
> Freshly ground black pepper
> Kosher or coarse salt
> Parmesan cheese, grated

1. Heat 2 tablespoons of the oil in a Dutch oven over medium-high heat. Add the sausage and sauté until it is browned, about 10 minutes.

2. Stir in the tomatoes, carrots, celery, onion, zucchini, and garlic. Bring to a simmer. Add the water, bring to a boil, reduce the heat, and simmer, covered, for 20 minutes.

3. Add the cabbage, basil, parsley, rosemary, chickpeas, and orzo. Simmer, uncovered, for 15 to 20 minutes longer, stirring frequently, until the pasta is tender.

4. Taste, then season with pepper and salt. Remove the rosemary sprig.

5. Serve hot. Drizzle each serving with some of the remaining 2 tablespoons of olive oil and sprinkle with the Parmesan.

Serves 6 to 8

Acorn Squash Stuffed with Sausage

This is virtually a complete meal in one dish. A tossed salad is about all that is needed to complete the fixin's. We like it with country-style breakfast sausage or a sweet Italian sausage.

    2 large acorn squash
    2 teaspoons light brown sugar
    1 pound fresh pork sausage, removed from its casing
    ½ cup fresh breadcrumbs
    1 large egg, well beaten

1. Preheat the oven to 375°F (190°C).

2. Cut each squash in half horizontally and scrape out the seeds and pith. If needed to make the squash halves sit flat, cut a small slice from the bottom. Sprinkle the cavity of each squash with ½ teaspoon of the brown sugar.

3. Pour 1 inch of water in the bottom of a baking pan and arrange the squash, skin-side down, in the pan. Bake, uncovered, for 20 minutes.

4. Meanwhile, combine the sausage, breadcrumbs, and egg in a large bowl. Mix well.

5. When the squash has baked for 20 minutes, remove it from the oven and stuff one-quarter of the sausage mixture into each of the squash halves.

6. Return the squash to the oven and bake for 30 minutes longer, or until the sausage is cooked through and crisp on top. Serve hot.

Serves 4

Capusta

This Polish dish is traditionally served with rye bread or over boiled potatoes.

    2 tablespoons vegetable oil
    1 large onion, chopped
    1 pound Smoked Kielbasa (page 141), cut into 1-inch pieces
    1 small head cabbage, shredded
    1 cup tomato juice
    Freshly ground black pepper (medium grind)
    Kosher or coarse salt

1. Heat the oil in a Dutch oven over medium-high heat. Add the onion and sauté until it is translucent, about 10 minutes.

2. Add the kielbasa and sauté for 5 minutes.

3. Stir in the cabbage, tomato juice, and pepper and salt to taste.

4. Cover and cook, barely simmering, for 1 hour. Serve hot.

Serves 4

Bratwurst with German Potato Salad

German potato salad derives its distinctive flavor from bits of crisp-fried bacon and some of the drippings from that bacon. This recipe is just as flavorful, if not more so, and probably somewhat more healthful, too, since vegetable oil is used to cook the sausage. Mixing the sausages and potatoes with the dressing while they are hot helps the mixture absorb the dressing better.

    6 large boiling potatoes, peeled
      and sliced
    3 tablespoons vegetable oil
    1 pound Bratwurst (page 115)
    1 large onion, thinly sliced
    ¼ cup cider vinegar
    Freshly ground coarse black pepper
      (coarse grind)
    Kosher or coarse salt

1. In a large pot of salted water, bring the potatoes to a boil. Reduce heat and simmer until the potatoes are tender, about 15 minutes. Drain the potatoes and transfer them to a large bowl.

2. Meanwhile, heat the oil in a large skillet over medium-high heat. Add the bratwurst and sauté the sausages until they are browned and cooked through, about 20 minutes. Remove the sausages with a slotted spoon. Wearing an oven mitt, slice the bratwurst and add to the potatoes. Add the onions and stir gently to combine.

3. Discard all but 2 tablespoons of the drippings in the skillet. Pour the vinegar into the skillet and scrape up any sausage pieces. Pour the mixture over the potatoes.

4. Taste the salad and add pepper and salt to taste.

5. The salad can be served warm or chilled.

Serves 6

Bubble and Squeak

A traditional English favorite that should surely get an award for "Best Recipe Name," this beloved combination of potatoes and cabbage gets even tastier with bits of sausage mixed in. The dish evolved as a way to use up leftovers, so feel free to get creative about your additions. Using lard gives the dish the most traditional flavor, but you can substitute olive oil if you prefer.

    1 tablespoon lard or olive oil
    ½ to 1 pound fresh sausage, removed
      from its casings
    1 small onion, thinly sliced
    2 cups chopped cooked cabbage
      (see Note)
    2 cups chopped cold boiled
      potatoes or mashed potatoes
    Freshly ground black pepper
    Kosher or coarse salt

1. Heat the lard in a large cast-iron skillet over medium-high heat until melted. Add the sausage and sauté, crumbling it with the back of a spoon as it cooks, until it is cooked through and browned, about 10 minutes. Remove the sausage with a slotted spoon and set it aside.

Every summer our area becomes a showcase for ethnic cuisines. The Italians have their field (or feast) days of Saint Anthony; the Czechs, Slavs, Russians, Ukrainians, Poles, and Greeks each have their own weekend of feasting, partying, dancing, and gaming — not to mention imbibing.

For one weekend a year, a public picnic area, a grassy field, or a church parking lot becomes Little Italy, Little Prague, or Little any one of many varied cultures and cuisines. The beer and wine flow freely. The music lasts until the wee hours of the morning.

Always the public is invited. And always — without reservation — the charcoal fires in the makeshift brick and cinderblock pits are kept burning to accommodate the barbecued chickens, steaks, and sausages that keep the revelers reveling, holding hunger at bay and, for several days at least, making life's problems blow away on the wood smoke–scented breeze. A soft summer's night, music, dancing, ice cold beer trickling down your throat, a hot sausage spurting juice on the first bite: It may not be heaven, but it sure comes close!

Good times and good food belong to the same brotherhood. Regardless of the nationality, people parade the best of their cuisine during times of partying and feasting. And one ingredient seems to play an important part in every one of them: the sausage.

2. Sauté the onion until it is softened, about 5 minutes.

3. Stir in the sausage, cabbage, and potatoes. Add pepper and salt to taste. Press the mixture down into the hot fat.

4. Cook over medium-low heat for about 15 minutes, until the mixture is browned on the bottom. Turn to brown the other side and cook for about 10 minutes longer.

5. Cut into wedges and serve hot.

NOTE: If you don't have cooked cabbage on hand, cook some by adding 1 pound sliced cabbage to a large pot of boiling water. Cover the pan and gently boil until tender, about 7 minutes. Drain thoroughly.

Serves 4

Cheddared Leeks
with Sausage

Nearly any variety of fresh sausage will go well in this recipe, but we especially like Mustardy Beef Sausage.

- 1 tablespoon vegetable oil
- 1 pound fresh sausage, removed from its casing
- 10 medium-sized leeks
- 1 cup grated Swiss or Cheddar cheese
- Freshly ground black pepper (medium grind)
- Pinch of cayenne pepper
- Kosher or coarse salt

1. Heat the oil in a large cast-iron skillet over medium-high heat. Add the sausage and sauté, crumbling it with the back of a spoon, until it is cooked through and browned, about 10 minutes. Remove the sausage with a slotted spoon and set it aside.

2. Preheat the broiler. Lightly grease a broiler pan.

3. Cut off the green tops of the leeks to within 2 inches of the white part. Wash well and steam over boiling water until crisp-tender, about 10 minutes.

4. Arrange the leeks in the broiler pan. Layer the cooked sausage on top of the leeks. Sprinkle on the grated cheese, cayenne, and black pepper and salt to taste.

5. Broil for 5 minutes, or until the cheese is bubbly and lightly browned.

6. Serve immediately.

Serves 4

Sausage and Lentils

Lentils are a staple legume in the Middle East, India, and parts of Europe, where they are always dried rather than eaten fresh. Use the larger brown lentil for this recipe. To make this into a vegetarian dish, substitute one of the vegetarian sausages in this book, such as the Wild Mushroom Sausage.

- 1 pound Polish kielbasa or other fresh sausage, cut into 1-inch pieces
- 6 cups water
- 1 tablespoon vegetable oil
- 1 large sweet onion, thinly sliced
- 2 cups dried lentils
- 1 tablespoon chopped fresh parsley
- 1 teaspoon grated lemon or orange zest
- 1 teaspoon crushed mint leaves
- 1 tablespoon tomato paste
- Freshly ground black pepper (medium grind)
- Kosher or coarse salt
- 1 cup dry white wine

1. In a Dutch oven over medium-high heat, cook the sausage pieces and ¼ cup of the water until the water evaporates. Add the oil and continue cooking until the sausages are lightly browned, about 10 minutes.

2. Add the onion; cook 5 minutes.

3. Stir in the lentils, the remaining 5¾ cups water, and the parsley, lemon zest, mint, tomato paste, pepper and salt to taste, and the wine. Bring to a boil.

4. Reduce the heat and simmer, covered, for 45 minutes, until the lentils are cooked through. Serve hot.

Serves 4

Sausage with Onions, Peppers, and Mushrooms in Wine Sauce

This recipe makes an excellent buffet dish for a party. It is easy and quick to prepare. Serve it with party rolls to allow guests to make miniature sandwiches.

- 2 pounds hot or sweet Italian-style sausage links
- 2 tablespoons olive oil
- 2 large sweet onions, thinly sliced
- 2 large red or green bell peppers, cored, seeded, and cut into strips
- 1 pound fresh mushrooms, thinly sliced
- 1 cup dry white wine

1. In a large skillet, over medium-high heat, panfry the sausages in the olive oil until they are well browned, about 20 minutes. Remove them with a slotted spoon and set aside.

2. In the same skillet, sauté the onions and peppers until they are tender-crisp, about 5 minutes. Remove them with a slotted spoon and set them aside.

3. Sauté the mushrooms until they give up most of their liquid, about 5 minutes. Drain the fat from the skillet.

4. Cut the links into ½-inch-thick slices and return them to the skillet along with the onions and peppers.

5. Add the wine and cook over medium heat until the liquid is almost evaporated, about 20 minutes. Serve hot.

Serves 4 to 6

Spanish Rice with Chorizo

Most Spanish rice recipes call for browned ground beef, but the addition of chorizo gives this recipe more flavor.

- 2 slices bacon, diced
- 2 tablespoons vegetable oil
- 1 pound fresh Chorizo (page 63), cut into 1-inch pieces
- 1 medium-sized onion, chopped
- 1 sweet bell pepper, seeded, cored, and chopped
- 2 cups tomato sauce
- 2 cups cooked rice
- Freshly ground black pepper
- Kosher or coarse salt

1. In a large skillet, cook the bacon until it is crisp, about 10 minutes. Remove it with a slotted spoon and drain it on paper towels. Drain off the fat from the skillet.

2. Heat the vegetable oil in the skillet. Add the chorizo and sauté until the pieces are browned, about 15 minutes. Remove with a slotted spoon. Drain off all but 2 tablespoons of the drippings.

3. Sauté the onions and peppers in the remaining drippings until they are tender-crisp, about 5 minutes. Return the bacon and chorizo to the skillet, add the tomato sauce, and bring to a simmer.

4. Stir the rice into the mixture in the skillet and cook to heat through. Then season with pepper and salt to taste. Serve hot.

Serves 4

Scalloped Potatoes with Sausage

Scalloped potatoes are a home-cooked favorite. The addition of sausage turns this popular dish into a main dish. Any spicy fresh sausage works well in this recipe.

> 1 pound fresh sausage, in links
> 3 tablespoons butter
> 2 tablespoons all-purpose flour
> 3 cups milk
> Pinch of cayenne pepper
> Freshly ground black pepper (medium grind)
> Kosher or coarse salt
> 6 large russet potatoes, peeled and thinly sliced
> 1 onion, sliced thinly

1. In a medium-sized skillet over medium-high heat, cook the sausage in just enough water to cover the bottom of the pan until the links are lightly browned, 15 to 20 minutes. Remove the sausages and set them aside until they are cool enough to handle. Cut them into ½-inch-thick slices.

2. In a saucepan, melt the butter over medium-low heat and whisk in the flour to make a roux. Add the milk, a little at a time, stirring, until the mixture thickens, about 10 minutes. Add the cayenne and the black pepper and salt to taste. Remove the sauce from the heat.

3. Preheat the oven to 425°F (220°C). Lightly grease a 2-quart casserole.

4. Layer the sauce, potatoes, onion, and sausage, in the casserole, beginning and ending with sauce.

5. Bake, covered, for 40 minutes. Uncover and bake an additional 20 minutes, or until browned. Serve hot.

Serves 4

Zucchini Stuffed with Sausage

More often than not, when our gardens overflow and we've had our fill of something, that something is zucchini. It's not that we plant too much; it's just that zucchini plants have a mind of their own, and they don't know when to quit. Consequently, we're always looking for new ways to fix this tasty summer squash. Here is one recipe that you can put to good use when your garden explodes with too much zucchini.

> 2 small to medium-sized zucchini
> 2 tablespoons olive oil
> 2 pounds sweet Italian sausage, removed from its casing
> ¼ cup finely chopped onion
> 2 cloves garlic, minced
> ¼ pound fresh mushrooms, chopped
> 1 can (6 ounces) tomato paste
> ¼ cup grated Romano cheese
> 2 tablespoons chopped fresh parsley
> ¼ cup dry white wine
> Freshly ground black pepper (medium grind)
> Kosher or coarse salt
> 2 tablespoons grated Parmesan cheese
> Olive oil

1. In a large pot, bring to a boil enough water to cover the zucchini. Add the zucchini to the pot and cook for 10 minutes. Remove the zucchini, pat dry, and set aside.

2. In a large skillet, heat the oil over medium-high heat. Add the sausage and sauté, crumbling it with the back of a spoon as it cooks, until it is cooked through and browned, about 10 minutes. Add the onion, garlic, and mushrooms and sauté 5 minutes longer. Drain off as much fat as possible and remove the skillet from the heat.

3. Slice each zucchini in half lengthwise. Scoop out the flesh with a spoon. Be careful not to puncture the skin. Chop the removed flesh and add it to the sausage mixture.

4. Add the tomato paste, cheese, parsley, wine, and pepper and salt to taste. Cook over medium heat for 5 minutes.

5. Preheat the oven to 325°F (165°C). Grease a baking sheet.

6. Place the zucchini halves on the baking sheet and divide the sausage mixture among the halves. Sprinkle the Parmesan cheese evenly on top and dribble a little olive oil on each.

7. Bake, uncovered, for 30 minutes, until the zucchini is tender. Serve at once.

Serves 4

SAUSAGE AND BEER: A MATCH MADE IN HEAVEN

*In Heaven there is no beer, /
That's why we drink it here . . .*
Sausage lovers know that sausage and beer are a heavenly combination, and not just on a hot summer day. For optimum flavor, here are some surefire combinations:

Sausage	Wash It Down With . . .
Summer sausage or cervelat	Kölsch (dry pale-gold ale)
Weisswurst	Weissbier
Andouille	Stout
Hot Italian	Porter
Mild salami	Real ales
Bratwurst	Cream ales
Wieners and ring bologna	Oktoberfest-style amber beers
Any mild sausage	Pilsner
Linguiça or garlic sausage	Steam beer
Kielbasa	Vienna beer
Spicy poultry sausage	Münchener
Bockwurst	Bock

METRIC EQUIVALENTS AND CONVERSION

Unless you have finely calibrated measuring equipment, conversions between U.S. and metric measurements will be somewhat inexact. It's important to convert the measurements for all of the ingredients in a recipe to maintain the same proportions as the original.

General Formula for Metric Conversion

Ounces to grams	multiply ounces by 28.35
Grams to ounces	multiply grams by 0.035
Pounds to grams	multiply pounds by 453.5
Pounds to kilograms	multiply pounds by 0.45
Cups to liters	multiply cups by 0.24
Fahrenheit to Celsius	subtract 32 from Fahrenheit temperature, multiply by 5, then divide by 9
Celsius to Fahrenheit	multiply Celsius temperature by 9, divide by 5, then add 32

Approximate Metric Equivalents by Volume

U.S.	METRIC
1 teaspoon	5 millileters
1 tablespoon	15 millileters
¼ cup	60 milliliters
½ cup	120 milliliters
1 cup	230 milliliters
1¼ cups	300 milliliters
1½ cups	360 milliliters
2 cups	460 milliliters
2½ cups	600 milliliters
3 cups	700 milliliters
4 cups (1 quart)	0.95 liter
1.06 quarts	1 liter
4 quarts (1 gallon)	3.8 liters

Approximate Metric Equivalents by Weight

U.S.	METRIC
0.035 ounce	1 gram
¼ ounce	7 grams
½ ounce	14 grams
1 ounce	28 grams
1¼ ounces	35 grams
1½ ounces	40 grams
1¾ ounces	50 grams
2½ ounces	70 grams
3½ ounces	100 grams
4 ounces	112 grams
5 ounces	140 grams
8 ounces	228 grams
8¾ ounces	250 grams
10 ounces	280 grams
15 ounces	425 grams
16 ounces (1 pound)	454 grams
1.1 pounds	500 grams
2.2 pounds	1 kilogram

METRIC	U.S.
1 gram	0.035 ounce
50 grams	1.75 ounces
100 grams	3.5 ounces
250 grams	8.75 ounces
500 grams	1.1 pounds
1 kilogram	2.2 pounds

Weight Conversions of Common Ingredients

1 pound salt = 1½ cups
1 ounce salt = 2 tablespoons
1 pound sugar = 2¼ cups
1 ounce cure = 1½ tablespoons

Spice Weights and Measures

This table is for approximate weights and measures of various spices and is intended as a handy compilation in estimating quantities. To use the chart, if a recipe calls for 1 ounce of allspice, then you would use 5 level tablespoons.

SPICE	¼	½	¾	1	2	3	4
	CONVERSION TO TABLESPOONS						
Allspice	1.25	2.5	3.75	5	10	15	20
Basil	1.5	3	4.5	6	12	18	24
Caraway	1.25	1.75	2.66	3.5	7	10.5	14
Cardamom	1	2	3	4	8	12	16
Celery, ground	1	2	3	4	8	12	16
Cinnamon	0.88	1.75	2.63	3.5	7	10.5	14
Cloves, ground	1	2	3	4	8	12	16
Coriander, ground	1	2	3	4	8	12	16
Cumin	1	2	3	4	8	12	16
Dill, whole	1	2	3	3.9	7.8	11.7	15
Fennel, whole	1	2.25	3.33	4.5	9	13.5	18
Garlic powder	0.75	1.5	2.25	3	6	9	12
Ginger	1.25	2.5	3.75	5	10	15	20
Mace, ground	1.33	2.75	4	5.5	11	16.5	22
Marjoram	1.5	3	4.5	6	12	18	24
MSG	0.5	1	1.66	2.2	4.4	6.6	9
Mustard	1	2	3	4	8	12	16
Nutmeg	1	2	3	4	8	12	16
Onion powder	1	2	3	4	8	12	16
Oregano	2	4	6	8	16	24	32
Paprika	1	2	3	4	8	12	16
Parsley flakes	3	6	12	16	32	48	64
Pepper, black	1	2	3	4	8	12	16
Pepper, ground	0.93	1.85	2.75	3.7	7.4	11.1	15
Rosemary, ground	1.75	3.5	5.25	7	14	21	28
Sage, ground	2.5	5	7.5	10	20	30	40
Salt	0.5	1	1.5	2	4	6	8
Savory	1.33	2.75	4	5.5	11	16.5	22
Thyme	1.75	3.5	5.25	7	14	21	28
Turmeric, ground	1.17	1.75	2.66	3.5	7	10.5	14

CONVERSION FROM OUNCES

Source: North Dakota State University Extension Service

Resources

Supplies for Making Sausage
(Casings, premixed cures, grinders, stuffers, smokers, seasoning packs, and other necessities)

Allied Kenco
Houston, Texas
800-356-5189
www.alliedkenco.com

Chop-Rite Two, Inc.
Harleysville, Pennsylvania
800-683-5858
www.chop-rite.com

Eldon's Sausage and Jerky Supply
Kooskia, Idaho
800-352-9453
www.eldonsausage.com

L.E.M. Products, Inc.
Harrison, Ohio
877-536-7763
www.lemproducts.com

The Sausage Maker
Buffalo, New York
888-490-8525
www.sausagemaker.com

The Sausage Source
Bennington, New Hampshire
800-978-5465
www.sausagesource.com

Stuffers Supply Company
Langley, British Columbia
604-534-7374
www.stuffers.com

Herbs and Spices

Pendery's World of Chiles & Spices
Dallas, Texas
800-533-1870
www.penderys.com

Penzeys Spices
Brookfield, Wisconsin
800-741-7787
www.penzeys.com

General Information on Sausage Making

Every state in the United States has one. They are called County Agents, part of the vast Cooperative Extension Service that is linked to your state university and all of its resources, as well as to the USDA. To call your County Agent, check the phone book under Cooperative Extension or your county government listings.

Agriculture and Agri-Food Canada
Ottawa, Ontario
613-759-1000
www.agr.gc.ca

U.S. Department of Agriculture
www.usda.gov

Useful Web Sites
In addition to the Web sites of the suppliers listed above, there are many good resources on the Web.

DeWied International
www.dewied.com
Largest producer of hog casings in North America; wholesale only, but good source of information

National Hot Dog & Sausage Council
www.hot-dog.org
Fun facts from the meat industry, even though we know you prefer homemade hot dogs.

International Natural Sausage Casing Association
www.insca.org
All about natural casings.

National Center for Home Food Preservation
www.uga.edu/nchfp
University of Georgia's food preservation site.

Food Safety
www.extension.iastate.edu/foodsafety
Iowa State University's food safety site.

The Art and Practice of Sausage Making
www.ag.ndsu.edu/pubs/yf/foods/he176w.htm
North Dakota State University

Nitrite in Meat
www.extension.umn.edu/distribution/nutrition/DJ0974.html
University of Minnesota

Processing Meat in the Home
www.extension.umn.edu/distribution/nutrition/DJ0972.html
University of Minnesota

Meat Preparation Fact Sheet: Focus of Sausages
www.fsis.usda.gov/Fact_Sheets/sausage_and_food_safety/index.asp
USDA: Food Safety and Inspection Service

Food Safety Throughout the Food System
http://foodsafety.cas.psu.edu
Penn State

ACKNOWLEDGMENTS

In preparing this revised edition, I consulted with home sausage makers, sausage suppliers, sausage-making teachers, food-safety experts, and chefs in the United States and Canada. Their generous advice, cheerful and illuminating conversations, and prized sausage recipes made the work enjoyable and contributed immensely to the scope of the book. Many of the people I talked with are profiled in this book. Special thanks for their time and patience in answering questions and offering ideas go to Rick Brown of The Sausage Source in Hillsboro, New Hampshire; Dr. Willis Wesley, Supervisor of the Minnesota State Meat Inspection Program in St. Paul, Minnesota; pharmacist Susan Harris of The Apothecary Shop in Keene, New Hampshire; and Chuck Miesfeld of Miesfeld's Market in my beloved hometown of Sheboygan, Wisconsin, where all the children are weaned on bratwurst and summer sausage.

Thank you, too, to my encouraging and helpful editor, Dianne Cutillo of Storey Publishing, who is always willing to talk or correspond about the minutiae of sausage making.

— Susan Peery

Index

Note: Page references to charts are in **bold** type; those for illustrations are in *italic* type.

Other Storey Titles
You Will Enjoy

Basic Butchering of Livestock & Game, by John J. Mettler Jr., DVM.
Clear, concise information for people who wish to slaughter their own meat for beef, veal, pork, lamb, poultry, rabbit, and venison.
208 pages. Paper. ISBN-13: 978-0-88266-391-3.

CloneBrews, by Tess and Mark Szamatulski.
One hundred and fifty recipes to brew beer that tastes just like premium commercial brands.
176 pages. Paper. ISBN-13: 978-1-58017-077-2.

Dave Miller's Homebrewing Guide, by Dave Miller.
A simple yet complete overview of homebrewing that is clear enough for the novice but thorough enough for the brewmaster.
368 pages. Paper. ISBN-13: 978-0-88266-905-2.

Fish Grilled & Smoked, by John Manikowski.
One hundred and fifty recipes for preparing fresh and saltwater fish in the kitchen and at the campsite.
264 pages. Paper. ISBN-13: 978-1-58017-502-9.

A Guide to Canning, Freezing, Curing & Smoking Meat, Fish & Game,
by Wilbur F. Eastman Jr.
A no-nonsense approach to preserving your own meat, from making beef jerky to building your own smokehouse.
240 pages. Paper. ISBN-13: 978-1-58017-457-2.

Home Cheese Making, by Ricki Carroll.
A classic primer to making artisanal-quality cheeses and other dairy products, as well as cooking with cheese.
288 pages. Paper. ISBN-13: 978-1-58017-464-0.

These and other books from Storey Publishing are available wherever quality books are sold or by calling 1-800-441-5700.
Visit us at *www.storey.com*.